CONTEMPORARY
▪ PERSPECTIVES ▪
ON MASCULINITY

Second Edition

CONTEMPORARY ∎ PERSPECTIVES ∎ ON MASCULINITY

Men, Women, and Politics in
Modern Society

KENNETH CLATTERBAUGH
University of Washington

WestviewPress
A Division of HarperCollins*Publishers*

Copyright © 1990, 1997 by Westview Press, A Division of HarperCollins Publishers, Inc.

Published in 1997 in the United States of America by Westview Press, 5500 Central Avenue, Boulder, Colorado 80301-2877, and in the United Kingdom by Westview Press, 12 Hid's Copse Road, Cumnor Hill, Oxford OX2 9JJ

Library of Congress Cataloging-in-Publication Data
Clatterbaugh, Kenneth C.
   Contemporary perspectives on masculinity : men, women, and politics in modern society / Kenneth Clatterbaugh. — 2nd ed.
      p.   cm.
   Includes bibliographical references and index.
   ISBN 0-8133-2700-8 (hc). — ISBN 0-8133-2701-6 (pb)
   1. Men's movement—United States.   2. Men—United States—Attitudes.   3. Masculinity (Psychology)   4. Sex role—United States.   I. Title.
HQ1090.3.C54   1997
305.31—dc20   96-43123
                                                                               CIP

The paper used in this publication meets the requirements of the American National Standard for Permanence of Paper for Printed Library Materials Z39.48-1984.

10   9   8   7   6   5   4   3   2

Contents

▪ Preface to the ▪ Second Edition

It has been more than five years since I wrote the first edition of *Contemporary Perspectives on Masculinity: Men, Women, and Politics in Modern Society*. In that time there have been significant changes in both academic and popular thinking about men and masculinity. First, there is a considerable body of new literature in both books and magazines that addresses a common set of issues. Second, the area of men's studies is now considerably stronger and more professional. Third, Robert Bly's *Iron John*, the top-selling nonfiction book of 1991, created a media sensation about the so-called men's movement. Fourth, the secular men's movement, for all these changes, has clearly begun to wane. Fifth, a prominent and rapidly growing evangelical Christian men's movement has captured the attention of the mass media and hundreds of thousands of North American men.

My own thinking about what is loosely called "the men's movement" has progressed. I have always been aware that this aggregate movement is just that: a collection of incompatible separate movements. But I am now much more aware of what these components have in common and how they have shared certain ideas and themes. And the balance of power within the movement has certainly shifted from a powerful profeminist perspective to an antifeminist stance. I argue in the final chapter that in spite of its profeminist beginnings, this aggregate movement's net effect has been to undermine feminism and to shore up patriarchal institutions and thinking.

This deep transformation in the aggregate movement makes it even more difficult for me, who continues to hold a socialist profeminist perspective, to present the various perspectives fairly. As I remarked in the first edition, it remains for the reader to judge whether I have been successful.

Kenneth Clatterbaugh

▪ Acknowledgments ▪

I am, as always, indebted to many students, friends, and colleagues, and to my spouse, Linda Heuertz, without whose help and conversation this second edition would never have been completed. The following acknowledgments of specific help are not in any particular order.

Various men's organizations and publishers have been especially generous in providing material for this book. I have particularly benefited from discussions with Michael Dash, Susan Jeffords, Jean Roberts, Stokley Towles, and my senior thesis students. John Boler, the chair of my department at the University of Washington, has given me solid support, and the university granted me leave time to finish this project. Richard Majors, Michael Kimmel, and Larry Icard have written material that is invaluable, and Michael Kimmel has also overseen the publication of several papers whose content found its way into this book.

K. C.

■ ONE ■

Introduction to the Men's Movement

Since the early 1970s, North Americans have been reading about a men's movement. We have been treated to images of men gathering in support of the feminist cause, coming together to denounce feminism, standing around roaring campfires and shouting "ho," and gathering in football stadiums and praying to become better men. What these images indicate is that the men's movement is not a single movement but is rather several movements that have been gathered under a single description. Because these movements are collected under a single description—one that each movement often claims for itself—the academic literature as well as the mass media are not particularly discriminating in their references to the parts of the whole. There is a need, therefore, for a more systematic identification of the component movements in the aggregate called "the men's movement."

As a social philosopher I tend to view the components of the aggregate movement as a set of sociopolitical perspectives. The way men live, how we see ourselves, and how we are seen are issues of great social importance. But these perspectives on men are also political: They offer an agenda for society as a whole. And each perspective is continually contentious in its discussion of other perspectives. With the exceptions of the first edition of this book and William G. Doty's *Myths of Masculinity* (1993), which draws heavily upon my own categories, there has been little sustained work on the categorization of perspectives on men and masculinity. Since the identities of groups are not static, a remapping of the perspectives on men is needed: Groups change their principles, accent different principles, and new groups appear as old groups disappear. This new edition of my book is my effort to survey once again this shifting territory.

To identify and to understand a sociopolitical perspective we need four kinds of information: that perspective's description of social reality, its explanation of why that reality exists, its vision of what should replace it, and its agenda for achieving that end (Wasserstrom 1980:52). Accordingly, I organize the treatment of each perspective around the following central questions:

1. What is the social reality for men in modern society?
2. What maintains or explains this social reality?
3. What would be a better social reality?
4. How can we achieve this better reality?

These four central questions do more than help us to identify perspectives on men and masculinity: They offer a logical structure for discussion and critique as well. Although all perspectives describe, explain, and evaluate social reality as well as set an agenda appropriate to those evaluations, there is sharp disagreement among them as to what is the correct description of social reality and how it should be changed. We find wide differences, for example, regarding the nature of the masculine social role or the impact of the contemporary feminist movement on men, and these, in turn, have led to disagreements over whether and how society ought to change. In addition to these disagreements within the components of the men's movement, there are also criticisms of the movement as a whole. Thus, our task in this book is both descriptive and evaluative.

This book takes up about eight major perspectives that dominate contemporary discussions of men and masculinity. I call these perspectives the *conservative, profeminist, men's rights, mythopoetic, socialist, gay, African American,* and *evangelical* perspectives. In subsequent chapters each of these perspectives will be described and evaluated. But before we begin this examination, let us return to the four central questions that constitute our framework for discussion.

1. What is the social reality for men in modern society?
The social reality for men in North American society is to be masculine or, more accurately, to adopt one of the many *masculinities* that are available to men. There are many ways of being a man, although masculinities are not all equally approved or equally condemned, and not all masculinities are approved by the same people. Throughout this book we shall be discussing men and masculinity, but it should never be thought that there is a single masculinity that applies to all men. The task of describing male reality or men's masculinities is a difficult one, regardless of the sociopolitical perspective; it is especially difficult when there is so much disagreement over what it means to be a man.

In discussing masculinity we will find it helpful to distinguish among four components. First, there is the question of what men are—the *masculine gender role*. This is a set of behaviors, attitudes, and conditions that are generally found in men of an identifiable group. For example, if men in this group tend to behave aggressively, aggressiveness is a part of their masculine gender role; if they tend to value rational discussion or to do certain kinds of work, then that, too, is a part. Distinct masculinities are social roles that belong to *identifiable* groups of men who exist in reasonably specific historical, ethnic, or religious situations. Within the conditions that determine a masculinity, I include privilege or lack of privilege. Thus, if some men are generally treated as more suited for political office, then that privilege is included in their masculinity. If some men are disadvantaged in being selected as the custodial parent—gay men, for example—then that, too, is an element in their masculinity or social role.

Second, there is the question of what people think men are—the *stereotype of masculinity*. A stereotype is a general idea of what most people consider to be the masculine gender role. If it is widely believed that men are wealthy, then that belief is part of the gender stereotype, regardless of whether it is part of the gender role.

The gender role and the stereotype are quite distinct. If we were interested in the masculine gender role, we would have to study an identifiable group of men. If we were interested in the stereotype of masculinity, we would have to survey people and ask them what they thought was typical of those men. The stereotype of what men are and the role that men actually play need not agree; in fact, there is considerable evidence to suggest that gender stereotypes are inaccurate. "Gender stereotypes . . . may not be based on statistically significant differences in behavior between the sexes but, at best, are exaggerations of a grain of truth" (Basow 1986:12).

Third, there is the question of what people think men should be—the *gender ideal*. The gender ideal is a widespread notion as to what the gender role for men should be. If it is widely believed that men of a certain age and means should be married, then that is part of their gender ideal. Obviously, what people think men should be may be quite different either from what men are or from what people think men are. Stereotypes and ideals, too, are historically situated; they reflect the ideas of specific groups about what men (of specific groups) are and should be.

Roles, stereotypes, and ideals tend not to become too disparate, however, because stereotypes are partially formed through perceptions of roles, and ideals and stereotypes serve as guides in developing gender roles (Basow 1986:13). Sociologists or social psychologists may question the accuracy of stereotypes and ideals in relation to actual social roles; but of importance to us is what a particular perspective is claiming when it describes masculinity. Is the perspective clear about the group of men being identified? Is it clear about the differences among role, stereotype, and ideal?

Certain masculinities are favored socially or come closer to the gender ideal. Boys are taught to adopt these social roles and ideals. Certain collections of behaviors, attitudes, and conditions (certain masculinities) are favored and rewarded, others are ignored, and still others are punished. Masculinities that are favored are *dominant* or *hegemonic* masculinities. These masculinities may vary from subculture to subculture, but they are dominant in the sense that they are favored and actively promoted throughout society, and those who appear to exemplify them are most likely to be placed in positions of power and trust. Thus, there is a strong set of similarities among the powerful men who sit in boardrooms, in legislatures, and in other responsible positions. And there are strong similarities among men who are excluded from positions of power and prestige. Of course, there are exceptions and there are changes, but there are also rules of thumb that favor certain sets of behaviors, attitudes, and conditions: For example, to be articulate, loyal, heterosexual, white, and wealthy are favored characteristics of hegemonic masculinities.

Fourth and finally, there is the subjective process each person goes through in arriving at his or her gender. One's *gender identity* is the self-definition of gender to oneself. Obviously, what an individual is as well as what an individual thinks he or she should be may itself vary from the more generalized gender role, stereotype, and ideal. Each of us is an individual, and how we are and how we think we are gendered is often a big part of that individuality.

Our eight perspectives disagree sharply in their descriptions of masculinity, largely because they differ on what to include in the masculine gender role. In other cases, they do not agree on the gender ideal. (Of course, any disagreement about these components of masculinity entails a difference in its description.)

The description of masculinities from some of these perspectives gives great weight to certain dynamic processes operating on men, including economic patterns, changing stereotypes and ideals, the media, social structures such as the military, and social movements such as the feminist or other liberation movements. Without fail, however, each perspective expresses an opinion about feminism and how it does or does not affect male reality. But feminism is not a unified theory. Within the profeminist perspective, for example, there are both radicals and liberals, and within the socialist perspective there are both classical Marxists and socialist feminists (Jaggar 1983; Tong 1988). A careful student of the diverse feminisms will notice that many of these perspectives offer only a superficial understanding of feminism. They either embrace all feminism or reject all feminism; seldom do they draw any fine distinctions. Thus, when advocates of a perspective on masculinity make claims about feminism, we must first discover, to the extent possible, what they have in mind before we can begin to understand or critique it.

The eight perspectives under study here are divided according to the masculinities that they consider important and in terms of their assessments of the impact of feminism. When I identify each perspective's description of the social reality of the American male, I shall accordingly focus on these two dimensions.

2. What maintains or explains this social reality?

Raw descriptions of reality are not very interesting in themselves. Unless we can explain that reality, unless we have some theory about how it comes about and what maintains it, we have not really come to an understanding of it. In the perspectives under study, the accounts of masculinity go beyond mere description and offer an explanation of the forces that create and maintain it. Typically, some aspect of male reality is identified as the maintaining cause.

The advocates of some perspectives, for example, believe that masculinities are primarily a manifestation of male biology; others believe that they are primarily learned and socially reinforced through ideals and stereotypes. I stress the word *primarily* because most of the eight perspectives posit one underlying cause or pattern that shapes male reality more than any other. Thus, one perspective may agree with another regarding the general list of causes of masculinities but disagree about which ones are most significant. A biological conservative, for example, may agree that gender ideals are a factor in shaping masculinities but argue at the same time that genetically determined tendencies toward certain behaviors are much more influential. In other words, if gender ideals could be changed and genetic tendencies were to remain the same, male reality would remain unchanged. Many of the disagreements among our eight perspectives are actually differences over the best explanation of masculinities.

The importance of such an explanation is not just that we gain understanding by learning why something is the way it is. We also need to know which causes, if any, are most crucial in maintaining male reality if we hope to affect it.

3. What would be a better social reality?

With this question we make a significant move from description and explanation to evaluation. To answer it a perspective must look at the described male reality and judge whether certain dimensions of it are good or bad. It must also survey the alternatives and determine which of them are possible and which desirable. For those that are undesirable or unjust, it must offer replacements. These replacements are usually defended with the argument that they would create a better society. For example, adherents of the profeminist perspective point to the oppression of women as the greatest societal ill; but they may conceive of that oppression in terms of inequality, violence, or an unfair division of labor. In its place they would offer a society of equal opportunity, safety, and equal pay for equal work. They also disagree among themselves about whether the net benefits for men will be positive or negative: Some argue that there must be an overall loss of male benefits in order to dismantle male domination; others argue that the long-term benefits will outweigh the short-term losses. Of course, *all* profeminists believe that when the gains for women are added in, society will be better off.

4. How can we achieve this better reality?
The description of reality tells us where we are, the explanation tells us why we are there, and the assessment of that reality tells us where we want to be. The answer to the fourth question, finally, tells us how to get there. The selection of strategies toward a better society must conform to four conditions: (1) The strategies must be feasible; they must be actions that individuals or groups can initiate. (2) They must have, or be likely to have, the desired result. (3) In reaching the desired result, they must not violate moral principles or individual rights. And (4), when there is conflict between individual rights or moral principles, an agreed adjudication of this conflict must be arrived at.

Consider, as an example, the effort to set an agenda for pornography. Suppose that we have already described, explained, and evaluated this issue. That is, we have found that the use of pornography is widespread, that it is caused by a learning process that links violence and sexuality, and that it is socially harmful to men and to the women and children victimized by men who use pornography.

Assuming we have reached the above conclusions, the agenda-building question remains: What can we do to ensure that men will use pornography less? As one strategy, we might impose severe penalties on anyone caught using pornography. But such a strategy might interfere with basic freedoms; and, in any case, given the number of pornography users, policing that many men would not be feasible. Suppose we were to ban the public display of pornography and place zoning limits on the stores in which the pornography could be sold. But, although availability may expedite the use of pornographic materials, it is hardly the cause of such use; and diminished availability is unlikely to reduce use significantly, as communities that have tried to restrict availability have discovered. Another strategy might be to elect a censorship board that would prevent the publication of pornographic books or the making of pornographic films. Such an agenda, however, would be impermissible to anyone committed to the right of free expression, even though some have argued that pornography so harms individuals that justice for victims and potential victims supercedes the pornographer's right of free expression.

As we have seen, each of these strategies encounters a serious challenge from the four conditions previously noted. A fourth strategy, one that would avoid the above pitfalls, is to educate men about healthy sexuality and the harm that comes from pornography while socially empowering those persons who are most likely to be victimized by its use.

Our simplified example illustrates the difficulties in finding an agenda, even when there is general agreement about the description, explanation, and evaluation. The agenda-building task becomes even more complicated when perspectives disagree in some of their answers to the first three questions.

One of the purposes of this book is to help the reader look critically at the conservative, profeminist, men's rights, spiritual, socialist, gay, black, and evangelical perspectives. The task is not an easy one, however. In the first place, the perspectives often rest on hidden assumptions about human nature, social change, and right versus wrong. These assumptions can be buried so deeply that they are seldom made explicit, let alone defended. Second, the perspectives are dynamic. As "moving targets," they change with new information from the social sciences; they shift in their emphases and borrow from one another. Indeed, the process of distinguishing among these perspectives is sometimes a matter of subjective judgment.

For these reasons, the criticisms and responses in each chapter are not definitive; in most cases, they reveal only the beginnings of a long and complex debate. Thus, the fact that a critique follows each perspective does not mean that the perspective fails on those grounds; and the fact that a response follows each criticism does not mean that the criticism has been satisfactorily and definitively answered. Ultimately, the reader must work out, to his or her own satisfaction, the adequacy of each criticism and each response.

Obviously, adherence to any one of the perspectives will yield criticisms of the others. For example, from the profeminist perspective, no other perspective that denies men are privileged relative to women can be satisfactory. Interperspective conflicts such as these are frequent, and many of them will be noted in the critique sections of each chapter.

However, there are some general criteria that do not depend on adoption of any particular perspective; these criteria tend to be the minimal standards to which any perspective must conform if it is to be credible. Many of the criticisms invoke these criteria, at least implicitly, and they offer a good starting point to the reader who is interested in a critical look at each perspective.

CLARITY

The perspectives presented in this book have been put forth by people who aspire to persuade us of the truth of their views. But before we can settle the truth or falsity of a position, we must *understand* it. Indeed, if a claim is presented in such a way that it has no clear meaning, we are not in a position to say whether it is true or false. That is, if it does not succeed in saying something, it does not succeed in saying something true or false. So a first requirement of any perspective is that it be stated clearly enough that we can grasp its meaning.

Lack of clarity often arises from ambiguity or the imprecision of basic ideas or concepts. A key term may stand for two or more distinct ideas, or a concept may be ill defined. It is not uncommon, for example, to find authors who confuse the terms *woman* and *feminist*.

Having a requirement of clarity does not mean that these perspectives must aspire to the rigor of a mathematical proof. Many concepts that are important to sociopolitical discussions have a certain vagueness or are in the process of being defined. But a perspective gains clarity even when it demonstrates an awareness of the shortcomings of its basic ideas and the need to refine them further.

PROPER USE OF EVIDENCE

Once we have established that a position is sufficiently clear, we can turn to an evaluation of the evidence or to the reasons set forth in support of its claims. If an author asserts that men always dominate women, we want to know what evidence there is for that conclusion. Some authors simply stipulate claims without offering evidence for them. In some cases they offer no evidence, because they believe that the claims are self-evident; as the diversity of perspectives reveals, however, there is never much agreement about what is self-evident. In stipulating claims or assuming self-evidence, authors too often try to establish by sheer authority or emphatic statement something for which the rest of us need a reason. Such stipulated "truths" deserve our notice but not our assent; they may be true, but the author gives us no reason for thinking so.

Then, too, a perspective may offer only that evidence which supports its own point of view. Such an approach to evidence is grab-bag; one reaches into history and science and selects only the favorable examples.

For example, if a researcher believes that most criminals are wrongfully convicted, and then collects in a large volume only those cases in which criminals have been wrongfully convicted, his or her belief will seem to be supported by that selected evidence. The perspectives covered in this book are much more than disinterested theories about masculinity; they are positions of advocacy out to win converts. Thus there is the danger they they, too, provide selected evidence. The reader is urged to keep this fact in mind throughout.

The reader will also notice that I frequently use the definite article and the singular to refer to the various general types of perspectives—for example, the women's movement, the men's movement, the conservative perspective, the black viewpoint. By following this practice I do not mean to suggest that such points of view are single, monolithic entities. Quite the contrary; I use the singular to designate an aggregate in which there are many divisions and points of view.

THE EIGHT PERSPECTIVES

It is time now to present a brief sketch of the eight major perspectives to be presented in subsequent chapters. Each perspective encompasses a general category, within which there are many voices. I have tried to choose those voices that are in the mainstream of each particular view. Where there is more than one important subgroup to be represented, I have identified them and indicated some of their similarities and differences. Although some of these perspectives have roots in the social philosophies of the nineteenth century, each has emerged and taken form in response to modern feminist movements as well as to other components in the aggregate men's movement. Furthermore, the order in which these perspectives are presented is a rough approximation of the order in which they appeared historically. That they are presented in the order in which they appeared is important in understanding both the ways they influence one another and the aggregate effect of these movements. Thus, although each perspective is part of the contemporary men's movement, it also occupies a particular historical and ideological place within that aggregate movement.

1. The Conservative Perspective

Moral conservatives admire and protect social institutions and practices that they find grounded in the traditions of society. Such traditions are, for them, natural and best as well as time-honored. In North American society these traditions include different roles for men and women. Men are the providers and protectors; women are homemakers and caregivers.

Many moral conservatives divide the world into the public sphere, which includes politics and business, and the private sphere, which means the family. Men are naturally dominant in the public sphere, and women are naturally dominant in the private sphere. Violations of traditions are likely to lead to social unraveling and moral crisis. Thus, the moral conservative rejects the demand for less stringent roles for men and women. An irony of the moral conservative public counterattack on feminism is that it was led by a conservative woman, Phyllis Schlafly, whose writings and public appearances were instrumental in defeating the ratification of the Equal Rights Amendment (Gilder 1986:101ff.).

Biological conservatives often agree with moral conservatives that traditional roles for men and women are natural. However, biological conservatives do not ground their belief in the sanctity of tradition but in the biologies of male and female. The science of sociobiology, which first appeared in the 1970s, argued that social institutions and practices are significantly determined by the genetic predispositions of men and women. If men rule in the public sphere, it is because men are predisposed to do so; if women stay at home more often, then that, too, is their biological inclination. But although sociobiologists agree that social practices are indebted to biological imperatives, they disagree as to the extent of those imperatives. Thus, some argue that it is futile to try to change gender roles, others argue that there is much about our gender roles that can be changed relatively painlessly, and still others argue that only the most tyrannical measures will enforce equal gender roles on men and women.

Both moral conservative counterattacks and sociobiological critiques of feminism appeared in the 1970s; they were the first wave of resistance to the contemporary feminist movement. And although these two forms of conservatism depend upon different assumptions, they both argue in the same direction. Furthermore, many moral conservatives draw upon biological arguments to bolster their claims that what is traditional is natural.

2. The Profeminist Perspective

Concurrent with conservative resistance, a movement of men sympathetic to feminist analyses and agendas appeared in the early 1970s. These men took the label *profeminist* rather than feminist because they recognized the personal experience of being a woman as an important component of being feminist. Profeminist men reject the claim that traditional masculinities are either biologically grounded or necessary to social stability. For them, masculinities are created and maintained through male privilege and its corresponding oppression of women, although they allow that traditional masculinity is also harmful to men.

Radical profeminists follow the lead of radical feminism in holding that masculinity is created and maintained by misogyny and violence against women, and that patriarchy is the social and political order in which this masculinity exists. To counter the patriarchal order, radical profeminists believe that it is necessary to repudiate masculinity and to replace it with new behaviors and attitudes that are informed by feminist values. That is, men may unlearn patriarchal behaviors by working against violence, learning to take on more caretaker roles, and helping to create noncompetitive, nonhierarchical organizations.

Liberal profeminists follow the lead of liberal feminism in maintaining that masculinity is a set of limitations that are imposed on men, much as femininity is a set of limitations that are imposed on women. These limited ways of behaving are encouraged by a system of rewards, punishments, and social stereotypes and ideals. Both men and women are prevented from self-realization by these restrictive roles. The best way for men to combat sexism is to break through their own limitations and to become fully human, just as women have had to struggle to overcome the limitations of femininity. The model for liberal profeminist men is the liberal women's movement—specifically, the National Organization for Women (NOW).

3. The Men's Rights Perspective

In the late 1970s many men, some of whom had been in the profeminist ranks, began a new movement that has come to be known as the men's rights perspective. This perspective concurs with the profeminist view that masculinity is damaging to men but with the gigantic difference of the belief that the principal harm in this role is directed against men rather than women. Indeed, the premise of all men's rights literature is that men are *not* privileged relative to women. Since male privilege is a cornerstone of every feminist perspective, the men's rights perspective is in this assumption irrevocably antifeminist.

Having denied that men are privileged relative to women, this movement divides into those who believe that men and women are equally harmed by sexism and those who believe that society has become a bastion of female privilege and male degradation. Whereas the women's movement has created new options for women, men have not been given the same range of choices. Thus, a new sexism has been born, a sexism that thrives on male bashing and male blaming. The agenda of the men's rights perspective is to bring about an understanding of the new sexism and to create laws that protect men against current injustices in such areas as divorce, child custody, affirmative action, domestic violence prosecution, and sexual harassment.

4. The Mythopoetic Perspective

In the late 1980s and early 1990s a new perspective appeared, one built around the writings and workshops of the poet Robert Bly. Men gathered to read poetry, drum, and speak of their emotional and psychic wounds. This perspective was founded on the neo-Jungian conviction that masculinities derive from deep unconscious patterns or archetypes. These patterns are best revealed through a tradition of stories, myths, and rituals. Men and women are essentially different kinds of beings who respond to different kinds of deep needs.

Bly believes that the women's movement has successfully tapped into the unconscious minds of women and found a way to unleash women's energy but that men have yet to find a positive and vigorous way of doing the same. Bly is implicitly critical of feminism because he believes it wounds men and holds out a kind of spirituality that is antagonistic to the deep masculine. Simply stated, Bly believes that modern men are overly feminized. Bly's movement has created several sympathetic submovements, such as the new warrior movement, that stresses wilderness experiences as forms of male initiation into manhood. The therapeutic nature of Bly's work also stimulated twelve-step movements that treat the behaviors of masculinity as addictions.

Bly's spiritual approach was quickly challenged from another neo-Jungian movement that had roots in the Wicca tradition, a pre-Christian pagan religion centered on an earth goddess with lesser deities. This voice, exemplified by John Rowan, argues that masculinity is overly influenced by a lack of feminization. In the Wicca tradition, the deep masculine should be controlled by the Great Goddess, often identified with various female deities such as Isis, Demeter, Kali-dra. Thus, this view is openly humanistic and feminist: It teaches that men have been cut off from a feminine understanding of themselves.

5. The Socialist Perspective

Sexism within the Left/liberal movements of the 1960s and 1970s emerged as an obvious problem by the 1970s. Different leftist men responded to the charges that women were clearly being discriminated against in leftist organizations. Some argued that the women's movement was a bourgeois phenomenon that only served to divide the working class. Others began to directly address issues affecting women, both within their own organizations and within society as a whole. Unions began to understand their own histories of sexism; some political organizations formed women's caucuses and produced special publications for women members. A few profeminist socialist men began to explore masculinity in light of socialist assumptions and feminist critiques.

From this point of view, masculinities are grounded in economically determined class structures. In patriarchal capitalism masculinities are determined by who does what work, who controls the labor of others, and who controls the products of that labor.

6. Gay Male Perspectives

Gay men stand, along with black men, as one of the two most oppressed groups of men in North America. Gay men have long been considered feminized males—men who lack some crucial component of masculinity. Thus, most gay men have struggled with the questions of masculinity. They have asked of the masculinities that emerge in their own community whether they are truly masculine or some feminized version of hegemonic masculinities. And gay men have challenged both the viability of hegemonic masculinities and the morality of these masculinities. They have further challenged the very distinction between what is masculine and what is feminine. Perhaps because of the centrality of these questions in their lives, gay men have been involved as participants and antagonists in every perspective on men and masculinity. Gay men have much to teach straight men about their fears of male intimacy and friendship and about overcoming their homophobia. Indeed, most gay perspectives list homophobia as one of the principal causes of dominant masculinities.

7. African American Men's Perspectives

The component of race and ethnicity is frequently discussed within the predominantly European American men's movements as well as by men of many nationalities: Chicano, Japanese, Jewish, and so on. But perhaps the best-developed critique of other perspectives and the role of racism in shaping masculinities occurs in the writings of African American men. The 1980s and 1990s have produced a considerable literature, particularly in books and essays, that warns that black men are becoming an endangered species. All these authors agree that black men experience a unique set of difficulties that derive from history and societal racism. But the voices within this movement vary greatly in how they describe the reality of African American men and the extent of racism's effects. Whatever their differences, however, almost all African American perspectives note that antiblack racism is a formative feature of hegemonic masculinities. Thus, they challenge both the viability and the morality of such masculinities.

8. Evangelical Christian Men's Movement

The leaders of the Promise Keepers often see themselves as the heirs of the waning secular men's movement. They believe they offer what has been lacking in the earlier movements. Promise Keepers is a religiously conservative movement. Based on a literal reading of the Bible, the movement teaches that men should be fathers and providers as well as the heads of their families. In what is a concession to feminism, this movement concedes that men have not been good providers and fathers. Men are to women as Jesus was to the Church. Men are also by nature sinners and dependent upon God. Indeed, having a personal relationship with Jesus is a foundational principle of Christian evangelism. Society is taken to be in moral crisis in part because men have abdicated their responsibilities and in part because women, influenced by feminism, have taken on the man's role.

Common Ground

For all of their differences, the components of the men's movements have many similarities. Each begins with a feminist viewpoint, whether or not it is ultimately opposed or endorsed. Some endorse specific principles of feminism: For example, that there should be no discrimination against women who work, though particular remedies for that discrimination, such as affirmative action, may be opposed. Each movement finds some significant parallel between women and men. Moral and biological conservatives see women as supreme in the domestic sphere and men as supreme in the public sphere. Evangelical Christians see men related to women as Jesus was related to the Church. Men's rights advocates are especially attached to the view that for every discrimination against women there is a comparable discrimination against men. Profeminists find that both men and women are restricted in their gender roles. Mythopoetics try to create a spiritual movement for men that can stand beside the spiritual movement for women. Black social theorists side with black feminists in identifying racism as the driving force in their lives; gay men find comparable common ground with lesbian feminists. Each movement claims that its agenda is in the best interests of men and women and eagerly solicits endorsements from prominent sympathetic women. At the same time, each movement tries to be supportive of men and to find ways to address issues of concern to men.

STRUCTURE OF THE BOOK

In identifying how the eight major perspectives answer the four basic questions, we will find it useful to consider the perspectives in a parallel manner. Chapters 2 through 9 of this volume are thus organized under the following headings: (1) Historical Sketch and Primary Sources, (2) Description and Explanation of Male Reality, (3) Assessment of Male Reality and Agenda for Change, (4) Critique: Criticisms and Responses, (5) Summary and Conclusions, and (6) Suggested Reading.

The historical sketch and primary sources section will include some very brief remarks about the history of the perspective and a description of the primary sources to be used in the ensuing discussion. The primary sources are selected writings that I consider to be the best and most available representatives of each perspective; they are also the most frequently cited sources in that chapter.

The reader will see that the description and explanation section of each chapter contains the perspective's answer to the first two central questions (What is the social reality for men in modern society? What maintains or explains this social reality?). In most of the writings, the answers to these two questions naturally occur together anyway. This second section will be subdivided under the two headings of *masculinities* and *feminism*, reflecting the importance of these topics within each perspective.

The third section of each chapter presents the perspective's answers to the third and fourth questions (What would be a better social reality? How can we achieve this better reality?). The focus here will be on evaluative and agenda-building tasks.

The fourth section of each chapter presents a number of criticisms and possible responses. Both interperspective criticisms and challenges to the clarity of the perspective and its use of evidence are featured here. At this point, I must remind the reader that these criticisms and responses constitute only the beginning of a critical discussion, only a direction for debate, rather than a definitive critique that, in many cases, would require an entire chapter or book to delineate.

In the fifth section of each chapter I shall briefly state my conclusions about the major strengths and weaknesses of the perspective in question. Although I try to present a fair picture of each perspective, I do not believe that they are all equally meritorious. It is in this section, therefore, that the reader can most easily discover my own conclusions about each perspective.

The section entitled "Suggested Reading" offers a list of further readings for a more thorough consideration of the perspective covered in that chapter. Although the primary sources are not repeated in this section, they are highly recommended to the reader who intends to study that perspective in depth.

We are now ready to apply our framework to the eight perspectives that have been identified. This book can be thought of as a map of contemporary perspectives on masculinity, in which major regions, contested areas, and unexplored territories are described. Like any map, it will need to be redrawn as new boundaries are formed. In its current form, however, it can serve as a guide to the past, the present, and the immediate future.

▪ TWO ▪

The Conservative Legacy

The conservative position . . . boils down to one overriding fact: There is no engine of progress, security, and social advancement as powerful as the family, particularly the bourgeois family whose customs and ethics defined Western civilization during the two centuries before the Great Unraveling of recent decades.
—William J. Gribbin, "Washington Abandons the Family"

The building block of nearly all human societies is the nuclear family . . . of an American industrial city, no less than a band of hunter-gatherers in the Australian desert. . . . In both cases . . . the women and children remain in the residential area while the men forage for game or its symbolic equivalent in the form of money.
—Edward O. Wilson, *Sociobiology*

HISTORICAL SKETCH AND PRIMARY SOURCES

Conservatism is the proper starting place for any systematic discussion of masculinity. As the most influential perspective in both the nineteenth and twentieth centuries, it constitutes the legacy from which other perspectives either borrow ideas or try to distance themselves. At the core of conservatism is a defense of the traditional gender roles whereby the masculine role of protector and provider is appropriate to men and the feminine role of childbearer and caregiver is appropriate to women. These are the roles of men and women in the traditional family, which conservatives believe is the building block of a moral society.

There are many varieties of conservatism. In this chapter we shall examine two forms that have been influential since the early 1970s. I call

17

them "moral conservatism" and "biological conservatism," respectively. Moral conservatives hold that there is an absolute set of values (i.e., a natural law) that is exemplified in the social order built around the traditional family, and that the preservation of the traditional family is necessary to the continuation of that order. Biological conservatives believe that the traditional social roles reflected in the nuclear family are the most consistent with the biological natures of men and women. Both forms of conservatism have long and intertwined histories going back to the late eighteenth and nineteenth centuries. In Chapter 9 we shall introduce a third variety of conservatism, evangelical conservatism, which has become prominent in the 1990s and whose origins are more properly in the twentieth century.

Moral conservatives usually claim Edmund Burke (1729–1797) as their founder. Burke rejected the rational utopianism of the Enlightenment, with its confidence that human reason can restructure society, and instead put his trust in what he called "prejudice"—the wisdom of a society's traditions as embodied in the family, church, and community. For Burke, society is inherently differentiated and unequal. Moreover, attempts to eradicate inequality, such as those made during the French Revolution, only yield a totalitarian state devoid of morality and consumed by the selfish pursuit of power. Women, according to Burke, are "naturally" suited to their roles as mother and wife, and men are "naturally" suited to their roles as protector and provider. And the "appropriateness" of these roles is evidenced by the "wisdom" found in tradition.

Most biological conservatives point to Charles Darwin (1809–1882) as their founder. They find in Darwin's theory of evolution an explanation of the different social roles of men and women. Every organism struggles to survive and reproduce. Society is made up of individuals whose ancestors were biologically successful—that is, whose genes survived into future generations. Individuals pursue different strategies, some of which have greater success than others. Human behavior in society is the result of the more successful strategies as selected in the evolutionary process. If men tend to be traditionally masculine and women traditionally feminine, it is because these behaviors have allowed them to be biologically successful. These behaviors have become innate to men and women precisely because those who tended to behave differently did not survive.

George Gilder's *Sexual Suicide* (1973), our first primary source for moral conservatism, is a detailed, passionate, and influential defense of moral conservatism by the contemporary conservative who writes most about men and masculinity. Since its publication in 1973, *Sexual Suicide* has been updated and expanded in individual articles in the *National Review*; it was also republished in 1986 under the title *Men and Marriage*. Our second primary source is David Blankenhorn's *Fatherless America* (1995). Blankenhorn takes the moral conservative view espoused by Gilder and extends that perspective to the controversies surrounding the role of men in the family. Robert Nisbet's *Conservatism* (1986) is our third primary source. Nisbet neatly sums up many of the underlying philosophical assumptions of the moral conservative's world view. His general scope complements Gilder's and Blankenhorn's specific focus on traditional gender roles.

Although there are several varieties of biological conservatism, I shall discuss only one—sociobiology. This theory originated with Edward O. Wilson's *Sociobiology: The New Synthesis* (1975) and his Pulitzer Prize–winning *On Human Nature* (1976). Since the mid-1970s sociobiology has become a widely taught theory, a frequent topic in the popular press, and a subject of heated debate among social theorists. Wilson defines sociobiology as "the systematic study of the biological basis of all social behavior" (Wilson 1975:2).

Two primary sources merit inclusion here: Pierre L. van den Berghe's *Human Family Systems—An Evolutionary View* (1979) and David P. Barash's *Sociobiology and Behavior* (1982). Both van den Berghe and Barash closely follow Wilson's path, but their textbook approach systematizes much of the material that is more casually presented by Wilson. Barash primarily explores animal behavior, whereas van den Berghe looks at human societies.

DESCRIPTION AND EXPLANATION OF MALE REALITY

Masculinity

Both forms of conservatism are *essentialist*; that is, they attribute intrinsically different natures to men and women. The social roles of masculinity and femininity are considered by conservatives to be manifestations of these intrinsic natures. Although the moral and biological conservative approaches do not always concur regarding the means by which these social roles are created, they do agree that male and female natures put constraints on the types of behaviors and attitudes that are generally available to men and women.

The moral conservatives' view of masculinity is familiar to anyone exposed to American middle-class values. Men, in their civilized role, are believed to be providers for families, protectors of women and children, and fathers to their children (Gilder 1973:103–114; Gilder 1986:190; Blankenhorn 1995:102). Men compete with each other and enjoy taking risks; they are the initiators of sexual encounters; and they are socially and politically more powerful and more influential than women. Men may enjoy their families, but childcare and domestic work are not high priorities for them; they need "masculine-affirming" work in order to feel that they are contributing to society. They enjoy sports both as participants and as spectators. And, finally, they are wary of emotional expression and tend to depend upon women for the satisfaction of their intimate emotional needs.

According to moral conservatives, society must encourage these behaviors and attitudes in men because such a social order constrains male nature in ways that are beneficial to society (Blankenhorn 1995:114–115). Indeed, the conservative view of unsocialized, unconstrained male nature is not very flattering. In an interview with Michael McLeod, Gilder states that men are "barbarians." By this he means that they tend naturally toward "short-term gratification" rather than toward "perpetuating the species" or "transmitting values to future generations" (McLeod 1986; Gilder 1986:39–47). Male nature with respect to civilization is "empty," "undirected," and a "limp nullity"; it has no "agenda or civilized role inscribed in it" (Gilder 1973:18, 19; compare Blankenhorn 1995:17). Blankenhorn prefers "narcissistic" as the summation of male nature before it is "domesticated" into a civilized role (Blankenhorn 1995:102, 115, 225). Left alone, male nature produces violent and destructively competitive behavior (Gilder 1973:97–98, 263; Gilder 1986:13).

Gilder offers two arguments to support his characterization of male nature as barbaric. First, he points to all-male societies, such as the Marine Corps, as examples of the violent, destructive, and competitive world of men left to their own natures; they are societies without "nurturance," "love," or "commitment to the future" (Gilder 1973:275). Second, he argues that the lives of single men exemplify male nature unfettered by the social constraints of marriage and family. "The single man is disposed to criminality, drugs, and violence. He is irresponsible about his debts, alcoholic, accident-prone, and susceptible to disease. Unless he can marry, he is often destined for a troubled life" (Gilder 1986:30). It is single men, Gilder reminds us, who account for 90 percent of all violent crimes (Gilder 1973:5, 208; Gilder 1986:188). Blankenhorn tends to argue that a careful examination of the statistics about male violence shows that it is not so often husbands as it is single men outside of marriage who batter partners and molest children (Blankenhorn 1995:35–42).

But masculinity, in its gender role and associated stereotype and ideal, is the civilized veneer that society imposes on men in its effort to control their antisocial nature. It is a "social contrivance" and "cultural invention" that is produced and maintained by external constraints (Gilder 1973:98, 203). Unless men act in a civilized manner, as fathers, protectors, and providers, society is deprived of their positive contributions and subject to the negative impact of their natures. "Only socialized males can usually contribute to the great corporations and bureaucracies . . . in modern societies" (Gilder 1973:210). "The crucial process of civilization is the subordination of male sexual impulses and psychology to long-term horizons of female biology. . . . It is male behavior that must be changed to create a civilized order" (Gilder 1973:24; Gilder 1986:188). As Blankenhorn puts it, "Fatherhood must domesticate masculinity" (Blankenhorn 1995:225).

A society intent on domesticating male nature must meet three conditions. First, there must be women in this society. Whereas male nature is antisocial and empty of values, female nature is filled with promise and the values of civilization (Gilder 1973:14, 20, 97–99). The differences between men and women transcend the physical plane (Gilder 1973:246). "Women control . . . the life force in our society and our lives . . . [and determine] the level of happiness, energy, creativity, and solidarity in the nation" (Gilder 1973:27; Gilder 1986:183). Second, women must exercise their erotic power over men; that is, they must offer sexual gratification to the male in exchange for his agreement to her demands for monogamy, marriage, and his roles as provider and protector (Gilder 1973:38, 98; Gilder 1986:18). Third, society must support women in their efforts "to secure these commitments from males" (Gilder 1973:78). It does so by investing "marriage with ceremonial sanctity" and by providing a role for males that is affirming and yet connects them to the family (Gilder 1973:78, 111, 263; Blankenhorn 1995:230–231). The masculine-affirming role is compatible with male nature in that it involves risk taking, independence, and competition; but it channels what could be antisocial expressions of these male tendencies into *socially beneficial* ones (Gilder 1973:97, 109, 213–214).

In sum, moral conservatives see masculinity as a triumph of civilization over nature, requiring that women have power over men and that men make the greater sacrifice. "When appraising the real power of the sexes, it is difficult to conceive of a measure less pertinent . . . than the number of male Senators and millionaires. Most people enjoy their real gratification . . . in the domestic and sexual areas, where female power is inevitably greatest" (Gilder 1973:12–13; Gilder 1986:17–18). But "it is men who make the major sexual sacrifice. The man renounces his dream of short-term freedom and self-fulfillment in order to serve a woman and family for a lifetime" (Gilder 1986:32).

The sociobiological conservatives' account of masculinity begins with a different set of assumptions. The human male is no different from males of other species in that he is subject to the evolutionary process of natural selection. During this process, individuals reproduce at different rates, some more successfully than others; and more copies of their genetic material reach future generations (Barash 1982:392). According to the theory of sociobiology, each individual male has two properties that are important in predicting his eventual success. The first is his *fitness;* the second, his *inclusive fitness.*

The fitness of an individual is a number representing the expected number of offspring of that individual in a certain environment. In the limiting case where the male is sterile, this number is zero. Fitter individuals are more likely to be represented in succeeding generations relative to that environment. On the other hand, the inclusive fitness of an individual is a number representing the *sum* of his fitness and the fitness of his relatives (kin), whereby the relatives are valued less as they become more distant (Barash 1982:392). Thus, a sterile man whose sister has two children possesses a greater inclusive fitness than a sterile man whose second cousin has two children. In both cases, his inclusive fitness is a positive number, even if his fitness is zero; and his genetic material is represented in succeeding generations. As David P. Barash has concluded, "The central principle of sociobiology [is] . . . that individuals will tend to behave in a manner that maximizes their inclusive fitness, their success in projecting copies of their genes into succeeding generations" (Barash 1982:45–46).

As society is a group of interacting individuals who are trying to be biologically successful, the masculine social role is simply a set of strategies for maximizing inclusive fitness (van den Berghe 1979:12–13; Wilson 1976:20–23). In looking at human society biological conservatives find men to be "aggressive, hasty, fickle, and undiscriminating" (Wilson 1976:125–126). Male nature is shaped by the strategies that have increased inclusive fitness. These strategies include male social and political dominance, male disinterest in childrearing, men as protectors and providers, men as initiators, aggressors, and competitors, and men as promiscuous (polygynous)—that is, sexually involved with several women either serially or at the same time (Wilson 1976:125, 128–131; van den Berghe 1979:142, 197). Behaviors such as male aggression were "fashioned during our long evolutionary childhood, when such behavior might well have maximized the fitness of those doing so" (Barash 1982:354).

Sociobiological conservatives offer a different story from that of moral conservatives as to why men behave as they do. The sociobiological account is that men and women pursue different strategies because men produce far more sperm than women produce eggs. Once a woman contains a fertilized egg, she cannot be reimpregnated. So, if she is to maximize her inclusive fitness, she must invest considerable effort in bringing the fetus to term and raising the child to self-sufficiency. In so doing she automatically reproduces copies of the father's genes. The father, on the other hand, is free to impregnate another female and thereby to increase his inclusive fitness. Furthermore, if he can compete successfully with other males and control more resources he will attract more females, who in turn will promote their own biological advantage by becoming his "property" (Wilson 1976:126; van den Berghe 1979:62).

Biological conservatives, unlike moral conservatives, do not ascribe to females (human or otherwise) "erotic power" over males. Rather, they believe that males have the power to initiate and maintain sexual partnerships. Indeed, they even describe rape as a reproductive strategy among the male's bag of "dirty tricks" (Wilson 1976:125; van den Berghe 1979:107, 126, 143; Barash 1982:269). In short, biological conservatives do not question the universality of male dominance in contemporary society (Wilson 1976:126; van den Berghe 1979:196–197).

The conservative perspective holds that men are everything that many feminist writers have condemned; they are aggressive, dominant, and competitive (cf. Millett 1970:42–43). For moral conservatives, the worst of these tendencies can be overridden and channeled into civilized forms, if women are sufficiently feminine and society backs them up. But for biological conservatives these tendencies are the result of natural selection; they are reproductive strategies that work. According to moral conservatives, civilization must triumph *over* male nature; for biological conservatives, civilization *is* the triumph of male nature.

Feminism

Moral conservatives recognize that there are different feminisms—specifically, radical feminism and liberal feminism (Gilder 1973:153, 201). But it is to the liberal feminists, represented by such organizations as the National Organization for Women, to which moral conservatives usually refer when speaking of "feminism" (Gilder 1973:153–161). According to these conservatives it is the liberal feminist agenda—including the Equal Rights Amendment; affirmative action goals in the workplace, the military, and the major political parties; court decisions favoring the right of women to choose an abortion; sex education in the schools; a national daycare program; and increased welfare for poor women with children—that is effectively weakening the traditional roles of men and women.

As noted, moral conservatives see masculinity as a triumph of culture over nature. The civilized male role depends directly on external constraints that control men's natural inclinations. Because the male social role is a "cultural contrivance," Gilder considers this role to be especially "vulnerable" to the liberal feminist agenda; it is the "Achilles' heel of civilized society" (Gilder 1973:203). Feminists, he maintains, have targeted this weakness in the traditional social order and are thereby damaging men's opportunities to assume the masculine role.

Let us look at two cases in which the male role is subverted by liberal feminism, according to the conservative perspective. Specifically, we shall examine the moral conservative view of the struggle by feminists to give women control over their own bodies in matters of sexuality, reproduction, and economic independence.

For liberal feminists a woman's right to control her body includes her right to choose whether she is sexual, with whom, how, and whether that sex is ultimately procreative or attendant to her own needs. According to Betty Friedan, women have been enduring sexual objects for male satisfaction and, when needed, the vessels for male procreation (Friedan 1963:255). This objectified role is oppressive to women and precludes a richer and more mature relationship with men (Friedan 1963:263).

Such thinking strikes moral conservatives as a form of sexual liberation, as a reflection of the belief that sex need not be restricted to procreative sex within the heterosexual marriage. Gilder, in particular, claims that when sex loses contact with its procreative source, it "becomes increasingly promiscuous and undifferentiated, homosexual, and pornographic. . . . It becomes in essence a form of sensuous massage" (Gilder 1973:45). The bonding between men and women that is so essential to the family is lost; and, ultimately, all forms of sexual liberation undermine this bonding (Gilder 1973:33). Moreover, as society gives way to unmarried mothers, lesbians, and female masturbation, men turn away from family and toward cathartic sports, violence, and drugs (Gilder 1973:110–111, 240–241).

For Gilder, the male nature, under the best of conditions, is hard to domesticate; men will not submit to civilization if their short-term gratifications can easily be met without it. And the feminist agenda, with its openness to nonprocreative sexual freedom for women, helps to create precisely the conditions under which men can avoid commitment and family. At present, Gilder maintains, women are losing their "erotic power over men" and society is succumbing to "the male pattern of insecurity, dominance, and group aggression" (Gilder 1973:276; see also Gilder 1973:6, 63, 111, 114). Feminism is thus damaging the very foundations of society, weakening the power of women, and making masculinity unattractive to men (Gilder 1973:265, 277).

From the outset, liberal feminism has advocated greater androgyny in social roles; that is, women are encouraged to achieve greater economic independence while it is hoped that men will take over an equal share of domestic labor within the home. In an early 1970s leaflet entitled *Who Cares About Women's Rights*, NOW urges women toward parity with men in employment, pay, credit, insurance pensions, fringe benefits, and Social Security. In a 1970 press release, NOW asserts that "the care and welfare of children is incumbent on society and parents. We reject the idea that mothers have a special child care role that is not to be shared equally by fathers" (Griswold 1993:245).

For conservatives such as Gilder and Blankenhorn, both prongs of this feminist agenda are recipes for disaster. As to women making equal economic contributions, Gilder argues that it would take an economic miracle to create enough jobs without displacing employed men to accommodate the millions of women who might wish to enter the work force. Gilder argues that "men . . . drop out virtually in proportion to the entry of women . . . into the work force" (Gilder 1973:188). Contributing to this decline in the motivation of men to work are the "college girls" who come into the workplace and "exorcise" the "rites and symbols" that make work "masculine affirming" (Gilder 1973:188). In the end, Gilder concludes, it is the upper classes that benefit from double incomes and spousal part-time work. For the lower- and middle-class men who need to work at least full time to make ends meet and the women who have poor employment prospects, male unemployment and underemployment are the results of women entering the work force (Gilder 1973:194–195; Gilder 1986:94–95). Poorer women will find it increasingly difficult to keep their men at home; they will be forced to take low-paying work and to abandon their role of domesticating their husbands and sons (Gilder 1973:25, 71–72, 195–196; Gilder 1986:94–95). Ultimately, policing the growing number of antisocial (unemployed) males will become "the chief concern of the state" (Gilder 1973:196).

Both Gilder and Blankenhorn also see a growing state of fatherlessness in a society committed to economic androgyny (Gilder 1986:95; Blankenhorn 1995). But Blankenhorn also explicitly sees moral decay in a society where men try to be androgynous parents along with women. Blankenhorn labels those who support the ideal of equal parenting as advocates of the New Father philosophy (Blankenhorn:114–115). Behind this philosophy, "The ideal of androgynous fatherhood—fatherhood without masculinity—emerges as the animating principle of the contemporary New Father model" (Blankenhorn 1995:117). But Blankenhorn argues that "the New Father philosophy of breadwinning is antithetical to the basic psychosocial dynamic of fatherhood. The onset of the 'parental emergency' requires dual mobilization. The mother mobilizes to nurture the child. The father mobilizes to nurture the mother and provide for his family" (Blankenhorn 1995:114–15). But this "New Father model is a mirage. It purports to be about fatherhood, but it is not. There is no father there. The New Father is a missing Father" (Blankenhorn 1995:102). In short, a father's role is in the masculine affirming roles of provider and protector. To try to share this with a woman or to try to take over the nurturing of children is to abandon one's "natural" role and thereby leave such a family fatherless. The historical results of the attempt at androgynous fathering in combination with the sharing of economic provider roles with women is the breakdown of civilization—youth violence, domestic violence, child sexual abuse, poverty, and teen pregnancy are the results (Blanken-horn 1995:27–48).

Some biological conservatives are equally worried about the impact of feminism. For them, feminism can only create social costs and tyranny as legislation and policy confront the biological foundations of gender. Steven Goldberg argues that women will bear the "brunt of this process" (Goldberg 1993:277). If women move into the "superfamilial areas" such as business, politics, and social leadership, they will suffer from a strong sense of not doing what they ought to be doing. If women end up competing with men in these areas, they will lose (Goldberg 1993:229). Thus, the feminist liberal agenda misleads women and promises what it cannot deliver. Michael Levin similarly argues that "moral prescriptions and social programs cannot be concocted in an empirical vacuum. It is senseless to try to make the sexes conform to an . . . ideal if they cannot conform to it. What is obviously unattainable cannot be the object of rational human effort" (Levin 1980:25). Goldberg and Levin are much more deterministic than are their sociobiological counterparts; in other words, they believe that in virtually any environment men will be masculine and women feminine in traditional ways. At the same time, they seem to fear more than do other biological conservatives the social dangers of trying to alter these predispositions.

The biological conservatism of Edward O. Wilson, Pierre van den Berghe, and David P. Barash is more cautious. These sociobiologists are willing to give social learning a greater role in the creation of gender roles, and thus they open the door for some feminist reforms. But their attitude remains skeptical; they do not believe that feminist goals are easily met or that the feminist agenda has produced substantial changes in traditional gender roles, even in the most experimental of human societies. As Wilson puts it, "I am suggesting that the contradictions [i.e., the failures of the kibbutz movement to successfully move men and women into nontraditional roles] are rooted in the surviving relics of our prior genetic history, and that one of the most inconvenient and senseless but nevertheless unavoidable of these residues is the modest predisposition toward sex role differences" (Wilson 1976:135). Barash and van den Berghe echo Wilson's thesis: "To a limited extent, sexual roles can be modified in the direction of equalization of parental load, but even the most 'liberated' husband cannot share pregnancy with his wife. In any case, most societies make no attempt to equalize parental care: they leave women holding the babies" (van den Berghe and Barash 1977:813). Van den Berghe's skepticism about the impact of feminism is obvious: "Neither the National Organization for Women nor the Equal Rights Amendment will change the biological bedrock of asymmetrical parental investment" (van den Berghe 1979:196).

ASSESSMENT OF MALE REALITY AND
AGENDA FOR CHANGE

From the moral conservatives' view of feminism we can derive an idea of their assessment of male reality. Gilder, for instance, maintains that we are heading toward a "sexual suicide society." Moral conservatives believe that women's independence from men and from traditional social roles has resulted in a dramatic increase in the number of antisocial males. That is, feminist gains for women have come at the costs of making the masculine role unattractive or unattainable for men, expanding the power of the state to regulate individual lives, and increasing the disparity between rich and poor. In short, claim the conservatives, the feminist agenda has made it more difficult for women to keep men at home.

The moral conservatives' vision of a feminist future is cataclysmic: Feminism is leading to "an act of genocide that dwarfs any in human history" (Gilder 1973:265). At stake, they insist, is the family, in which social values are created and reproduced; it is being attacked through its weakest link—masculinity, the male role. And the end of the family is the end of civilization. Blankenhorn, as we have noted, considers fatherlessness brought about through the New Father philosophy, easy divorce, and welfare payments that replace the father to be "our most urgent social problem" (Blankenhorn 1995). Gilder perceives the damage to society to be so great that he must seriously ask: "Will we manage to maintain our most indispensable condition of civilization—an obstacle to totalitarian usurpation—the human marriage and family?" (Gilder 1973:278).

Of course, feminism is not the only source of the social unraveling of masculinity; moral conservatives also blame liberals, big government, big business, utopian planning, and the impact of these factors on the conditions of work. For example, men often find their civilized role unattractive because the workplace itself is filled with abuses of power, inhuman treatment, "monotony," and "impotent dependency" (Gilder 1973:206). A man is often "doomed to a lifetime of tough and relatively unremunerative labor in support of his family," causing him to be absent from the family in a "hostile environment" (Gilder 1973:113, 242). The male worker is totally "replaceable," and his value is set not by his humanity but by the market (Gilder 1973:106; Gilder 1986:172).

Moral conservatives offer a lengthy agenda to prevent social unraveling; much of the rhetoric of that agenda is centered on the restoration and preservation of the traditional family. Gilder, for one, is emphatic in his criterion for sound social policy: "The society is chiefly an assemblage of families. . . . Unless we take this reality into account, our politics will fail to achieve its goals—will fail to foster the happiness and fulfillment of our citizens. A sound social policy will devote itself to promoting the creation and maintenance of family connections" (Gilder 1973:151). In addition to the usual urgings on behalf of the family, Blankenhorn suggests that all legislation and policy be tested as to whether it strengthens or weakens the institution of marriage. He further suggests that sperm banks be available only to married couples (Blankenhorn 1995:231, 233). The conservative author William Gribbin argues that there can be no "recovery in economics, defense, and international affairs," no reversal of the social disintegration of "abortion, pornography, violence, drug abuse, and the general collapse of theistic norms" until "the bourgeois social order" is reestablished (Gribbin 1986:61). Conservative think-tanks such as the Heritage Foundation and the Free Congress Foundation call for "a conservative opportunity society, in which the dynamism of innovation is sustained by moral order, strong family life and the continuous tradition of Western culture" (Calamai 1988). Similar themes are repeated by conservative women's groups such as the U.S.-based Eagle Forum (whose spokesperson is Phyllis Schlafly) and Real Women in Canada.

The moral conservatives' agenda calls for three kinds of measures. In the first category are those measures that undo the damage of existing (antifamily) programs. Conservative attempts to end affirmative-action programs, welfare structures, access to abortion, and sex education all fall within this first category. Second is the concerted effort being made to block new policies that might further weaken the traditional family. Conservative resistance to the Equal Rights Amendment, comparable-worth legislation, and legislation that extends nondiscrimination laws to gay men and lesbian women are examples. Finally, there are the positive measures intended to strengthen the family, such as greater tax exemptions for children, severe penalties for males who fail to support children, tax breaks for families that choose church-affiliated schools, tax credits for full-time homemakers, and support for family businesses.

Ultimately, many of these conservative measures are attempting to shore up the traditional masculine role with its associated ideals, inasmuch as these ideals are perceived to be most damaged by contemporary feminism. Men must have opportunities to work, to be primary providers, and to take risks (i.e., as entrepreneurs), hence society must exert strong external constraints (rewards and punishment) in order to keep men at home. Men are the focus of the conservatives' social policy for the simple reason that they are assumed to have natural antisocial tendencies. Men, therefore, are seen as the core of the problem.

For conservatives, utopia is never just around the corner. Even if a "conservative opportunity society" were created, it could never be a utopia. Human nature, especially male nature, is too flawed; men have a tendency to degenerate even under optimal conditions. In any case, moral conservative thinking involves a deep distrust of utopian planning (Gilder 1973:141). It is characteristic of such planning to assume that human problems can be solved from the top down, using human reason and the coercive powers of the federal government. Indeed, one of the central complaints of conservatives against feminists and liberals is that they have enlisted the power of the federal government in civil rights laws, affirmative-action legislation, and welfare laws—in other words, that they are engaged in social engineering based on utopian planning (Nisbet 1986:105). Even right-wing antichoice activists are guilty of violating this conservative principle when, for example, they try to pass legislation banning abortions rather than leaving such decisions to the "local" community. (The recent Webster decision by the Supreme Court, giving greater power to the states in setting the criteria for abortion, is a conservative as opposed to right-wing view.)

According to moral conservatives, healthy social change occurs through the agency of individuals in small family and community units; it occurs because these individuals trust their experiences and their feelings rather than some grand social vision (Nisbet 1986:29–31). The true constitution and wisdom of society are found not in the reasonings of academics but in the feelings and actions of the community. Paradoxically, the restoration of the family can come about only through the family. "Individuals grow and gain in strength not principally through government, but rather through other institutions . . . like family, church, school, civic associations" (Bennett 1988:39).

Whereas moral conservatives see civilized society on the brink of disaster and the traditional male role as eroding at an alarming rate, biological conservatives tend to find universality and stability in human society. Efforts at change have been made and are being made, but these have failed and will fail. Women are left holding the baby while men provide for them.

Unlike moral conservatives, sociobiologists do *not* claim that the traditional roles of males are morally preferable or that women *should* be dominated socially and politically. But biological conservatives do argue that it is neither realistic nor rational to try to change what is so well established in our ancestral infancy. Thus, they come to the conclusion that it is wrong to try to eliminate practices based on biology. Consider van den Berghe's dismissal of feminist ideology:

> Ideological passions unfortunately contaminate our way of looking at data and interpreting them. I am not suggesting that male dominance is good, but that it [simply] *is*. Nor do I deny that individual women can dominate over individual men. On the average, however, males are dominant and the more dominant have, throughout our past evolutionary history, been the more re-

productively successful. . . . Women can try to assert their dominance, but it is often at the cost of disrupting existing pair-bonds. Not surprisingly, many women never try. (van den Berghe 1979:197–198)

Compare that passage to Goldberg:

There's a sense, of course, in which none of this matters. Whatever their beliefs, men and women are still men and women, and beliefs that require the impossible are not taken seriously by reality. But the attitudes and values held by men and women do determine whether they live their lives on a dance floor or a battlefield, and this is not such a little thing. (Goldberg 1993:283)

Edward O. Wilson prefers to talk about the role of sociobiology in developing social policies. But many of his comments about the proper social agenda contradict those of the moral conservatives. Wilson attacks the ideas that sex is for procreation and that masturbation or homosexuality is unnatural. Social policies, he claims, have too often been the result of the natural-law theory of the moral conservatives. "This theory is in error. The laws it addresses are biological, were written by natural selection, require little if any enforcement by religious or secular authorities and have been erroneously interpreted by theologians writing in ignorance of biology" (Wilson 1976:141–142). Specifically, and contrary to Gilder's remarks about homosexual men, Wilson argues that homosexuality is universal among human societies, that both gay men and lesbian women are well adapted in their social relationships, and that male homosexuals are upwardly mobile. Moreover, homosexuality is just another way for an individual to maximize inclusive fitness by giving up his or her own reproduction to aid in the raising of siblings. From which Wilson concludes: "It would be tragic to continue to discriminate against homosexuals on the basis of religious dogma supported by the unlikely assumption that they are biologically unnatural" (Wilson 1976:147).

Biological knowledge is essential for our assessment of social agendas. It allows us to see the costs of certain policies. Wilson, for example, allows that society could go a long way toward greater equality between men and women but that such equality could be achieved only at a cost. Every social order, even the present one, has costs that must be calculated. "There is a cost, which no one can yet measure, awaiting the society that moves either from juridical equality of opportunity between the sexes to a statistical equality of their performance in the professions, or back toward deliberate sexual discrimination" (Wilson 1976:147).

We can gain insight into Wilson's point by imagining the possible costs to a society that tries to eradicate male promiscuity, assuming that sociobiological theory is correct in its description of male sexuality. Inasmuch as men have a tendency toward promiscuity and women have a tendency to seek acceptance by dominant males, a society that intends to free itself of male promiscuity would have to implement severe measures of monitoring and punishing both men and women. And as the most promiscuous men are, in the sociobiological view, among the most powerful and productive, such measures of control would probably reduce productivity and result in their flight from that society. Thus, the biological knowledge of human tendencies helps us to determine that the price is high if we want to eliminate male promiscuity. For some social agendas it may be worth the cost; for others it may not. But Wilson contends that sociobiology does not involve itself in this final moral judgment.

> The evidences of biological constraint alone cannot prescribe the ideal course of action. However, they can help us to define the options and to assess the price of each. The price is to be measured in the added energy required for education and reinforcement and in the attrition of individual freedom and potential. . . . Since every option has a cost, concrete ethical principles will rarely find universal acceptance. (Wilson 1976:134)

The 1990s have seen the rise of new variations on conservative themes, and many of those who adhere to these variations have come to political power in Canada (Reform Party) and the United States (Republican Party). Crudely stated, such conservatives believe that economic matters should be decided by an unregulated market. They oppose federal regulations over industry, for instance in pollution control, affirmative action, worker safety, and sexual harassment laws. They also generally oppose international protectionism in favor of free trade. But on social and moral issues they favor federal interventions to strengthen the family, teach values in school, teach pro-America history, abolish abortions, support church schools, and encourage prayer in public schools. Thus, unlike classical moral conservatives, who are suspicious of federal intervention at any level of daily life, these neoconservatives strongly advocate federal intrusion in support of their values while also advocating a hands-off attitude regarding economic life. Such conservatives sometimes bolster their defense of traditional gender roles by appealing to sociobiological claims about male and female nature. Consider Newt Gingrich's famous remarks opposing equal roles for men and women in the military in his 1995 lecture "Renewing American Civilization" at Georgia's Reinhardt Junior College: "If combat means being in a ditch, females have biological problems staying in a ditch for thirty days because they get infections, and they don't have upper body strength. I mean, some do, but they're relatively rare. On the other hand, men are basically little piglets, you drop them in the ditch, they roll around in it, doesn't matter, you know. These things are very real" (quoted by Clarence Page, *Seattle Post-Intelligencer*, January 24, 1995).

In Nisbet's words this conservative movement "... is less interested in Burkean immunities from government power than it is in putting a maximum of governmental power in the hands of those who can be trusted. It is the control of power, not diminution of power, that ranks high" (Nisbet 1986:105).

CRITIQUE: CRITICISMS AND RESPONSES

Criticism 1

The sociobiological view of the extent to which social matters are influenced by biological factors is muddled and perhaps contradictory. On the one hand, Wilson often talks like a biological determinist—as when he claims that "the question of interest is no longer whether human social behavior is genetically determined; it is to what extent" (Wilson 1976:19). Wilson then goes on to say that human behavior is biologically determined to a greater extent than anyone has heretofore realized—a very strong claim given the history of science, which is riddled with claims of biological determinism of the most extreme kind. When van den Berghe looks at the extent to which human behavior is shaped by either genes or culture, he attributes only the most trivial behaviors to culture: For instance, Frenchmen shake hands more than do Englishmen (van den Berghe 1979:7). Thus, on the one hand, sociobiology characterizes genes as the major cause of important social behaviors.

On the other hand, Wilson and van den Berghe acknowledge that each individual is shaped in important ways by his or her environment, that biology and culture share equally in this formation (Wilson 1976:18; van den Berghe 1979:8). In one text, Wilson goes so far as to say that genes have given away most of their "sovereignty" (Wilson 1975:550). Thus we find that genes play a *slight* or at best *equal* causal role in the formation of social behaviors.

Such vacillation creates the impression that Wilson and others hold to both a "hard" and "soft" sociobiology, the former being much more deterministic than the latter (cf. Gould 1977:253). Hard sociobiology is defended by sociobiologists who want to stress the originality of their theory; the soft version is defended by the same scientists when faced by critics who point out the obvious cultural and learning components in human behavior. The upshot of this confusion is that one does not know what to make of the sociobiological claim that biology influences the social behavior. It is also much harder to separate Wilson from his unwanted allies who clearly espouse a rigid determinism, such as F. D. Winner in *Genetic Basis of Society* (1983) and Steven Goldberg in *The Inevitability of Patriarchy* (1974).

Response

The contradiction is more apparent than real. The sociobiological view is that genes and culture are equally important to social development. Wilson's apparently conflicting claims are made in different contexts. When Wilson confronts radical environmentalists who believe that all behavior is learned, he emphasizes the importance of genetic influence. When not concerned with such radical views, he is able to put more stress on the importance of culture in the formation of social behaviors. Certainly Wilson, van den Berghe, and Barash subscribe neither to the determinism of Goldberg and Winner nor to their belief in male supremacy. In fact, Winner and Goldberg cannot be described as sociobiologists; they are simply advocates of a crude, rigidly deterministic social Darwinism.

Criticism 2

The moral conservative view depends heavily on the concepts of "intrinsic nature," "inseparable traits," and "essence." But these concepts are so vague that the conservative view is finally unintelligible. As the philosopher and feminist critic Christine Pierce has noted:

> "Nature" and "human nature" must be among the most enigmatic concepts ever used. Often, when the "natural" is invoked, we are left in the dark as to whether it is meant as an explanation, a recommendation, a claim for determinism, or simply a desperate appeal, as if the "natural" were some sort of metaphysical glue that could hold our claims and values together. (Pierce 1971:242)

Gilder's writings, too, leave one wondering about what is natural, and what is included in male nature and female nature. On the one hand, he describes male nature as empty and not directed toward procreation (Gilder 1973:18–19), but, on the other, he says that men have an unconscious desire to procreate (Gilder 1973:99–100). Elsewhere he notes that there are no "human beings, just men and women" and that this is "the nature of things" (Gilder 1986:165). Does he mean that men and women are so different that they have no traits in common? A belief in such radical essentialism would account for his conviction that an androgynous society is "behavioral gibberish," because such a society would require "patterns of activity that so violate the inner constitution of the species that they cannot be integrated with our irreducible human natures"

(Gilder 1973:251). Yet, in another text, Gilder claims that many women do not have to adopt traditional roles, that they can perform work that is "essentially masculine" if they have the will and the skill to do so (Gilder 1973:262–263). Have these women accomplished the impossible task of integrating masculine work into their inner constitutions, then? We do not know because we are not told what these "irreducible human natures" are.

Gilder also vacillates on the question as to what degree nature shapes society. When he stresses the role of nature in shaping society, he refers to society as durable and virtually impervious to the feminist revolution ("men will remain men and women women"); but when he talks of society as a cultural contrivance, society is suddenly something very fragile and vulnerable to the feminist agenda (Gilder 1973:201–203).

We are thus left with a rather murky conservative view of *nature*. Sometimes what is natural is what "ought" to be: The nuclear family is natural; heterosexuality is natural. Sometimes what is natural is what derives from basic human needs: Marriage is unnatural for men, and homosexuality may well be as natural as heterosexuality. Without clarity in this area moral conservatism becomes confused and confusing—yet the perspective depends on this concept. That is, both the description and the explanation of social reality depend on a clear understanding of male and female *nature*; the conservative perspective holds that other perspectives such as feminism are wrong because they go against *nature*; and the conservative agenda seeks to restore what is *natural* in human relationships. Why should we give credence to any view grounded in such an enigma?

Response

What is natural is often controversial. If we are to understand nature we must look to the traditional wisdom of society. Of course, "human nature" cannot be fully explained, but it can be understood as part of that traditional wisdom. And, ultimately, we have the guidance of "Scripture" in helping us to know what is natural and unnatural (Gilder 1986; Nisbet 1986:35–36).

Criticism 3

Sociobiology attempts to explain a number of general behaviors—homosexuality, male dominance, war, rape, male hierarchies, differential parental investment, and so on. Sociobiologists consider such factors to be universal in human society and prevalent among nonhuman animals as well. The fact that a behavior is found in both humans and nonhumans is strong evidence that it contributes to biological success (i.e., helps to maximize inclusive fitness).

Critics such as Anne Fausto-Sterling argue, however, that this talk about universals is filled with "linguistic hat tricks." In its search for universals, sociobiology characterizes animal behavior indiscriminately and tends to "confuse the meanings of two different behaviors" (Fausto-Sterling 1985:161). Fausto-Sterling notes that sociobiologists apply the term *rape* not only to humans but also to animals and even to cross-fertilizing plants. She argues that such word use conflates meanings and anthropomorphizes animals but, worse yet, ignores the implication that rape is a crime that occurs when a woman is unable or unwilling to give her consent. Similar arguments apply to sociobiological extensions to the animal world of such terms as *slavery, war, communication,* and *altruism.* As applied to human beings, these words have political, legal, and consentual content that precludes their application to animals or plants. Description of animal behavior is a serious problem for ethologists who are usually very careful not to import human connotations; and when a common word is used, it is carefully qualified (Fausto-Sterling 1985:161). One can only speculate as to why sociobiologists are not more precise. If they were to offer reasonably rigorous definitions of terms like *rape* and *war,* they would lose many if not all of the "universals" between humans and animals—but these universals are the very objects whose explanation is the proud accomplishment of sociobiology.

Response

It is true that human rape is a crime and that failure to consent is part of the content of human rape, but in evolutionary theory these characteristics are irrelevant to the study of reproductive strategy. Barash responds to this criticism as follows:

> Some people may bridle at the notion of rape in animals but the term seems entirely appropriate when we examine what happens. Among ducks for example, pairs typically form early in the breeding season. . . . When this rite finally culminates in mounting, both male and female are clearly in agreement. But sometimes strange males surprise a mated female and attempt to force immediate copulation. . . . If that's not rape, it is certainly very much like it. (Barash 1979:54)

Furthermore, to note the universality of rape is not to endorse it or justify it; in fact a recognition of its universality is useful to writing informed laws to control it.

Criticism 4

Sociobiology offers a seemingly simple picture of male nature: Male aggression results in male dominance over females, and male competition creates hierarchies among human (and primate) males. As Wilson states, "The physical and temperamental differences between men and women have been amplified by culture into universal male dominance" (Wilson 1976:128). The same is true of "little brother species" such as chimpanzees and other primates with whom humans share certain genes (Wilson 1976:31). Through their greater aggressiveness, males come to dominate females, not just among humans but in the animal world generally (Barash 1982:339–359).

Yet studies of primates and humans offer a more complex picture. Different criteria of dominance yield different, nonoverlapping hierarchies among males as well as between males and females. Furthermore, dominance has not been correlated with greater access to resources, and it is by no means clear that the more dominant males mate more frequently or more successfully than the subordinate males, contrary to two very important sociobiological assumptions (Leibowitz 1979).

Nor do human aggression studies unequivocally support the sociobiological view. In the first place these studies often employ very different concepts of aggression. Some studies of children count only unprovoked attempts to harm as aggressive behavior, but others include rough-and-tumble play, defensive or self-protecting behavior, and even mock-aggression (Satzman 1979). Not all of these studies conclude that human males are more aggressive than human females. In their book *The Psychology of Sex Differences* (1974), Eleanor E. Maccoby and Carol Nagy Jacklin reviewed ninety studies on human aggression. They found that 33–50 percent indicated no significant sex-related differences in human aggression, 46 to 61 percent assessed males to be more aggressive, and 8 percent assessed females to be more aggressive (Fausto-Sterling 1985:148). Later studies of aggression are even less supportive of Wilson's suggestion that greater male aggressiveness is universal (Tieger 1980).

Philip Kitcher, in his detailed critique of sociobiology, offers another striking example of sociobiology's desperate pursuit of universals. First he cites David Barash's remark that "monogamy is . . . almost unheard of in primates" (Barash 1979:65). Next he notes that the "unheard of" social behavior among primates actually occurs in about 18 percent of primates (i.e., 37 out of the more than 200 species studied). Kitcher argues that sociobiologists use only selected information because they have an optimal strategy in mind even before they look at any evidence. Then, consciously or unconsciously, they see the world as consisting of such strategies; everything else is judged an exception. Thus, Kitcher concludes, "we arrive at a curious situation. . . . Wilson's grand generalization, the claim that 'in the large majority of animal species' males are assertive and fickle, females passive and coy, turns out to fragment. . . . We should have no faith in so gerrymandered a generalization" (Kitcher 1985:174).

Response

Sociobiologists may be guilty of exaggeration, but even their critics have to admit that most studies find that males are dominant and more aggressive and that fewer than 20 percent of primates are monogamous. There may be environments in which male aggression has evolved differently, and there may even be environments in which males are less aggressive than females: Neither assumption is contrary to sociobiological theory. And environments in which primate males are monogamous obviously do exist. But the male aggressive-dominance behavior and promiscuity noted by sociobiologists is supported by most studies and is true in most environments. Noting the prevalence of this behavior is not a case of selecting only the favorable cases; rather, it is a matter of identifying the gross patterns that command our attention as evolutionary biologists.

Criticism 5

Moral conservatism, too, can be charged with looking only at the favorable evidence and ignoring the unfavorable. Gilder, for example, makes much of the difference between socialized (married) males and unsocialized (unmarried) males (Gilder 1973:97). The latter, he claims, are responsible for violent crimes such as assault and rape, whereas the former are the providers for and protectors of women.

With the development of feminist social science in the 1970s, the traditional family has been subjected to new research. Apparently it does not shine so brightly for feminist researchers as it does for moral conservatives. The former contend that the traditional family is hardly a safe and secure place for women, and that blaming single men for virtually all assault and rape is misleading. In fact, women are subjected to greater risk of sexual assault or battery at home than outside (Martin 1976; Finkelhor and Yllo 1985).

Violence is and always has been part of the traditional family. Marital rape, for example, is rarely considered a crime; even now the vast majority of rape laws have a marital rape-exemption clause, following British Chief Justice Mathew Hale's dictum that "the husband cannot be guilty of rape committed by himself upon his lawful wife" (Russell 1982:17). Battering by the husband in the traditional family has also been considered an acceptable form of paternal discipline. *The Effects of Marriage on Property and the Wife's Capacity,* written in 1879, states that "acts which would amount to an assault if committed against a stranger may be legally innocent when committed by a husband against a wife" (cited in Langley and Levy 1980:36). Today, husbands who batter are rarely reported; if reported, rarely arrested; and if arrested, rarely convicted.

If violence against women is legitimized within the family and married men can assault women with greater impunity than unmarried men, then, of course, unmarried men appear to be the perpetrators of violence and married men the protectors of women. But male violence is endemic in the traditional family. Hence the conservatives have either been misled to overlook such violence or they are guilty of creating a mythical picture of family life.

Response

Violence in the home is largely the result of fatherlessness in the family, exemplified by the black families of the ghetto (Gilder 1973:120–121). Much of society's violence is due to the lack of support for the family; "the large number of broken or unconsummated families . . . creates dire problems. For broken families are ineffective in socializing males" (Gilder 1973:119). However, married women, far from fearing for their safety, have been shown to be happier, more creative, more community involved, and more intellectual than either working women or men (Gilder 1973:225).

Criticism 6

Blankenhorn and Gilder, in their efforts to justify the nuclear family, oversimplify in the extreme. Fatherlessness simply cannot be the determining factor of teenage pregnancy, juvenile delinquency, and other problems. Sweden, for example, has almost the same percentage of women-headed single families as the United States but only a fraction of the teenage pregnancy rate, delinquency rate, and other problems Blankenhorn and Gilder single out (Jones, Tepperman, and Wilson 1995:116, 173). Furthermore, Gilder's and Blankenhorn's efforts to blame such conditions on too much government support is challenged by the fact that Sweden and other countries with fewer social problems offer significantly more government support. Higher levels of support, better educational opportunities, and encouragement seem to be a better remedy than forcing fathers to stay in the home (Jones, Tepperman, and Wilson 1995:173–174). Other researchers have reached the same conclusion: Fatherlessness does not contribute to problems at school or delinquency—poverty and its resultant change of peer group does (Schwarz 1995).

Response

Blankenhorn concedes much of the above argument when he notes that the feminization of poverty amounts to the masculinization of irresponsibility (Blankenhorn 1995:115). The poverty and the change of peer group that result from fatherlessness is precisely why fatherlessness in modern society needs to be addressed. The United States is not Sweden: There is no dependable national welfare system for women with children; it varies from state to state and from presidential administration to presidential administration. Hence, fathers are more important in the United States than in Sweden, especially as regards the financial stability of the family (cf. Whitehead 1993).

SUMMARY AND CONCLUSIONS

For moral conservatives, civilization involves a set of practiced values that can be maintained only if male nature is domesticated—that is, directed away from its natural antisocial inclinations and toward the masculine roles of protector and provider. As feminism has set an agenda that makes it harder to domesticate male nature, it constitutes what conservatives see as a threat to civilization. Whereas feminists perceive the social order as a patriarchy that exhibits the worst aspects of male nature, conservatives see the social order as that which protects us from the worst aspects of male nature.

The strengths of moral conservatism derive in part from the fact that it is the "received wisdom" about men and women. In other words, the appeal of this perspective may have something to do with its familiarity. But moral conservatism also offers detailed instructions to men on how to deal with their work, their relationships, and their children—in short, how to be masculine. It attempts to explain such diverse matters as why men work hard, belong to all-male civic organizations, and do not want women bosses. It tries to explain why men are attracted to pornography and extramarital affairs; it also explains why these are wrong. It criticizes feminism at a time when feminist movements are challenging and changing traditional male behaviors and attitudes. The moral conservative vision is so entrenched in American beliefs that few, if any, public officials, social theorists, families, or individuals can escape its influence. Its strength lies not in the fact that it honors tradition but in the fact that it *is* tradition.

Although biological conservatives also claim to be on the side of "conventional wisdom," they argue that this wisdom is scientifically founded (van den Berghe 1979:197). Sociobiology claims to be founded on both realism and science, a feature that makes it attractive to many people. We engage in the kinds of behavior that we do because they work; they allow men and women to be biologically successful. These behaviors are neither easily disrupted nor rapidly changed. But there is the promise that if we legislate with human nature in mind, society will become more humane.

Although these two conservative approaches differ in many particulars, they agree that *traditional* behaviors are appropriate to men and women. Together they form a loose alliance. Both moral conservatism and biological conservatism suggest that we will be happier if we maintain the traditional roles—either because we will live in a more civilized world or because we will be true to our natural tendencies. But both also face serious problems and criticisms; their foundations are murky and confused. There is a considerable body of evidence which suggests that reality is not as the conservatives would have it. And there is always the lingering suspicion that conservatism in either form primarily serves the purpose of creating a rationale for the present social order. Perhaps men and women would not be happier or better off in a "conservative opportunity society"; that, at least, is the view of most of the remaining perspectives.

SUGGESTED READING

The historically oriented reader might enjoy Barker-Benfield's *The Horrors of the Half-Known Life* (1976), a book that gives the reader a clear picture of the gender roles, stereotypes, and ideals of nineteenth-century moral conservatives. It also points up many remarkable parallels to twentieth-century conservatives. Stephanie Coontz's *The Way We Never Were: American Families and the Nostalgia Trap* (1992) offers a more critical look at the history of American families; it is a good counterbalance to the somewhat rosy picture from which many conservatives operate. Her perspective contrasts sharply with Blankenhorn's. Stephen Jay Gould's *The Mismeasure of Man* (1981) gives an excellent account of the efforts to attribute different social roles to biological differences. Gould covers the nineteenth- and early twentieth-century versions of biological determinism. Carol Tavris's *The Mismeasure of Woman* provides a perfect complement to Gould. Tavris shows that the differences between men and women, apart from the obvious biological differences, are situational; for example, men tend to be more aggressive because they are placed in more situations where aggression is required.

Finally, readers interested in detailed critiques of sociobiology may find Anne Fausto-Sterling's *Myths of Gender* (1985) and Philip Kitcher's *Vaulting Ambition: Sociobiology and the Quest for Human Nature* (1985) especially insightful.

· THREE ·

Feminist Allies: Profeminist Men

Under patriarchy, men are the arbiters of identity for both males and females, because the cultural norm of human identity is, by definition, male identity—masculinity. And, under patriarchy, the cultural norm of male identity consists in power, prestige, privilege, and prerogative as over and against the gender class women. That's what masculinity is. It isn't something else.

—John Stoltenberg, "Toward Gender Justice"

Neither men nor women need be limited by sex-role stereotypes that define "appropriate" behavior. The present models for men and women fail to furnish adequate opportunities for human development.

—Jack Sawyer, "On Male Liberation"

HISTORICAL SKETCH AND PRIMARY SOURCES

Profeminist men began to lay the groundwork for this perspective in the late 1960s. Deeply affected by the ideas of feminism, they met in order to discuss the impact of feminism on their lives. Many of these men came to this interest in feminism through the direct influence of women with whom they were intimate. They all conceded that American society is sexist, that women are discriminated against and dominated by men, and that women are objectified sexually and excluded from many, if not most, areas of power that are open to men. They maintained that men's lives, too, are greatly affected by this system of male dominance and that men are competitive, emotionally isolated from one another and their families, and overly involved in work and sports. They rejected the conservative idea that traditional gender roles are either natural or necessary to civilized society.

These ideas about masculine behavior were already the conclusions of an active and diverse women's movement. The diversity of this movement corresponded to the diversity among the men who sought strategies to combat sexism. One wing tended to follow the radical feminists whereas the other sided with the liberal feminists, thus producing two coexisting profeminist traditions.

From the outset, the feminist movement had to confront the issue of male responsibility for the oppression of women and to contemplate the possibility of a role for men in the feminist struggle against sexism. The early radical feminists identified men as the problem: Men, they claimed, are the oppressors and the beneficiaries of patriarchy, and masculinity is intrinsically violent and woman hating. The "Redstockings Manifesto," which appeared in mimeographed form in New York on July 7, 1969, explicitly states that "all men oppress women" and that "all men receive economic, sexual, and psychological benefits from male supremacy" (Roszak and Roszak 1969:272–274). It also asserts that men have too much to lose to be reliable allies in the struggle against patriarchy.

From its beginnings liberal feminism has been more open to men. In the first place, liberal feminism does not identify men as the problem; rather, both women and men are seen as subjected to a mystique (born of social stereotypes and ideals) that prevents the realization of their full humanity. The feminine mystique channels women into the submissive role, and the masculine mystique channels men into the dominant role. According to Betty Friedan, one of the founders of liberal feminism, "the problem that has no name [is] simply the fact that American women are kept from growing to their full human capacities" (Friedan 1963:351). In an echo of Friedan's analysis, Jack Sawyer's paper "On Male Liberation" opens with the sentence: "Male liberation calls for men to free themselves of the sex-role stereotypes that limit their ability to be human" (Sawyer 1974:170). A second reason that liberal feminism is less distrustful of men than the radical feminist approach is that men have had an honorable place in the history of the liberal struggle for women's rights. In the 1970s men sat on the board of directors of NOW, and earlier liberals such as John Stuart Mill, Havelock Ellis, and Gunnar Myrdal had defended women's rights.

The initial response of both radical and liberal men who were sympathetic to feminist ideas was to form consciousness-raising (CR) groups in the late 1960s and early 1970s. These groups were independent of each other, but their members shared a belief in some form of feminism and a concern about their place as men in the feminist struggle. *Brother: A Male Liberation Newspaper*, a somewhat erratic publication that appeared in the early 1970s, provided a forum for men who identified themselves as antisexist. Very early, however, the radical wing came to reserve the term *anti-sexist* as a label for men who accepted radical feminism and the term *liberationist* for those who followed liberal feminism. These unilateral labels have never been accepted by liberal profeminists, however. As an example of this labeling process, *Brother: A Male Liberation Newspaper* was changed after the third issue to *Brother: A Forum for Men Against Sexism*.

Several profeminist pamphlets and journals also appeared throughout the 1970s and early 1980s. "Unbecoming Men," which originated in 1971 in a men's CR group, was published by Times Change Press. It focused on the difficulty and apparent hopelessness of learning to become less sexist and less masculine. An editorial board formed in 1979 commenced publication of *M.: Gentle Men for Gender Justice*, which was soon renamed *Changing Men: Issues in Gender, Sex and Politics*, still the major forum for profeminist men's writings. "Male Pride and Anti-Sexism," prepared in 1980 by the California Anti-Sexist Men's Political Caucus, attempted to define the politics of antisexism and listed resources available to men in California. And in 1983 New Society Publishers in Philadelphia produced a radical antisexist booklet entitled "Off Their Backs . . . and on Our Own Two Feet."

In the late 1970s and early 1980s profeminist men began to plan a national organization. The First National Conference on the Masculine Mystique, held in 1974, was strongly influenced by NOW. In 1975 the first Men and Masculinity (M&M) conference was held in Knoxville, Tennessee, under the auspices of the Women's Studies Program at the University of Tennessee. These conferences have occurred almost every year since at different locations, usually on college campuses. The fourth conference in St. Louis began a push for a national organization that would help to "provide for positive alternative masculine roles which are non-oppressive, and to oppose sexism" (National Organization for Changing Men n.d.). The National Men's Organization, which came out of the seventh M&M conference in Boston in 1981, became the National Organization for Changing Men (NOCM) in 1982 and changed its name again to become the National Organization for Men Against Sexism (NOMAS) in 1990. This is the largest national organization for profeminist men; it contains both liberal and radical wings and meets concurrently with each M&M conference. These profeminist groups constitute what is often referred to as the "profeminist men's movement," as distinct from other groups such as the men's rights movement or the mythopoetic men's movement.

The 1990s have seen the emergence of men's studies as an academic discipline. The Men's Studies Association (MSA), affiliated with NOMAS, and the American Men's Studies Association (AMSA) both maintain a scholarly approach to issues of men and masculinity. Both publish curricular materials for courses in men's studies. *masculinities,* an interdisciplinary quarterly, made its appearance in 1993, although it was previously published under the title *Men's Studies Review*. Its mission statement declares that it is "an interdisciplinary quarterly, dedicated to publishing high quality scholarship in the broadly defined field of gender studies, with a particular focus on men and masculinity." *The Journal of Men's Studies* seeks "to publish scholarly material in the field of men's studies, recognizing the varied influences of class, culture, race, and sexual orientation on defining men's experiences." Both journals include articles from a variety of disciplines, including literature, sociology, culture studies, philosophy, and psychology.

Much of the early profeminist writing is no longer in print, but two important books are fortunately still widely available and can serve as primary sources. *A Book of Readings for Men Against Sexism* (1977a) is a collection of radical writings from the 1970s edited by Jon Snodgrass, and *Men and Masculinity* (1974) is a collection of early liberal feminist writings edited by Joseph H. Pleck and Jack Sawyer. Both volumes contain personal accounts of experiences in men's consciousness-raising groups, important manifestos, and theoretical essays.

Both the radical and the liberal wings of profeminism are well represented in contemporary men's writings and organizations. (The liberal wing is somewhat more prolific, in terms of both the number of books that advance this point of view and the number of adherents.) Two primary sources published more recently are *Beyond Patriarchy* (1987a), edited by Michael Kaufman, and *The Making of Masculinities* (1987a), edited by Harry Brod. Both Kaufman and Brod are sympathetic to radical feminism. On the whole, however, most of the essays in *Beyond Patriarchy* assume a radical perspective, whereas the essays in *The Making of Masculinities* have a more liberal tone. Michael S. Kimmel and Michael A. Messner's *Men's Lives* (1992) offers an updated collection of writings on men and masculinity. This collection includes many of the best essays from *Changing Men* and from other profeminist writers.

Although these primary sources cover most of the ideas that are important to the profeminist perspective, many other works need to be cited. The reader will find numerous references to these works in the sections that follow.

DESCRIPTION AND EXPLANATION
OF MALE REALITY

Masculinity

At the core of radical profeminism is the belief that the political and social reality in which we live is best described as "patriarchy," and that it is within this structure that masculinity is culturally produced and reproduced. But some authors claim that there is nothing natural or biologically necessary about either patriarchy or traditional masculinity (Stoltenberg 1977:75; Lee and Daly 1987:31; Kimmel 1994:119–120).

Patriarchy is a difficult concept; in radical writings it is often used as a synonym for *sexism, male supremacy,* and *male domination.* Here are two sample definitions from that literature: (1) Patriarchy is "the systematic domination of women by men through unequal opportunities, rewards, punishments, and the internalization of unequal expectation through sex role differentiation" (Kokopeli and Lakey 1983:1). (2) "Patriarchy . . . is . . . a cultural norm of masculinity perpetuated by the sexual politics of heterosexual men" (Stoltenberg 1977:76–77).

As used in this chapter, however, *patriarchy* is a radical profeminist term connoting male domination through violence or the threat of violence for the benefit of men. That domination includes the authority to define values and social roles such as "femininity" and "masculinity" as well as the ability to control and enforce those definitions (cf. Stoltenberg 1977:75; Kaufman 1987b:7). In later chapters other definitions of *patriarchy* will be discussed.

The masculine gender role, for radical profeminism, is a set of behaviors, attitudes, and conditions supported by stereotypes and ideals that maintains a system of power and benefit for men. Prominent among male behaviors are violence and aggression: male violence against women, male violence against other males, and male violence against self (Kaufman 1987b:6–23). Boys and men are taught to despise and control the values and behaviors that are not considered masculine. As feminine traits are clearly not included in this category, this hatred transforms male behavior and attitudes into violence and misogyny (hatred of women) (Schein 1977a:69–70). Ultimately, then, masculinity is power over women (Stoltenberg 1977:75; Kaufman 1987b:13). Moreover, boys and men are bonded together in their rejection of the feminine and in their collusions against women (Schein 1977a:132–133; Lyman 1992). At the same time, they miss out on being taught to see sensitivity in other men or to be sensitive toward other men; instead, they relate to each other as competitors in sports, in sexual conquest, and ultimately in war (Litewka 1977:24–25; Easlea 1987:197–204; Sabo 1992). "The struggle for a world without war must also be a struggle against patriarchy with its masculine character ideal" (Kokopeli and Lakey 1983:7).

Although not all forms of violence are overt, some radical writers believe that overt violence is the ultimate test of masculinity (Kokopeli and Lakey 1983:3; Kaufman 1987b). When the values of patriarchy are internalized (that is, when boys and girls are taught very early and thoroughly to want the things that patriarchal society demands), overt violence need not be used to maintain the patriarchal structure. But overt violence is always close to the surface. Patriarchal society requires sexualized male domination: "Rape is one of the most savage, and yet most accurate, metaphors for how men relate to women" (Lamm 1977a:52). Indeed, rape is hardly a rare behavior among men; if anything, according to some radical profeminists, it is the masculine norm (Lamm 1977a:53; Wandachild 1977:93; Schein 1977a:72–73; Kokopeli and Lakey 1983:2–3).

As radical profeminists have noted, many men benefit from their domination of women (Stoltenberg 1977:76; Kaufman 1987b). Women take care of men by doing their domestic labor, raising their children, and serving as their emotional and physical caretakers. Moreover, when women are paid a wage for their labor, it is often in caregiving fields such as nursing, teaching, and social work or in support positions such as clerical work. Such work keeps women in the role of caregivers and prevents them from competing with men for more prestigious work at better pay.

Although men thus benefit from being masculine in a patriarchy, the radical profeminist perspective asserts that they are also harmed by being masculine. "Sexism hurts men as well, by directing us to abandon our feelings of caring, equality and sensitivity" (California Anti-Sexist Men's Political Caucus 1980:4). Thus . . . "men have a lot to gain by fighting sexism. From what we have seen and experienced, men . . . feel relief and joy just from being freed from the roles that lead to the oppression of women" (Blood, Tuttle, and Lakey, 1983:13). The costs of masculinity translate for men into shorter lives, a higher suicide rate, alcoholism, and a higher incidence of stress-related diseases. Yet most profeminists are also quick to observe that "the emptiness, self-loss, powerlessness, and violations that women endure are far more insidious than our masculine role suffering. Even as incomplete, unalive human beings, we enjoy privilege and power: the world, God, and culture are all made in our own image" (Schein 1977b:131; compare Pleck 1992a:19–27).

At this point it is interesting to note two aspects of masculinity that moral conservatives and radical profeminists interpret in very different ways.

1. Masculinity is a social contrivance and, for that reason, is very fragile. It is maintained primarily by community social structures: "The family, school, sports, friends, church, clubs, scouts, jobs, and the media all play a role" (Kaufman 1987b:12–13). The moral conservatives and the radical profeminists agree that society constantly reaffirms the male social role. But whereas the former see masculinity as a social role continually imposed on men to control their naturally destructive tendencies, the latter see masculinity as a destructive social role that is continually imposed

on a naturally benign being in order to maintain a patriarchal social order. "The sexual politics of the family provides the psychological model for the power politics of the state" (Kokopeli and Lakey 1983:7). That is, males do not come into the world as misogynists, rapists, or batterers who seek to dominate women; they must be "trained" as such (Kaufman 1987b:8). And since the family helps to train men to dominate women, the breakdown of the family may have some "positive effects" (Kokopeli and Lakey 1983:7).

2. At the root of masculinity are the sexual relations between men and women; to change this relationship is to alter the entire social system (Gilder 1973:201). In the context of these sexual relations, moral conservatives see women as exercising the greater power, whereas radical profeminists believe that "male sexual functioning operates as the instrument of women's oppression and enforces male rule" (Snodgrass 1977a:12–13). Thus, the social reality that for profeminists is a sexually violent patriarchy is for moral conservatives a situation in which men sacrifice their natural tendencies to women's erotic power.

These differences between conservatives and profeminists betray some deep assumptions about human nature. Clearly, radical profeminist men reject the moral conservatives' premise that men are barbarians by nature. They also reject the idea that women are intrinsically morally superior to men. After all, if men and women were *naturally* superior or inferior, how could men overcome their nature, let alone be trusted allies in the women's movement? Historically, radical profeminist men have had to contend not only with these conservative ideas but also with the tendency in radical feminism to endorse them. As Alison Jaggar notes: "Contemporary radical feminist writings abound with references to 'the power inherent in female biology' and 'the creative power that is associated with female biology.' Mary Daly for instance, appears to endorse the 'native talent and superiority of women'" (Jaggar 1983:95). Thus, the radical profeminists, to avoid conservatism and to present themselves as possible allies, have adopted a liberal view of human nature to the effect that, apart from women's capacity to have children, there is no significant difference between men and women. That is, *all* humans have the capacity to reason and to be moral agents; and the gender differences that do exist are shaped by learning and socialization (Mill 1988:24).

Liberalism completely rejects any claim suggesting the natural moral superiority of women over men and asserts, instead, that all individuals have the same set of potentialities, such as the ability to reason. Special talents, such as musical ability, are distributed randomly among women and men. In addition, each individual has an intrinsic and equal worth as a human being and is thus entitled to freedom of speech, freedom from coercion, and the right to self-development (Gray 1986:x–xi, 45–56; cf. Jaggar 1983:33). Differences between men and women occur because their social roles are constrained by different ideals and stereotypes. Because each individual has equal value and the same basic rights, a social injustice occurs when an individual or group of individuals is denied these rights. Thus, when Betty Friedan identifies "the problem with no name" as the restrictiveness of the social role of femininity, she is pointing to the systematic denial of the opportunity to exercise these rights that afflicts women individually and collectively.

For liberal and radical profeminists alike, the masculine gender role is a set of limitations akin to the limitations of feminity; it is restricted by masculine stereotypes and ideals (Kimmel 1992:1–11). If women are limited by the need to work at home, the absence of sport facilities, and the lack of economic opportunities, men are equally limited by not being able to work at home, not being able to avoid athletic participation, and not being allowed to be economically dependent. And, just as women are socialized into being submissive, men are socialized into being dominant (Sawyer 1974:171). This socialization, which relies heavily upon gender stereotypes and ideals, blocks both men and women in very much the same way from becoming full human beings.

The "Berkeley Men's Center Manifesto," written in 1973, condemns the restrictiveness of masculinity and espouses the goal of becoming fully human:

> We, as men, want to take back our full humanity. We no longer want to strain and compete to live up to an impossible oppressive masculine image— strong, silent, cool, handsome, unemotional, successful, master of women, leader of men, wealthy, brilliant, athletic. . . .

> We are oppressed by conditioning which makes us only half-human. This conditioning serves to create a mutual dependence of male (abstract, aggressive, strong, unemotional) and female (nurturing, passive, weak, emotional) roles. (cited in Pleck and Sawyer 1974:173–174; cf. the National Organization for Men Against Sexism Statement of Principles 1992:553).

Masculinity is an acquired set of behaviors and attitudes that are maintained by a complex system of rewards and punishments; accordingly, much of the liberal profeminist literature deals with how this set of behaviors is learned. *Men and Masculinity*, for example, begins with a scientific as well as personal look at how boys come to be masculinized. As one author in this volume observes: "Demands that boys conform to social notions of what is manly come much earlier and are enforced with much more vigor than similar attitudes with respect to girls" (Hartley 1974:7). Indeed, most of the contributors note the relentless pressure on men to excel, as athletes, breadwinners, and scholars, and to rely on themselves rather than others (Candell 1974:14–17; Jourard 1974:21–29; Gould 1974:96).

Two other liberal profeminist classics appeared about the same time as *Men and Masculinity*—namely, Warren Farrell's *The Liberated Man* (1975) and Marc Feigen Fasteau's *The Male Machine* (1974a). Farrell lists the ten commandments of masculinity, which include not expressing feelings of emotion, not revealing vulnerabilities, not listening, condescending to women, controlling women, being a top breadwinner, and assuming no responsibility for housework (Farrell 1975:30). Fasteau's description of the masculine man is typical of this period:

> The male machine is a special kind of being, different from women, children, and men who don't measure up. He is functional, designed mainly for work. He is programed to tackle jobs, override obstacles, attack problems, overcome difficulties, and always seize the offensive. . . . He has armor plating which is virtually impregnable. His circuits are never scrambled or overrun by irrelevant personal signals. . . . His relationship with other male machines is one of respect but not intimacy. . . . In fact, his internal circuitry is something of a mystery to him and is maintained primarily by humans of the opposite sex. (Fasteau 1974a:1)

Early liberal views assumed a unitary masculinity to which all boys are assigned and from which all men are trying to break free (Kimmel 1987a:122). Most of the recent work by liberal profeminists, however, treats the masculinity as a *dynamic* entity that changes through history and through interaction with women and men of different generations and backgrounds. Masculinity also differs from subculture to subculture within modern society; black men, for example, are subject to a very different set of socializing influences than white men; they live in a different social reality and have a different masculinity (Franklin 1987:167–169). It is better, therefore, to speak of "masculinities," because the plural form acknowledges the fact that no single set of behaviors, attitudes, and conditions characterizes all men (Brod 1987b:4).

Social scientists have long assumed that the masculine ideal prescribes a *consistent* set of behaviors and attitudes to which all men must adhere if they are to be socially adjusted. Recent liberal studies argue, however, that this ideal is contradictory, virtually impossible to achieve, and violated by a very high proportion of well-adjusted males (Pleck 1981:9).

The causal role of stereotypes and ideals is emphasized in the liberal literature. In *A Choice of Heroes: The Changing Face of American Manhood*, for instance, Mark Gerzon outlines the stereotypes and ideals of masculinity throughout the history of the United States. The thesis of his work is the liberal idea that these images are restrictive of full human development. Gerzon argues further that stereotypes and ideals are "thrust upon us by marketing strategies," even though there is no single image, nor even a consistent image, of what it is to be a man (Gerzon 1982:6, 233).

Whereas liberal profeminists tend to find symmetry in the situations of men and women (inasmuch as both are restricted by gender roles), radicals find male power and privilege. Whereas radical profeminists place misogyny at the core of masculinity, liberals see misogyny as only one among several primary traits. In spite of these differences, however, contemporary profeminists agree that every man and every woman has a full complement of human abilities and that masculinity allows only a subset of these to develop.

Feminism

Radical profeminists clearly believe that their perspective provides the essential insights into gender role issues. As Schein has noted, "We must realize our debt to feminism and that, for most of us, our main motivation for dealing with sexism comes from women who have forced us to, and that feminism has already provided the theory, structure, and models for us" (Schein 1977b:132). Indeed, feminism has taught men a lesson that is both personal and painful: "We [men] are the ones who need the help; we are the ones who are the enemy; we are the ones who oppress and objectify women; and we are the incomplete, crippled human beings" (Schein 1977b:131). Yet not all radical profeminists agree. "Some people say that men are the enemy when it comes to fighting sexism. We do not agree; blame and guilt don't help in understanding why people function as they do or in getting them to change. . . . As men, we are all involved in the oppression women experience and we benefit from it each day. Yet this is no reason to fix blame on ourselves as 'the oppressor'" (Blood, Tuttle, and Lakey 1983:12).

Liberal profeminist writers are not tormented with the same guilt and distrust of self that is common especially among the early radical writers. The liberals see feminism as the impetus for men to examine their lives and critique the masculine mystique, much as women have critique the feminine mystique. As Sawyer puts it, "The women's liberation movement has stressed that women are looking for a better model for human behavior than has so far been created. Women are trying to become human, and men can do the same" (Sawyer 1974:173).

Feminism gave profeminist men the impetus to form men's consciousness-raising groups in the 1970s. These evolved into the support groups and the state and national organizations against sexism that exist today. "Anti-sexist consciousness raising is an activity which permits participants to see clearly the ways in which their individual situation reflects the total social process around them. It allows people to examine and come to understand . . . the devastatingly dehumanizing effects of patriarchy" (Hornacek 1977:125). Both wings of the profeminist movement have employed consciousness raising as a major tool to acquaint men with their own sexist behavior, to draw close emotional support from other men, and to nurture and encourage their antisexism (Hornacek 1977:124).

The participants in some radical men's CR groups were suspicious of themselves; they feared that exclusively male groups might become small patriarchal structures in which men would support one another in their misogyny (Schein 1977b:133). But CR groups took hold anyway, as flawed instruments by which to unlearn male power and privilege (Hornacek 1977:124). Such men's groups became focused on how men were affected by masculine stereotypes and harmed by the masculine role (Farrell 1975:201–216; Levine 1974; Weiss 1974). The emerging consensus among profeminists by the 1990s was that although men certainly had power, holding that power extracted a price: "Whatever power might be associated with dominant masculinities, they also can be the source of enormous pain. Because the images are, ultimately, childhood pictures of omnipotence, they are impossible to obtain. Surface appearances aside, no man is completely able to live up to these ideals and images. For one thing we all continue to experience a range of needs and feelings that are deemed inconsistent with manhood" (Kaufman 1994:149).

Liberal profeminism has always been closer than radical profeminism to mainstream North American feminism. Liberal books often enjoy forewords, endorsements, and other contributions from the liberal feminist leadership. For instance, Gloria Steinem's introduction to *The Male Machine* concludes: "This book is a complement to the feminist revolution, yet it is one no woman could write. It is the revolution's other half. . . . There will be male allies like this one; men who also want a world in which we can shed the crippling stereotypes of sex or race, and become the unique individuals we were born to be" (Fasteau 1974a:xv). Farrell's *The Liberated Man* (1975), too, was enthusiastically endorsed by Gloria Steinem as well as by Wilma Scott Heide, president of NOW from 1971 to 1974. And Betty Friedan endorsed Donald H. Bell's *Being a Man*, a classically liberal work that argues for a "self-created" masculinity relatively free of the traditional "male symbols, rituals, and practices" (Bell 1982:157).

For radical profeminist men, radical feminism constitutes a set of political principles that provide not only the correct analysis of masculinity but also the structures that maintain it. But these principles create tensions. Some men inclined to follow radical feminist theory are torn between wanting to take on the burden of changing themselves and distrusting themselves because they doubt that those who benefit from patriarchy will ever pursue genuine changes within it. For liberal men, liberal feminism stands as an exemplar of the needed analysis of masculinity. Since men experience their own limitations, they alone are in a position to describe and destroy the masculine mystique (Friedan 1992:572–579). Liberal feminists seem to agree, as did Gloria Steinem when she observed that *The Male Machine* is a book that no woman could write.

ASSESSMENT OF MALE REALITY AND AGENDA FOR CHANGE

We already have much of the profeminists' assessment of male reality and masculinity; it is inseparable from their discussions of how masculinity is created and maintained. As noted, this perspective has two wings that share the same national organization and journals. It is to this organization and these publications that we now turn in order to discover more about the profeminist assessment of masculinity—specifically, the National Organization for Men Against Sexism, *Brother: The Newsletter of the National Organization for Men Against Sexism*, and *Changing Men: Issues in Gender, Sex*, and Politics, as well as *masculinities*.

In its "Statement of Principles" NOMAS identifies itself as "an activist organization of men and women supporting positive changes for men." It notes that "traditional masculinity contains many positive characteristics" but that it also "contains qualities that have limited and harmed us." Among the most harmful qualities of traditional masculinity is "fear of homosexuality," which leads to injustices against gay men, lesbians, and bisexuals as well as to limitations for heterosexual men. NOMAS generally calls for an end to discrimination and violence against women and calls on men and women to "work together as allies to change the injustices that have so often made them see one another as enemies." Finally, it acknowledges the oppression of people by "race, class, age, religion, and physical condition." Its announced goal is to "change not just ourselves and other men but also the institutions that create inequality."

This statement is an interesting blend of radical and liberal points of view. It avoids such buzzwords as *patriarchy* and claims not that women are oppressed but that they lack full equality. It also avoids any suggestion that men are oppressed or need liberation. Men are "allies," not the enemy; and masculinity contains "positive characteristics." The statement also demands political action and a change of the "institutions" that create inequality. In this regard it is less radical than the original call that went out in 1981 to form an antisexist men's organization—a call that was the model for the "Statement of Principles." This earlier summons, a mimeograph entitled "Announcing a National Anti-Sexist *Men's* Organization," stressed the struggle against "patriarchal structure," spoke freely of the "oppression" of women, avoided the language of "pro-maleness," and even made the radical feminist claim that *all* injustices are "connected to the ancient patriarchal pattern."

Organizations and publications open to both wings of profeminism must make many compromises, but they can also reveal sharp differences. For instance, the radical wing frequently calls for direct action such as picketing or leafletting—especially against institutions that allow or condone violence against women. The more liberal wing, by contrast, focuses on political struggles such as the Equal Rights Amendment and on workshops, aimed at personal change, that help men escape the confines of masculine stereotypes and ideals. Moreover, this wing has dominated the national M&M conferences and the agendas of NOCM/NOMAS. The statement of purpose in the announcement for the Seventh National M&M Conference reads much like the "Berkeley Men's Center Manifesto":

> We can no longer accept mutually exclusive categories and stereotypes of what it means to be a man. Men are merely virile, rational, competitive, powerful, independent. . . . [We give] ourselves permission to examine facets of our lives which we have been taught to shut out by narrow views of masculinity. (Seventh National Conference on Men and Masculinity 1982)

The many workshops at these conferences that focus on personal growth reveal the impact of the liberal agenda. In *How Men Feel,* Anthony Astrachan states that of the 104 workshops scheduled at the 1985 Tenth National M&M Conference, the workshops on "sex roles, gay issues, and personal-growth topics" greatly outnumbered the political workshops (Astrachan 1986:293). Astrachan attributes this fact to the large proportion of therapists, counselors, and psychologists who attended these conferences. At the same time it is easy to see the liberal argument for helping men to end their isolation from one another, their inability to be intimate with other men, and their aggressiveness toward one another. If men cannot reveal their vulnerabilities, help each other with their burdens, communicate their needs, and stop competing, there is little chance of building a political profeminist men's movement. "We ought to want to break through these barriers for the pleasure of getting to know ourselves and each other better. Until we do, men's liberation will remain an idea instead of a movement" (Fasteau 1974b:21).

In his Action Day speech at a demonstration against male-perpetrated rape and violence (also part of the Tenth National Conference), John Stoltenberg's call for direct action revealed yet another side of NOCM's agenda:

> We *will* make a difference when we demonstrate our personal commitment to equality, when we are decisive in our stand for sexual justice, when we are

opposed to men's violence absolutely. . . . This is a difference we will make . . . by putting our lives on the line for a world that men don't dominate. . . . This is not about touchie-feely never-neverland. This is about our collective courage to face down male megalomania. This is not about helpless self-hate and self-blame. . . . This is not about learning to cry. . . . We are men who are going to learn to mobilize our rage against . . . men's violence. (Stoltenberg 1985a:9)

Some members of NOMAS believe that as important as personal growth workshops may be, they have not placed enough emphasis on political action. In commenting on Stoltenberg's talk, Billy Easton writes: "Throughout the history of M&M and NOCM, a conflict has existed between focusing on personal development or on political action. The Action Day signaled a greater commitment to political activism in the men's movement" (Easton 1985:39).

Let us now look at a concrete example of this tension in profeminist agenda building. In the fall of 1985 *Changing Men* provided a forum on pornography. The participants in this forum were divided between the radical and liberal perspectives. The radicals argued that pornography is "the social power of men over women acted out as eroticized domination and subordination" (Stoltenberg 1985b:47). But, they added, pornography is more than an erotic depiction. It is a practice that abuses real women and children in the process of producing the visual pictures that *teach* men to abuse women and children. It perpetuates the major myths that hold up patriarchy—that women like to be dominated and raped, that women are inferior and men are superior. In short, pornography perpetuates racial and class stereotypes and desensitizes men to violence. To attack pornography is thus to go to "the jugular of patriarchal power" (Wagner 1985:26).

In anticipation of a liberal objection based on the right of free expression, radicals also argue that pornography does not deserve the protection of free speech; it is the antithesis of freedom, as women lack freedom because of it (Stoltenberg 1985b:47). Freedom-of-speech arguments are simply defenses of the freedom of men to speak out in favor of silencing women. An example of legislation against pornography is the antipornography law written by Andrea Dworkin and Catharine MacKinnon, which allows women to take civil action where pornography has contributed to the denial of their civil rights (Dworkin and MacKinnon 1985:23). Indeed, such legislation can restore women's civil rights and help them to protect themselves against the harm of pornography.

The liberals' emphasis on individuality has emerged in their response to this initiative. They argue that to invoke even the possibility of civil action against a pornographer infringes the pornographer's right of free expression. Even if the harm of pornography is conceded, "censorship" in any form is too dangerous to justify such infringements; it is "too blunt and dangerous an instrument" to be used against pornography (Small 1985:7). The liberals also claim that there is already too much censorship against discussions about sex. "The messages of pornography are insidious in part because they are virtually the only messages most men get about sex. In the absence of free and open discussion of sexuality, porn speaks to men without rebuttal. . . . It flourishes in the darkness. It thrives on taboo" (Small 1985:45). An ordinance like the Dworkin-MacKinnon law would only feed that taboo and lengthen that darkness.

The *Changing Men* forum itself argued against such "legal" strategies as the antipornography ordinance. Its assertions, from deep within radical feminism itself, were unavailable to liberalism, given its trust in the political and legal system. The court system, the laws, and the judges, it claimed, are all unreformable instruments of patriarchy, and women's trust in the patriarchy to protect them from itself is naive and betrays an ignorance of history (Feminist Anti-Censorship Task Force 1985:12).

Today, NOMAS encompasses a number of task groups devoted to both the political and the personal issues of sexism. Included are task groups on sexual harassment, ending men's violence and pornography, fathering, gay rights, homophobia, racism, the military, men's studies, men's culture, men and mental health, men and spirituality, male-female relationships, and child custody legislation. These task groups sponsor educational activities, writing workshops, and direct support for feminist organizations and, in some cases, take direct action against institutions that contribute to violence aimed at women. Both the task group for ending men's violence and RAVEN, a St. Louis–based anti-violence group, produced *The Ending Men's Violence National Referral Directory*. As Michael Shiffman concludes in his article "The Men's Movement: An Exploratory Empirical Investigation," it is too soon to tell whether NOCM will "form a set of radical social practices, or will . . . travel down the liberal abyss" (Shiffman 1987:311).

In fact, the 1990s have seen a growing fracturing of NOMAS. One split in 1991–92 divided its men's task group into the Men's Studies Association, which remained within NOMAS, and the American Men's Studies Association, which wanted to keep men's studies independent of any activist ideology. The American Men's Studies Association is an effort "to recognize and respect the many voices emerging from among those working with and/or studying men and masculinity" ("AMSA Mission Statement"). AMSA remains closely associated with *The Journal of Men's Studies*. The Men's Studies Association remains committed to the principles of NOMAS, and its publication is *masculinities*. Thus, the former is not formally committed to profeminism, though its articles tend to be profeminist; the latter organization is firmly committed to a profeminism statement of principles. The split reduced the membership of the NOMAS task group in men's studies from some 359 members in June of 1992 to around 130 in 1993 and 1994. Approximately the same number belong to AMSA.

A second major controversy erupted when *Changing Men* published an article, "First Loves," describing a homosexual encounter between a seventeen-year-old and a twelve-year-old (Beane 1992). The publication of this article was challenged by Nikki Craft in the next issue. Her article, entitled "So Much Slime, So Little Time: The Transgression of Pro-Feminism" objects to "First Loves" and a certain advertisement from NAMBLA (North American Man-Boy Love Association), an organization committed to ending age constraints on consensual sex. The editors of *Changing Men* apologized for publishing the NAMBLA advertisement, claiming they were not aware of the content of the ad (Cote, Biernbaum, and Bresnick 1993). But a serious and bitter fight ensued over the publication of "First Loves." The *Activist Men's Journal* (AMJ), following the lead of radical feminism, attacked *Changing Men* and NOMAS in January 1993. Geov Parrish, coeditor of AMJ, argued, "Unless and until NOMAS adopts reforms that can institutionalize accountability and prevent future incidents such as its ass-covering paralysis and white male bonding frenzy in the Jeff Beane/*Changing Men* case ... North America still needs a continental organization run by and for pro-feminist activists" (Parrish 1993; cf. *Activist Men's Journal* 5:3 [November 1992]; 5:4, 5:5 [February 1993]; 6:5 [March, 1994]). *Changing Men* defended itself through an article by Michael Kimmel entitled "The Politics of Accountability," in which Kimmel pointed out, first, that Beane's account of his early sexual experiences was descriptive and not advocating such encounters—a point also made by Beane—and second, that freedom of expression protects such descriptions (Kimmel 1993:3; cf. Beane 1993). Kimmel concurred with the critics that Beane's article was not reflective of feminist principles in its consideration of his earlier behavior—a central aspect of profeminist consciousness raising. A further defense of NOMAS was provided by Jack Straton, Coordinator of the Child Custody Task Group, in a letter to AMJ in early 1993. Straton points out that NOMAS has always strongly opposed pedophilia and child sexual abuse. And once the controversy erupted, NOMAS established clear guidelines to prevent ads such as NAMBLA's from appearing in future issues. NOMAS also adopted a resolution that objected to the "dehumanizing and isolating" manner in which the editors of *Changing Men* and NOMAS were treated during the controversy (Straton 1993). The consequences of the controversy were a weakening of the profeminist movement, loss of membership in NOMAS, and the refusal of some members to run for NOMAS office (Cohen 1993).

These debates are illustrative of deep ideological differences within the profeminist perspective. These divisions within profeminism all center on what Kimmel calls "the politics of accountability" (Kimmel 1993). The first split within the Men's Studies Association was over which feminism men's studies should be accountable to. By keeping the Men's Studies Association within NOMAS, articles that did not fully concur with the generally liberal profeminist "Statement of Principles" could be rejected, even if they might be considered feminist by certain women. The American Men's Studies association clearly felt that any serious scholarship should be acceptable. This recognition of many voices is also a principle of some versions of feminism. Thus, the first split found NOMAS arguing for a more restricted accountability to those feminists who would embrace its own statement of principles. The second controversy, however, fell the other way. NOMAS supported a generally liberal feminist wing with many voices, whereas the *Activist Men's Journal* demanded accountability to radical feminism in the tradition of Andrea Dworkin, Nikki Craft, and John Stoltenberg. Such sectarian battles are an inevitable byproduct of a diverse and contesting set of feminist theories; the profeminist perspective is as divided as the feminism it would support. Profeminists, by definition, must be accountable to feminist leadership. The question profeminists face is: Which leadership?

In addition to building a national profeminist men's organization, liberals have been especially attracted to the formation of men's studies programs as a way of combating sexism; it is within such programs that the limiting stereotypes and ideals of masculinity can be examined and exposed for what they are. As Harry Brod notes in "The Case for Men's Studies," some of the arguments for men's studies are directly tied to the liberal analysis of the harms of masculinity (Brod 1987c:55). Brod defines men's studies as "the study of masculinities and male experiences as specific and varying social-historical-cultural formations" (Brod 1987c:40). If the liberal goal of fighting sexism by removing these harms and making men more fully human is to be realized, the male mystique must be dissected. Masculinity must be understood; it must be a subject of study just as femininity is. If it is not studied, the danger that it will remain the norm increases. Furthermore, as Pleck (1981) has argued, the existing theories of masculinity are inadequate partly because they do not examine male sexuality, work, and violence from a profeminist perspective. It would follow, then, that new directions need to be found if these powerful socializing forces are to be understood and controlled.

In the late 1980s and 1990s, men's studies as an academic area has grown significantly. Two new journals, *masculinities* and *The Journal of Men's Studies,* have provided scholarly outlets for papers from a variety of disciplines. Academic studies of men and masculinity have traditionally come from the social sciences, especially sociology, anthropology, and social psychology. To these traditional disciplines have been added a number of new areas. Historians E. Anthony Rotundo and Robert L. Griswold have written, respectively, *American Manhood: Transformations in Masculinity from the Revolution to the Modern Era* (1993), and *Fatherhood in America:*

A History (1993). A collection of essays edited by philosophers Larry May and Robert Strikwerda and entitled *Rethinking Masculinity: Philosophical Explorations in Light of Feminism* (1992), asks philosophical questions about sex differences, male friendship, pornography, and men's movements. Literary criticism, often in a postmodernist style, explores the discourse by which men and masculinity are constructed: Thus, we find David J. Ulbrich offering "A Male-Conscious Critique of Erich Maria Remarque's *All Quiet on the Western Front*" (1995), and Suzanne Harper's insightful essay "Subordinating Masculinities/Racializing Masculinities: Writing White Supremacist Discourse on Men's Bodies" (1994). Probably no area is more suited to the interdisciplinary approach of men's studies than is cultural studies. Books such as Susan Jeffords's *The Remasculinization of America: Gender and the Vietnam War* (1989) and James William Gibson's *Warrior Dreams: Violence and Manhood in Post-Vietnam America* (1994) are examples of the excellent work in this new area.

Although the academic study of men and masculinity is just coming into its own, the profeminist men's movement, which began as a political struggle in alliance with the women's movement, is having trouble maintaining its political momentum. Liberal profeminists follow the politics of liberal feminism, which have been characterized by Barbara S. Deckard as "let us in" in contrast to the radical feminist politics of "set us free." Thus, the political agenda of liberals usually involves working within existing social structures to eradicate sexism. Efforts to pass the ERA, to impose affirmative-action goals on corporations and universities, to elect more women to political office, to increase the numbers of professional women, to establish special sexual-assault units with the police and the prosecutor's office, and to place women studies programs in universities and colleges all fit within the liberal political agenda. Of course, there is nothing about liberalism that prevents liberal men from joining such causes: Men Allied Nationally for the ERA, for instance, was a national organization of men even before NOCM/NOMAS came to the fore.

But for liberal men who already have access to most of these institutions, the road to a better society is likely to appear as a personal journey rather than as a collective political action. It is not that the liberal feminists' political agenda fails to provide opportunities for liberal profeminist men to be politically engaged. Rather, the place of men in the social-political hierarchy often makes personal change more attractive, and their own faith in the system makes political action less urgent. As Laurel Richardson has observed of liberal profeminists: "Their privileged position within the system does not give them the structural advantage of challenging their own treatment as unfair. Most goals of the Men's Movement are not easily politicized" (Richardson 1988:247).

It may be precisely this question of how to get men politicized that leads some liberals to say that men are oppressed—a claim that is corroborated by the parallel they find between the restriction of women in their social roles and that of men in theirs. If women are oppressed by restrictive roles, why not men? Thus, some liberal profeminists do not hesitate to talk about the "oppressive dehumanizing sex roles" that afflict men or "the oppression we feel by being forced to conform to the narrow and lonely roles of men in this society" (Keith 1974:81; "A Men's Group Experience" 1974:161). The "Berkeley Men's Center Manifesto" declares that "we are oppressed by conditioning" and "by this dependence on women for support, nurturing, love and warm feeling" (Berkeley Men's Center 1974:173–174). In a variation on the radical claim that masculinity is power and privilege, one liberal essay even argues that "it can be oppressive to have to be these things" (David and Brannon 1976:27).

But to claim oppression itself is a political act has important consequences, and many liberal profeminists consciously avoid making such a claim (Clatterbaugh 1992). Talk of male oppression only aggravates the tension between radicals and liberals, inasmuch as radicals clearly deny that men are oppressed (California Anti-Sexist Men's Political Caucus 1980:5). And, as we shall see in the next chapter, it is primarily men's rights groups that talk of male oppression. Such talk alienates many feminists who see men as the paradigm of a nonoppressed group. For some, it is the willingness of liberals to talk about male oppression that has earned them the label "men's liberationists" (Ehrlich 1977:143).

Radical profeminists also encounter a problem when they join the radical feminist agenda. Radical feminism is not interested in reforming the patriarchy. Women's energies cannot be directed to helping men deal with patriarchy; women need to have a "womanspace" in which to achieve feminist values. Therefore, radical feminists often seek to build small feminist organizations that are outside of existing structures— women's bookstores, rape relief centers, battered women's shelters, and antipornography organizations (Jaggar 1983:275–282). Often men are not welcome in these womanspaces.

Radical men cannot build political agendas around their own oppression because radical feminism rejects the idea that men, too, are oppressed. Some radical profeminist men argue that men should take on childcare and other drudgery so that women will have more time for feminist causes. They also argue that men should take on the burden of changing their own masculinity so that women, who have enough to do, will not have the additional burden of changing men. But these arguments encounter resistance among radical feminists who assert that men are too sexually exploitive and violent to be trusted with childcare and too privileged to undertake their own change.

Some radical men's groups such as Boston's Organized Against Sexism and Institutionalized Stereotypes (OASIS) focus on gay and lesbian rights. Boston's "EMERGE: A Men's Counseling Service for Domestic Violence" and St. Louis's Rape and Violence End Now (RAVEN) are concerned with violence against women. Still other men, not just radical profeminists, have focused on ending the draft, eliminating the existence of nuclear weapons, and, especially, calling attention to the connection between masculinity and the military (Easlea 1987:195–213; Kokapeli and Lakey 1983:6–7, Fasteau 1974a:144–189). But the problem remains: how to politicize radical men into working in support of a movement from which they are excluded or which, at best, does not trust them.

Nowhere is the political frustration of the profeminist movement stated more clearly than in discussions of what should replace masculinity. Logically, there are many options. Men could adopt a new masculine social role with different behaviors and attitudes; they could become feminine; they could blend masculine and feminine behaviors and attitudes; or they could somehow transcend masculinity and femininity altogether. Liberals are often attracted to the idea that masculinity and femininity are complementary sets of traits found in everyone: Men who are masculine are simply persons who have been blocked by stereotypes and ideals from developing their feminine side; women who are feminine are simply persons who have been blocked by stereotypes and ideals from developing their masculine side. A person who develops both sets of traits is androgynous. For many liberals androgyny is what should replace masculinity (Fasteau 1974a:186, 196; cf. Ferguson 1977:45–69).

Radical profeminists seem divided on the question of androgyny as a replacement for masculinity, although they do want masculinity replaced. For instance, John Stoltenberg claims that ending sexism requires "a total repudiation of masculinity" (Stoltenberg 1977:80). But radicals almost universally reject the liberal conception of androgyny because they believe that what is masculine and what is feminine are already defined by the patriarchy. Thus, if radical profeminists are attracted to androgyny as an alternative to masculinity, they do not talk about it as a blend of the masculine and feminine. "We prefer to recognize the feminine/masculine dichotomy for the nonsense it is, and to abolish it, putting in its place androgyny, a single character ideal to which all can aspire" (Blood, Tuttle, and Lakey 1983:15). Radical feminists such as Janice Raymond have critiqued the liberal claim that androgyny is a blend of complementary qualities because masculine and feminine traits are as incompatible as the traits of slave and master, submission and dominance (Raymond 1981:63–64). And, finally, androgyny as a political goal undercuts the radical feminist belief that the situations of men and women are not symmetrical inasmuch as men have power over women (Raymond 1981:65).

In short, radical and liberal profeminists differ fundamentally over the most basic sociopolitical goals of their profeminist/antisexist struggle and in particular about their respective conceptualizations of the alternatives to being traditionally masculine. These differences further hamper their ability to launch a united antisexist movement.

CRITIQUE: CRITICISMS AND RESPONSES

Criticism 1

The men's radical profeminist movement, especially in its early writings, is characterized by an uncritical kowtowing to feminism. As Tim Carrigan and his colleagues have noted:

> The most striking thing about *For Men Against Sexism* is the massive guilt that runs through its major pieces. Authors bewail their own past sexism. . . . The book insists that men must accept radical feminism as the basis for their CR groups and have them started and supervised by women. . . . One gets the impression that being subject to constant criticisms by feminists is the emotional center of this book, and the response is to bend over backwards, and backwards again. . . . [But] a series of back somersaults is not a strong position from which to confront the patriarchal power structure. (Carrigan, Connell, and Lee 1987:163)

Response

The early radical feminist movement demanded that men (1) take feminism seriously and (2) acknowledge the harm done by male privilege and power. At this stage men were confronted with an angry feminism, a feminism that believed men controlled virtually every aspect of their lives.

It was natural for these men to feel guilty. But acceptance of that guilt was a necessary step in being radical profeminists. Of course, guilt and uncritical acceptance are not permanent features of this perspective. As one CR participant noted: "When I first joined a group, about four years ago, we did some 'guilt-tripping' at first—flagellating ourselves for the ways we were oppressing women—but we soon moved on to sharing other problems" (Katz 1976:294).

Criticism 2

Unlike NOW, NOCM/NOMAS has consistently failed to attract a mass following. Men tend not to stay with the movement; they take what they need and move on. Their lack of commitment derives from the assumptions that "feminist ideology is not directed toward men" and that it is "hostile to men." Thus "male feminists need to refine feminist ideology, to expand its interpretation so that it speaks to men as well as to women.

We need to define our experiences within the context of feminist ideology" (Wheat 1985:2–3). In short, men need to find a way to complete feminist analysis without appearing to reject feminism. Perhaps NOCM can best achieve this end under the auspices of NOW. By this means feminist men would gain not only access to a mass organization but also the credentials to be interpreters of feminism for men.

Response

This argument may be self-defeating. It is true that NOCM/NOMAS has not achieved the wide support of NOW. It may also be the case that this lack of appeal is due in part to the incompleteness of feminist ideology and in part to its angry rhetoric toward men. But to put NOCM/NOMAS under the control of a large women's organization would seem to work against the creation of a mass movement. Men have been able to belong to NOW since its inception, but they have not joined in significant numbers. An independent men's organization is probably going to appeal much more to men who are concerned about thinking through their own ideology; and radical profeminists would not be happy about an affiliation with a clearly liberal movement. Besides, an independent organization always has the option of giving strong political and moral support to NOW without being bound by the liberalism of that organization. Furthermore, many feminists have long been wary of men who become involved in women's organizations: "And watch out most of all for the 'liberationists' who try to move in on the women's movement itself. . . . The motives of this brand of male intrusion could hardly be more transparent. . . . The movement is too important to leave the definition of priorities, strategy, and tactics exclusively in the hands of women" (Grimstad and Rennie 1977:151).

Criticism 3

Many radicals do not see liberal profeminism as a political movement concerned with giving up male power. Lyttelton has pointed out that "men's liberation has no analysis of sexism as political. If both men and women are oppressed by sexism, who is the oppressor? Men's liberation wants the goodies without paying the price" (Lyttelton 1987:473). And as Lamm puts it:

> The men's movement has a line all right . . . creating awareness between, among, and about men and men's issues. . . . There is no mention of women. . . . There is no mention of feminism. There is no mention of male supremacy. There is no mention of woman-hating. . . . When women see a movement of privileged men uniting to talk among themselves . . . how do

they react? . . . Do they feel a little worried—having experienced all too well the politics and power of many other men's movements run by men of similar privilege? (Lamm 1977b:155–156)

Response

Radical profeminists criticize liberalism not for lacking a political analysis but for failing to accept radical feminist analysis. Liberalism holds that there are gross inequities between men and women, that both are subject to restrictive stereotypes and ideals, and that both are prevented by these limitations from their full humanity. Liberalism has a concrete political agenda aimed at reforming our sexist society: Liberal profeminists support the Equal Rights Amendment, men's and women's studies, equal opportunity, and affirmative action for women. Although there are problems involved in attracting men into these political projects, the consequences of the liberal political agenda will be improved interpersonal relations, a better understanding of the impact of social stereotypes on our lives, more freedom for men and women, and a real decline in the advantages of men over women. The struggle for equality is, in fact, a political struggle against male power.

Criticism 4

Radical feminists argue that the area of men's studies is just another patriarchal structure to keep men on center stage. According to Carol Ehrlich, "The Pleck-Sawyer bibliography indicates that MIT has an extensive archival 'men's studies' collection.' In its own way, this seems like the height of insensitive academic sexism: Women's Studies developed because all of academia already was 'men's studies'" (Ehrlich 1977:141).

Response

This objection rests on a misunderstanding of the profeminist conception of men's studies. According to Harry Brod, for instance,

The new men's studies . . . does not recapitulate traditionally male-biased scholarship. Like women's studies, men's studies aims at the emasculation of patriarchal ideology's masquerade as knowledge. Men's studies argues that while women's studies corrects the exclusion of women from the traditional canon caused by androcentric [male-centered] scholarship's evaluation of man as male to man as generic human, the implications of this fallacy for our understanding of men have gone largely unrecognized. (Brod 1987c:40)

As noted in the previous section there are many good reasons for feminism to welcome men's studies programs.

Criticism 5

Liberalism offers an inadequate solution to social injustices. This is a criticism that might be offered by radical profeminists, but it could also be given by socialists. In the first place, liberalism focuses on the individual and seeks ways by which the individual can escape the restrictions of the masculine gender role. This focus looks like a prescription for personal-growth strategies rather than for collective political action, however. The direction that liberal men's groups have taken is proof of that. Second, however, by following a liberal strategy, liberal men (who are inside the power structure) are saying, "let the women in, too." Liberalism is committed to equality, but that equality must be an equality of men and women, class by class. Do we want to end up with a liberal society of equal numbers of rich men and women, middle-class men and women, and a vast number of poor, equally divided between men and women? Liberal feminism offers not a restructured society but a society in which only the grossest inequities by sex are eliminated (Brod 1985:2, 5).

Liberalism asks men to give up some privileges, to allow equal and fair opportunity to women; but all the men get out of that loss of privilege is more competition for the limited resources of society. At least radical profeminism offers men a new set of values, such as freedom from competition, instead of more competition; and socialism offers men more control over their workplaces, not just the opportunity to accept a woman as boss or owner.

Response

Liberalism does offer something to men: It offers both the positive value of letting go of some of their limits and the opportunity to develop their human potential. Moreover, it offers these benefits without requiring men to accept the unworkable revolution demanded by socialism and radical profeminism. We have to start somewhere; and since society is a collection of individuals, why not start with individual change?

Criticism 6

Radical profeminism puts too much emphasis on male violence and, to that extent, paints a false or selective picture of masculinity. It thus restricts the focus of its political action to antiviolence organizations and limits support to feminist projects such as rape relief centers and antipornography organizations.

Response

The systematic pattern of male violence against women is always the most difficult to admit and to confront politically. In the first place, much of this violence has been institutionalized and thereby hidden (as in the case of rape laws that do not forbid a husband from raping his wife). Second, violence against women is so common that society has become desensitized. Third, men sometimes define even their well-being in terms of the oppression of women. Thus, their freedom to make and use pornography comes at the expense of women. Unless male violence against women is confronted, there can be no equality between men and women: "Sexual justice is incompatible with a definition of freedom that is based on the subordination of women" (Stoltenberg 1985b:47). This emphasis on the core issue of patriarchy has not prevented radical profeminists from working on other dimensions of the patriarchy such as racism and poverty; nor has it prevented them from working toward liberal reforms such as the ERA. Ultimately, a just society can emerge only when women are no longer sexually oppressed by men.

SUMMARY AND CONCLUSIONS

Liberal profeminism has encouraged new scientific studies concerning the socialization of men; it has also called attention to the diversity of masculinities throughout history and across different cultures. But because it sees masculinity as a stereotypically limited subset of human abilities, the issues that many liberals identify as "men's issues" are difficult to politicize. Liberal profeminism's ability to join in other struggles is further restricted by the claim of many liberals that white heterosexual men are not just limited by masculinity but oppressed in the masculine role; this claim tends to alienate other groups such as blacks and women who see such men as privileged and distinctly nonoppressed. Finally, liberalism does not offer men a new society: It tries to achieve more balanced access to power, but it does not challenge the values of capitalism, competition, and hierarchy.

In its promise of a new society of feminist values, radical profeminism expresses greater urgency about making major structural changes. It presents the masculine social role as intrinsically dependent on violence or the threat of violence. Patriarchy, the target of radical profeminism, is the social and political context that maintains masculinity. But its relentless emphasis on male sexual violence is perhaps too focused and may mistake symptoms for causes. Certainly sexual violence is one facet of patriarchy, but poverty and exclusion are facets, too.

Both wings of profeminism have launched major arguments against moral and biologically based conservatism. They have argued that masculinity is culturally created, not biologically mandated. They have argued that the traditional family is not the civilizing institution that moral conservatives claim it to be but, rather, is an institution that is oppressive to women and destructive of men's ability to be caring, loving partners to women. They have also turned their attention to traditional masculine-affirming activities such as sport, work, the military, and male sexuality and have demonstrated the dangers to men and women of the behaviors produced by these activities.

Because profeminism is heavily focused on the ways in which sexism oppresses women and harms men, and because no one has really experienced a nonsexist society, the profeminist's goal of a better society is only partially articulated. They have never quite clarified their vision of a replacement for traditional masculinity. Thus, compared to the conservative perspective, the antisexist stance seems idealistic and incomplete—even though it makes a powerful case for change.

SUGGESTED READING

Those interested in the growth of the profeminist perspective in the twentieth century may wish to consult two early books: Julius Fast's *The Incompatibility of Men and Women and How to Overcome It* (1971) and Michael Korda's *Male Chauvinism: How it Works* (1973). Of course, John Stuart Mill's *The Subjection of Women*, edited by Susan M. Okin (1988) is a classic statement of liberal profeminism in the nineteenth century. Joseph H. Pleck's *The Myth of Masculinity* (1981) is a now-classic critique of the treatment of masculinity in the social sciences. *Against The Tide: Pro-Feminist Men in the United States 1776–1990*, edited by Michael S. Kimmel and Thomas E. Mosmiller (1992), offers the reader a historical guide to individual men as well as an overview of the different motivations of men who adopt a profeminist stance.

The third edition of James A. Doyle's *The Male Experience* (1995) provides the reader with an overview of the social science literature dealing with men and masculinity. Harry Brod and Michael Kaufman's *Theorizing Masculinities* (1994) is a current collection of writings with a definite postmodern flavor.

The personal stories of several men who have been involved in the men's profeminist movement and an overview of the movement itself can be found in Anthony Astrachan's *How Men Feel: Their Response to Women's Demands for Equality and Power* (1986).

Douglas M. Gertner and Jeff E. Harris's *Experiencing Masculinities: Exercises, Activities, and Resources for Teaching and Learning About Men* (1994) gives the reader a good sense of a profeminist men's studies course. The two scholarly journals in profeminist men's studies are: *masculinities: Interdisciplinary Studies on Gender*, Department of Sociology, S 406 Social and Behavioral Sciences, State University of New York at Stony Brook, Stony Brook, NY 11794-4356; and *The Journal of Men's Studies: A Scholarly Journal About Men and Masculinities*, P.O. Box 32, Harriman, TN 37748-0032.

Further information can be obtained from the National Organization for Men Against Sexism, 54 Mint Street, Suite 300, San Francisco, CA 94103-1812.

▪ FOUR ▪

Counterattack: The Men's Rights Movement

The male . . . is oppressed by the cultural pressures that have denied him his feelings, by the mythology of the woman . . . by the urgency for him to "act like a man" . . . and by a generalized self-hate that causes him to feel comfortable only when he is functioning well in harness, not when he lives for joy and for personal growth.
—Herb Goldberg, *The Hazards of Being Male*

Sexism is discounting the female experience of powerlessness; the new sexism is discounting the male experience of powerlessness.
—Warren Farrell, *Why Men Are the Way They Are*

HISTORICAL SKETCH AND PRIMARY SOURCES

The men's rights perspective begins with the fundamental premise that men as men are subject to numerous generally unrecognized injustices of a legal, social, and psychological nature. The adherents of this perspective wish to act as advocates for men in a society they believe is generally oblivious to these injustices. Organizationally, this perspective represents a merging of the fathers' rights movement with the men's rights political movement.

The fathers' rights movement consists of men and some women who are concerned with a legal system that they believe discriminates against men, particularly in the areas of divorce and child custody. The issue of men's divorce and custody rights is as old as the earliest feminist groups. When liberal feminists were seeking arguments to convince men of the value of the Equal Rights Amendment, they identified divorce and child custody among the many areas in which the ERA would help men. The ERA would require the end of state laws and practices that assume the woman is the primary caregiver and the only parent capable of caregiving and that the man is merely the provider. If the ERA passed, it would no longer be legal for men to be exclusively responsible for paying child support; nor would there be adultery laws that punish married men but not married women. Federal laws could no longer fail to recognize the dependents of single males, and widowers, too, could receive child-support benefits in cases where the wife had been the primary breadwinner (Hayman 1976:297–321).

Men began organizing around these issues in the early 1970s. The Coalition of American Divorce Reform Elements was founded in 1971, and out of this arose the Men's Rights Association in 1973. The goals of the latter were "to cut the divorce rate in half [and] obtain equal rights for men" (Doyle 1976:47). In 1976 Richard Doyle, the founder of the Men's Rights Association, wrote *The Rape of the Male*. The thesis of this book is that the legal discrimination against men in divorce, custody, and marriage law amounts to male rape. Doyle, who is strongly conservative in his language, argues that there is a need for equal rights between men and women and for court decisions that promote and preserve the family. In 1977 he founded an international men's organization, MEN (Men's Equality Now) International, with approximately the same agenda as that of the Men's Rights Association. The 1980s witnessed a boom of such "fathers' rights" organizations—approximately 200 groups in almost every state, including Husbands Against Dirty Divorce (Seattle, WA), Fathers for Equal Rights (Jackson, MI), the Coalition of Paternal Rights Attorneys (Phoenix, AZ), and the Joint Custody Association (Los Angeles, CA). Under a variety of new leadership, the 1990s have seen the rise of new and larger fathers' advocacy groups. David Blankenhorn's National Fatherhood Initiative calls for a public debate on the importance of fathers. Groups like the American Fathers Coalition is a for-profit corporation that hires congressional lobbyists to advocate its agenda. Fathers United seeks to restructure divorce and custody laws, calling, for example, mandatory joint custody, unless one parent is unwilling or unable to parent, a guiding principle for all fathers' rights organizations.

The men's rights political movement encompasses both men and women, some of whom were once associated with various profeminist groups but became disenchanted with the feminist movement. These men and women believe that the women's movement wrongly blames men for the oppression of women and that such blame is counterproductive to ending sexism. They also deny that men live privileged lives. They argue that many states have laws that give men longer sentences for the same crimes as women have committed, grant tax benefits to widows but not to widowers, fail to recognize sexual assault except when it is committed by a man, and extend protective workplace requirements to women but not to men (cf. Hayman 1976:297–321). They also argue that feminism seriously misconstrues male and female reality and has instituted an agenda that only makes things worse for men. Along with adherents of the profeminist men's movement, they express a concern for the costs and hazards of the masculine role.

There are two milestone publications for the men's rights movement. One is Herb Goldberg's *The Hazards of Being Male* (1976); the other is an article, written in 1984 by Richard Haddad, that amounts to a manifesto. It is entitled "The Men's Liberation Movement: A Perspective," and although it identifies itself as antisexist, it rejects both liberal and radical feminism as possible starting points for an analysis of men's social reality.

By 1977 men had begun to organize into small groups devoted to men's rights issues. Several chapters calling themselves Free Men were begun in the late 1970s; the members of many of these groups, situated mostly in the east, came together in 1980–1981 to launch the "Coalition of Free Men." This national organization featured psychologist Herb Goldberg as one of its advisers. Its publication, *Transitions,* remains a major forum for the men's rights perspective. In 1977 Fred Hayward established Men's Rights Incorporated, which is ideologically close to Free Men. Its purpose is not so much to educate, however, as to challenge legal and policy discriminations against men. The "news releases" of that organization constitute another major forum for the ideas of this perspective.

In 1980 the two sides of this perspective came together to form an umbrella organization, the National Congress for Men (NCM), now the National Congress for Men and Children (NCMC), whose motto is "Preserving the Promise of Fatherhood." The National Congress for Men consists of representatives of many of the fathers' rights groups together with those of Men's Rights Incorporated and the Coalition of Free Men. Men's Rights Incorporated is politically dominant in NCM, whose national meetings were held somewhat erratically in the 1980s. The NCM negotiated unsuccessfully toward inclusion of MEN International in 1982. Within NCM/NCMC there has been an ongoing division between those who wish to continue the focus on fathers' issues (custody and divorce) and those who wish to look more at the general issues of discrimination against men. At the group's 1988 annual meeting in Chicago this division resulted in a rather low turnout of the men most concerned with fathers' rights (Men's Rights Incorporated, January 1989, "News Release"). In the ensuing years, however, fathers' rights have moved to the fore within most men's rights organizations. Most of the statement of principles for today's NCMC are standard issues for fathers' rights organizations: These principles call for the encouragement of public support for fathers, joint custody, equality in child custody litigation, visitation rights to both parents, equitable-finance child-support guidelines, affirmation of men's rights to choose traditional or contemporary masculine roles, equality of men and women, and fairness in courts (The National Congress of Men and Children, Membership Application).

Just as the profeminist movement has been factionalized in the 1990s, so too has the men's rights movement split into diverse factions. One wing of this movement is an admittedly backlash movement. This movement stridently attacks feminism and portrays men as the true victims in today's society. The editor of *The Backlash!* says to women "Get over it! Because the real victims today are men!" (Houtz 1995). *Liberator,* a publication of the Men's Rights Association; M.E.N. International Incorporated; American Fathers' Rights Conference; and others make a stronger claim, arguing that patriarchy is civilization (Novak 1991). The language of this wing is of unashamed support for traditional males, male anger, and denunciation of feminism. A second wing of the men's rights movement has labeled itself the "gender reconciliation" movement. Following the writings of Americans Aaron Kipnis and Warren Farrell but born in Edmonton, Alberta, the Movement for the Establishment of Real Gender Equality (MERGE) publishes *Balance* "to promote the vision of full equality and understanding between the sexes." The fundamental premise of this wing is that both men and women are victimized and rendered powerless in different ways—something members of both genders need to recognize and acknowledge (*Balance* 1:1:1, 8–15; cf. Farrell 1993:27–101).

Men's rights groups and their representatives are not usually participants at national M&M conferences. Their agenda is opposed by NOMAS, and their organizations are not listed in profeminist directories. They do, however, have influence among men both inside and outside the profeminist men's movement. Fred Hayward was invited for the first time to present a workshop at the 1988 M&M conference in Seattle. Whereas many in the profeminist movement consider the men's rights perspective to be antifeminist, men's rights partisans claim to be the *true* antisexist movement. The two groups also disagree strongly both about the rights of gay men and about the relevance of the gay experience to understanding masculinity. Warren Farrell, a founder of the liberal profeminist wing, experienced a conversion to the men's rights perspective in the mid-1980s. Because of his profeminist perspective, he boycotts the M&M conferences. Farrell has served on the board of Men's Rights Incorporated and is listed as a board member of NCMC. His two books, *Why Men Are the Way They Are* (1986) and *The Myth of Male Power* (1993) have become primary texts for the reconciliation wing of this perspective.

There has been an increase in writings from the men's rights perspective in the late 1980s and 1990s. Further support for this point of view comes from regular columns in *Playboy* by Asa Barber and occasional columns in other men's publications such as *Esquire* (Stein 1994). There has been a proliferation of small-circulation publications such as *The Backlash!, Men's Advocate, Rogue Male Majority, Transitions, The Liberator,* and *Heterodoxy.* Most view themselves as politically incorrect and proud of it. In trying to present an overall picture of the various voices in this perspective, Farrell's books are central, but for historical accuracy one must also go back to Herb Goldberg's *The Hazards of Being Male: Surviving the Myth of Masculine Privilege* (1976). Whereas Farrell is better known to contemporary readers, Goldberg's books really provide the ideological foundation for this perspective and anticipate all the major points found in Farrell's writing—Goldberg is the originator of the expression "free man." In addition to the two books by Farrell and one by Goldberg, three other books serve as primary sources. *Men Freeing Men: Exploding the Myth of the Traditional Male,* edited by Francis Baumli (1985), collects some of the best writing of the 1980s; here the Goldberg influence is most obvious. Aaron Kipnis's *Knights Without Armor* (1991) serves as an important example of the writings of the reconciliation wing of the movement. And Andrew Kimbrell's *The Masculine Mystique* (1995) offers a slightly different explanation for and solution to the afflictions of men than do other writers in this perspective.

DESCRIPTION AND EXPLANATION
OF MALE REALITY

Masculinity

It is tempting to say that Goldberg, Farrell, Kipnis, Kimbrell, and others who share this perspective perceive the structure of masculinity and the costs of the masculine social role exactly as the liberal profeminists see it. Men block their emotions and are distanced from other men, angry and violent toward women, not playful or spontaneous, ignorant of their physical and psychological needs, and comfortable only when "in harness" (Goldberg 1976:45–60; Kipnis 1991:1, 35–59; Kimbrell 1995:45–130). Certainly some observers of contemporary perspectives on masculinity find a fairly complete agreement between the men's rights groups and the profeminists. "Here, then, are two groups [Free Men and profeminist men] which talk about the male role in identical ways, but draw different political implications from their analyses (Interrante 1982:20; see also Astrachan 1986:304).

But, although they see many of the same costs in being masculine, the profeminist and men's rights perspectives perceive masculinity in significantly different ways. For radicals the masculine gender role is a set of behaviors and attitudes, prominent among which are violence and woman hating, that allows men to have power over women. For liberal profeminists the masculine role is a set of behaviors and attitudes that is limited by rigid social stereotypes of what it means to be a man. For men's rights proponents the masculine gender role is a set of behaviors, attitudes, and conditions, prominent among which are overwork and guilt, that allow men to cope with the condition of their powerlessness in the face of the considerable power of women. According to the men's rights perspective, then, traditional masculinity is essentially a defensive posture by which men try to cope with their reality of powerlessness (Goldberg 1979:6; cf. Farrell 1993:27–41).

The men's rights analysis of the development and formation of masculinity in some ways agrees more with that of the moral conservatives than with that of the profeminists. Men's rights advocates claim that the male is subject to the power of women and develops an ongoing dependency on them, first as a son raised by his mother and then as a man drawn to the eroticism of women. "The male is deeply dependent on the female from conception on. The roots and explanations for this lie in early social and emotional conditioning" (Goldberg 1976:13). In his essay, "The Men's Liberation Movement: A Perspective," Richard Haddad echoes this belief: "Esther Vilar has spoken of it quite bluntly. . . . Women run the show by raising their male children to please women, to protect them, and to crave their praise. They raise their female children to keep men in harness, as they do, by rewarding a man's good behavior by dispensing sexual favors" (Haddad 1984:16; cf. Diamond 1985a:80; Farrell 1986:120–131). George Gilder could have written these passages, except that he would have *applauded* the women's role of keeping men in harness.

A consequence of this dependency on women is that men are isolated from other men. When men turn to women for their nurturance and to express their feelings, they become less comfortable with other men as emotional intimates (Williamson 1985a:104; Diamond 1985b:105; Bauer and Bauer 1985a:292; Kipnis 1991:58; Farrell 1993:368–370). That is, the reliance on women as emotional caretakers makes men afraid of other men (i.e., homophobic). Add to this the male fear of admitting fear, and men will not look for help to their best source of empathy and self-knowledge—other men. Hence, *Men Freeing Men* contains the frequent suggestion that women need to listen to men and men need to listen to one another (Baumli 1985: Preface; Sides 1985a:296).

The masculine gender ideal is contradictory; it reveals the powerlessness of men in the face of social reality. Any boy or man who tries to abide by that ideal fills his life with no-win situations. For example, a boy grows up to find that many of the values he acquired from his mother are no longer acceptable. If he is to become a man, he must disown these "feminine" values (Goldberg 1976:87). The same is true in other aspects of his life—his playfulness, his need to form intimate male friends, choosing a masculine ideal to emulate, being a good father, being an authority, being a breadwinner, and even attempting to grow personally. In each case he faces condemnation and high costs regardless of how he chooses.

> Men are told to be gentle, while gentle men are told they are wimps. Men are told to be vulnerable, but vulnerable [men] are told they are too needy. Men are told to be less performance oriented, but less successful men are rejected for lack of ambition. The list of contradictions is seemingly endless. (Hayward 1987:12).

When there are no right choices, when male socialization pushes men in conflicting directions, and when society condemns whichever direction is chosen, the situation is one of powerlessness. The core idea of the men's rights position is that this powerlessness shows that men are *not* privileged or first-class citizens relative to women. "The conventional notion that men are somehow more privileged than women is starting to look like a bad joke" (Kipnis 1991:11). From Goldberg's subtitle *Surviving the Myth of Masculine Privilege* to Farrell's *The Myth of Male Power,* the idea of male powerlessness is central. Contrary to the profeminist view that men are generally privileged relative to women, the men's rights description of male reality is one of powerlessness and victimization (Farrell 1986; Farrell 1993:27–28; Kimbrell 1995:xiv).

This shift from viewing men as powerful and privileged introduces three significant changes in the men's rights description of men's social reality. The first is a focus on the evidence for the claim that men are powerless. Here there is general agreement. Men are pressured to be good providers; failure in this area is seen as failure as a man—these pressures keep men in harness (Goldberg 1976:148–149; Kimbrell 1995:176–208). Men are the expendable sex: Men are expendable as cannon fodder in war, as workers who are maimed and killed on the job, as parents in the home (except as providers), as homeless who are left to fend for themselves, and as victims of violence (Farrell 1986; Kipnis 1991; Farrell 1993:105–234; Kimbrell 1995). Men's lives are sufficiently miserable that men lead women in committing suicide successfully (Farrell 1993: 164–179; Kimbrell 1995:6–7). Various explanations are given for these afflictions. Some authors, as noted, stress the power of women over men— the enslavement of men by women; others stress the economic enclosure of men—declining wages and working conditions; still others focus on the negative images of men put forth by feminists and the media. In the end, the men's rights conclusion is that men are powerless and that it is not their fault.

The second shift is a tendency to explain the undesirable behaviors and attitudes of masculinity in terms of this powerlessness. This explanation of masculinity in terms of powerlessness is virtually the entire thrust of

Farrell's *Why Men Are the Way They Are* and *The Myth of Male Power.* Consider:

> Men's first incentive to change, then, comes with redefining power; it comes with understanding their experience of powerlessness (while not denying the female experience of powerlessness). Men do not change by being persuaded that one component of power means "men have the power." That just keeps men blind to real power. (Farrell 1986:15)

> Fortunately, almost all industrialized nations have acknowledged these female experiences [of powerlessness]. Unfortunately, they have acknowledged only the female experiences—and concluded that women have the problem, men are the problem. Men, though have a different experience. A man who has seen his marriage become alimony payments, his home become his wife's home, and his children become child-support payments for those who have been turned against him ... feels desperate for someone to love but fears that another marriage might ultimately leave him with another mortgage payment, another set of children turned against him. ... When he is called "commitment-phobic" he doesn't feel understood. (Farrell 1993:27–28)

> When a man tries to keep up with payments by working overtime and is told he is insensitive, or tries to handle the stress by drinking and is told he is a drunkard, he doesn't feel powerful but powerless. When he fears a cry for help will be met with "stop whining," or that a plea to be heard will be met with "yes, buts," he skips past *attempting* suicide as a cry for help, and just *commits* suicide. Thus men have remained the silent sex and increasingly become the suicide sex. (Farrell: 1993:28)

In an earlier version of this theme, Robert Sides, in a letter to *American Man*, a publication of the National Coalition of Free Men, takes issue with another author's criticism of certain male behaviors and attitudes. "I fear Levenson buys in too readily to the idea that men freely choose to be 'bad boys.' ... Personally I feel he's not angry enough. He's not dealt with why men do what they do (to get love, female attention, etc.) ... only that they must stop what they are doing" (Sides 1984:2). This shift from blaming men for their behaviors to explaining these behaviors through their powerlessness is a clear demarcation of the men's rights view from the profeminist view.

Third, whereas expressions of guilt are common in the profeminist writings, men's rights advocates often call for anger against the injustices inflicted upon men rather than guilt or apology:

> I am angry because in my rush to select a career ... so I could demonstrate to my parents ... and the rest of the world that I was a "mature and responsible adult male," I abandoned some dreams I am now sorry I never pursued.

I am angry because I was never really convinced that I had the option of not getting married. . . .

I am angry because of the . . . defensive and sometimes self-righteous denial of most of the women in my life that they had anything at all to do with my conditioning. . . .

I am angry because women have been blaming and dumping on men for close to fifteen years now. . . .

I am angry that in the name of eliminating sex-stereotyping, feminism has reinforced some of the most fundamental and devastating stereotypes of all: the man as predator . . . stalking . . . powerful . . . base and insensitive . . . exploitive and untrustworthy. . . .

I am angry over the hypocrisy of too many women I know. . . .

I am angry because of the broken bodies and spirits of good men who spend their lives locked in a death dance. . . . (Haddad 1985a:285–286)

Astrachan has labeled the men's rights movement the "no-guilt wing" of the men's movement—he might have named it "the angry men's movement" (Astrachan 1986:304).

Much of the anger within the men's rights movement is due to the perception by its members that many women, the mass media, society in general, and especially feminists engage in the practice of perpetuating negative stereotypes of men, or male bashing, "the mean-spirited mockery and categorical denunciation of American men" (Kammer 1992:64). In *The New Male*, Goldberg notes that men are labeled "oppressor, victimizer, abuser, user, exploiter, chauvinist, sexist pig," whereas women are the "helpless victim" (Goldberg 1979:141). Farrell devotes a lengthy chapter to the "new sexism" that makes men the "enemy," that "distorts" male reality, that arises from a "deep-seated anger toward men" (Farrell 1986:191–237). Kimbrell notes that the current masculine mystique "inevitably leads to the degradation of men"; men are perceived as the source of the world's woes: "Violence and racism . . . war, the environmental crisis, and poverty, are seen as the direct result of masculine values" (Kimbrell 1995:18–19). Kipnis singles out the media, citing a Men's Rights Incorporated study, and notes that "men have been notably silent about being so frequently depicted as inept, impotent buffoons or aggressive, dominating, alcoholic, child-abusing, raping, sexist, greedy, wife-beating, power-monopolizing, narcissistic, unfeeling jerks" (Kipnis 1991:69). In short, from the men's rights perspective, "male" has become a four-letter word (Kammer 1992).

The economic contractions of the late 1980s and early 1990s have also begun to draw the attention of men to this perspective. No writer is more effective at using these facts to illustrate the difficulties of being male in the 1990s than Kimbrell:

> Men in the unskilled-labor market have seen their wages drop over 25 percent over the last decade. Real wages for men under twenty-five have experienced an even more precipitous decline. Over the last two years, wages paid male high school graduates were 26.5 percent less than in 1979. . . . College-educated men over forty-five have also seen their yearly pay descend by 18 percent over the last five years. In each of these categories women have experienced an increase in annual real wages. During the 1980s the number of men (twenty-two to fifty-eight years of age) who were working full-time, year-round declined by over 10 percent. By 1990 the number of men working full-time year-round . . . was declining by 1.2 million each year, while the number of women working full-time was increasing by 800,000. . . . (Kimbrell 1995:164)

The result of male bashing, guilt, double messages, and declining work opportunities is that masculinity has become lethal and oppressive. Men have become the "suicide sex" (Farrell 1993:164–179; Kimbrell 1995:6–7, 13; Kipnis 1991:40). Or, in their efforts to be manly, men simply take unacceptable risks, neglect their physical and mental health, suffer low self-esteem, or simply die younger than women. In the language of Men's Rights Incorporated, "The most basic human right is the right to survive. . . . Demographic statistics make it incontestable that men's liberation is more a 'survival' issue than women's liberation. The present difference between male and female life expectancy is 7.7 years. Contrary to popular myth, (1) the differential is caused by sexism [the male sex role and its costs] and (2) the differential is growing" (Men's Rights Incorporated 1985:1; cf. Kimbrell 1995:3–13). Probably no one has said it better than Goldberg:

> By what perverse logic can the male continue to imagine himself "top dog"? Emotionally repressed, out of touch with his body, alienated and isolated from other men, terrorized by the fear of failure, afraid to ask for help, thrown out at a moment's notice . . . when all he knew was how to work. . . . The male has become an artist in the creation of many hidden ways of killing himself. (Goldberg 1976:181–182)

Feminism

It would be an understatement to describe the men's rights perspective as simply nonfeminist; yet it is an oversimplification to say that it is simply antifeminist. Most feminist themes are repeatedly targeted by men's rights advocates as ridiculous, counterproductive to social change, and harmful to men. At the same time, this perspective shares with feminism a rejection of the conservative ideal of the traditional gender roles. But the men's rights perspective rejects these roles not because they give men power over women but because they give women power over men—and they are lethal to men. And, the men's rights analysis of masculinity shares with the profeminist analysis a deep concern over the costs of the masculine role; in fact, men's rights advocates go even further than liberal profeminists in citing a parallel between the social realities of men and those of women.

For Farrell and Goldberg, feminism has achieved much of what it started out to achieve: It has shattered the expectation that women will continue to be traditionally feminine. "The female . . . can readily move between the traditional definitions of male or female behavior and roles. She can be wife and mother or a business executive" (Goldberg 1976:4; cf. Farrell 1987:24). Men's options have not changed along with the changes that have occurred for women; men are stuck in the same traditional gender roles as providers, protectors, and competitors for women's attention. As Goldberg puts it, "The male in our culture is at a growth impasse. He won't move—not because he is protecting his cherished central place in the sun, but because he can't move" (Goldberg 1976:3).

Some advocates of this perspective see the feminist movement as having evolved from a human liberation movement for both women *and* men into a women's lobby working against the interests of men. As Tom Williamson has reported in *Men Freeing Men*, Warren Farrell, who prior to 1974 was on the board of directors of NOW but as of 1990 is on the board of the National Congress for Men, saw the women's movement of the late 1960s and early 1970s as "a voice for human rights." He now sees it as a special interest group for women only (Williamson 1985b:322). John Gordon echoes these feelings: "The single clearest thing about feminism today is that it has become a lobby, tactically and morally indistinguishable from the American Dairy Association or the National Rifle Association. It looks after one special interest group, fudges and lies and wheedles and bullies in that group's interest, and doesn't give a fig for any idea of fairness" (Gordon 1985:279). *Balance*, a publication of MERGE, sees itself as reclaiming a lost principle of feminism. "This society needs a new vision of equality between the sexes. . . . The ideal of full two-way justice, once endorsed by feminism, has in recent times been pushed aside. . . . " (*Balance* 1994 [Spring]).

For other advocates of men's rights, feminism was *never* concerned to liberate men; on the contrary, they believe, it has actively conspired to keep men in their traditional roles (Haddad 1985a:286–287).

Does the Women's Movement promise to liberate men from this role? To the contrary . . . the feminist message is that men do not provide enough [child support, alimony]! What is especially disconcerting to men is that feminism has reinforced traditional demands upon men at the same time that it has deprived us of the traditional tools to meet those demands. Not only are we still expected to protect, but we are asked to forego those traits (violence and emotional distance) which were so helpful in performing this role. Not only are we still expected to provide, but we are told to forego those aids (better access to jobs and high pay scales) which were helpful in performing that role. (Hayward 1988:22–28)

The feminist movement has thus accentuated the contradictions in the traditional masculine provider role and, in so doing, has placed more guilt on men. Publications like *The Backlash!* and *Liberator* clearly see their role as the repudiation of feminism. The full title of *The Backlash!* is *The Backlash! . . . Against Negative Male Stereotypes*. Most of each issue is devoted to correcting what are taken to be feminist lies and distortions.

The different attitudes toward feminism between the reconciliation wing and the backlash wing of the men's rights movement result in more than just a difference in tone. According to Goldberg, Farrell, and Kipnis, it is not that feminism has failed men but that men have failed to understand feminism. Feminism never held out the hope of liberating men, although many men, including Farrell and Kipnis, thought at one time that it would (Kipnis 1991:62–64; Farrell 1993:12). "There is . . . a commonly expressed notion that men will somehow be fried as a by-product of the feminist movement. This is a comforting fantasy for the male but I see no basis for it becoming a reality. It simply disguises the fear of actively determining his own change" (Goldberg 1979:183). But whereas feminism is not aimed at saving men from the harms of masculinity, it does offer lessons for men in learning how not to accommodate and not to be afraid of expressing their anger (Goldberg 1976:5–7; Goldberg 1979:183). Farrell puts the matter thus: "I am a men's liberationist (or 'masculinist') when men's liberation is defined as equal opportunity and equal responsibility for *both sexes*. I am a feminist when feminism favors equal opportunities and responsibilities for both sexes. I oppose both movements when either says our sex is the oppressed sex, therefore, 'we deserve rights' (Farrell 1993:19). Feminism has set a tone from which men must learn (Farrell 1993:18).

But for men who are part of the backlash wing, feminism is not something from which they can learn but rather something that must be overcome and purged. Their reason is simply that from the beginning feminism has gotten it all wrong. For example, John Gordon argues in *The Myth of the Monstrous Male—and Other Feminist Fables* that from its earliest writings feminism has been committed to male bashing:

The four feminist books that have had the widest impact have been *The Feminine Mystique, Sexual Politics, Against Our Will,* and *The Women's Room.* Of those four, three operate from the assumption that women's woes are traceable to the nature of the male libido: *Sexual Politics* is about heterosexual pornography, and how it is paradigmatic of the relation between men and women; *Against Our Will* is about rape, and how it is paradigmatic of the relation between men and women; *The Women's Room* opens with an attempted rape and concludes with a successful one, and features a cast of men who typically dabble in writing sadistic pornography. (Gordon 1982:xv)

In the early writings of Goldberg, he, too, notes the "mixture of facts, half-truths, hyperbole, sweeping generalizations and the fiery adjectives" by which Gloria Steinem "castigates, in wholesale fashion, the entire male sex" as sexual abusers of children (Goldberg 1979:104–105). Farrell includes a chapter entitled "What I Love Most About Men" because he believes that "praise of men is an endangered species" (Farrell 1986:287).

For all its harshness toward feminism, most men's rights writing reserves a good bit of derision for profeminist men as well. Goldberg describes feminism's impact on these men: "They have introjected the voices of their feminist accusers and the result is an atmosphere that is joyless, self-righteous, cautious, and lacking in a vitalizing energy. A new, more subtle kind of competitiveness pervades the atmosphere: the competition to be the least competitive and most free of the stereotyped version of male chauvinism" (Goldberg 1976:5). Many profeminists have taken on "a basically guilt and shame-oriented approach to the male" (Goldberg 1976:4). Kipnis argues that feminized men (profeminist men) are driven by the fear of being shamed by women.

> Feminized men often seem to feel that responding to women's pain is the primary agenda for men's work. . . . They have embraced the cult of the female victim and are apologetic for men in their historical role as victimizers. It is as if they feel guilty, by gender association, for all past abuses committed by men, and need to present themselves to women in a way that seeks absolution for those sins. They also clearly fear the power of women to shame them. (Kipnis 1991:81)

Kipnis is kind to profeminists; consider Adams's characterization of profeminist men:

> In the humanist community, feminism is like a never-ending ideological "ladies' night." All sociological theory and rhetoric are on the house. And if that's not enough, then a woman can always hit on the male-feminists to treat her to some more. "Hey, sailor . . . buy me a rationalization for being angry at you and treating you any way I want, and I'll show you a good time by relieving some of your guilt." And the sailor trades away his own rela-

tionship with himself for a little sign of approval from some angry women. (Adams 1985:289).

Although the adherents of the men's rights perspective are united in their belief that feminism enhances male guilt, increases masculine binds, and promotes myths and negative images of men, they are not united in their support for the feminist goal of ending traditional gender roles. Richard Doyle, representing the fathers' rights wing, believes that feminism has destroyed the traditional male authority and weakened marriage such that marriage and divorce have become ways for women to acquire power and resources (Doyle 1976:65, 175–182). In a passage where he contradicts Goldberg's analysis of healthy marriage and healthy male roles, Doyle argues that men should be providers and in control:

> Women have an elemental need for masculine authority. A good husband must fulfill his demanding role. Men have various needs in a mate: wife, mistress, and friend. A good woman will fulfill all these equally demanding roles. Marriage is like a dance. There can be only one leader, and most women want their man to be it. (Doyle 1976:204)

The tension between the Doyle wing, which is the backlash wing, and that of groups like Men's Rights Incorporated is significant. Although Doyle may have been in the minority in the 1980s, the men's rights perspective has been inching toward accommodation with the conservative perspective. This accommodation has come about because of the growing stress on the importance of fatherhood in the family and the promotion of fathers' rights issues in the conservative political agenda. In its efforts to change divorce and custody laws, the men's rights position concurs with the conservative position in claiming all manner of social evils stem directly from the growing number of fatherless children and woman-headed households (Kimbrell 1995:145–175; Farrell 1993:333–351; Novak 1991:1). Kimbrell notes in "A Manifesto for Men" that "the men's movement must be at the forefront in educating parents on the potential risks posed to children in single-parent families. . . . The public must be made aware that children who grow up with only one parent are at an increased risk for emotional problems, of becoming high school dropouts or teen mothers, and having difficulty in finding a steady job as compared with children raised with both parents" (Kimbrell 1995:316). Blankenhorn could not have said it better. But, as Blankenhorn points out, the primary way in which men parent is as providers and protectors of families. Thus, the men's rights position is a short step away from endorsing traditional masculinity. Indeed, of the principles of NCMC, the right to choose to be traditionally masculine is one. How can this endorsement square with the men's rights view that most traditional evils, such as shorter life expectancy, are due to men trying to live the traditionally masculine life? Either the men's rights view must abandon this claim and thereby join the conservative ideology or hold onto it and argue against conservatives that traditional fatherhood is not the path toward a better society. To date, in efforts to shore up its antifeminism with conservative support, there has been little recognition of this tension in the men's rights movement (see however Kimbrell 1995:296).

Regardless of the differences over the importance of traditional male roles, there is general agreement among men's rights advocates that men and women are in parallel situations: Both are subjected to limited sex roles and both are relatively powerless in certain situations. The Coalition of Free Men agrees: "For every women's issue there is a corresponding men's issue" (Coalition of Free Men n.d.). Most writers also agree that the masculine role is deadly for men. "Because of the inner pressure to constantly affirm his dominance and masculinity, [a man] continues to act as if he can stand up under, fulfill, and even enjoy all the expectations placed on him no matter how contradictory and devitalizing they are" (Goldberg 1976:7). One of the most controversial claims of the men's rights movement is that men are equally as likely as women to be victims of domestic violence (Farrell 1986:228; Men's Rights Incorporated 1985; Farrell 1993:228; Kimbrell 1995:162–163). Citing the work of researchers M. Straus, R. Gelles, R. L. McNeely, and G. Robinson-Simpson, these studies conclude that women act violently toward men with the same degrees of violence and frequency as men act violently toward women (McNeely and Robinson-Simpson 1987). This parallel between men and women should call for enough shelters and treatment programs for both sexes, though in fact it is only violence toward women that receives most of the attention (Farrell 1993:228).

Some feminist leaders have been won over to the men's rights perspective. Karen DeCrow, past president of NOW, became a member and board member of the National Congress for Men. As a keynote speaker at the annual meeting in 1982, she made the following statement:

> There should be no men's movement. . . . neither should there be a women's movement. . . . It should be recognised that sex discrimination affects men's lives as negatively as it does women's lives. What is really needed is a joint effort of men and women to eliminate sex role stereotypes. It should not be hard to understand that the same sexism that imposes a compulsory military registration for males, implying them to be disposable in society, is the same sexism that implies fathers are dispensable after divorce. (DeCrow 1982)

DeCrow offers ringing endorsements of *Men Freeing Men:* "Every man should read this book—so should every woman. *Men Freeing Men* . . . is brilliant, thorough, and will become, I predict, a classic in our understanding of human relations." Of *Why Men Are the Way They Are,* she writes "A revolutionary understanding of equality, power, women and men. I loved this book!" (DeCrow 1982).

Naomi J. Penner, a founder of both the Coalition of Free Men and one of the early chapters of NOW, sees a need for the men's rights perspective inasmuch as women have made gains but men have not. She concludes: "If I were a man . . . I would be angry at having fewer options. I realized that always having to take the initiative and have the responsibility is very burdensome" (Penner 1985:304).

In a remarkably succinct statement, Asta Bowen summarizes the parallel between the situations of men and women that provides the core of this perspective:

> Just as sexism reduces women to sexual objects, it reduces men to financial objects. Just as women have been exploited as sexual and emotional commodities, men are exploited as cogs in the economic machinery, expendable war fodder, and providers who must never fail. . . . The sex-object status that women have found so demeaning is no different from the money-object status that men, too, have every right to reject. (Bowen 1989)

As we shall see in the next section, it is the communication of this parallel and the education of people to this point of view that constitutes the primary agenda of the men's rights perspective.

ASSESSMENT OF MALE REALITY AND AGENDA FOR CHANGE

The goal of the men's rights movement is to free men from the double binds of masculinity as well as from the social and legal injustices aimed at them—that is, to liberate them from "the restrictive roles in which they find themselves, and to foster the conditions under which they can define and choose for themselves the behaviors and relationships with which they are most . . . free" (Haddad 1985a:283). Speaking about a rally for the ERA, Frederick Hayward writes:

> The rally served to raise public awareness about men's issues. . . . Men, as well as women, need to free themselves from having to live out traditional sex roles (and end the draft). Men, as well as women, need to receive equal opportunity to pursue non-traditional sex roles (and enact joint custody legislation). Men, as well as women, need to make their own decisions about parenthood, receive more effective health care, and be freed from the threats of violence. (Men's Rights Incorporated, June 1982, "News Release")

Ultimately, the vision of this movement is the equal treatment of men and women in "all matters social, emotional, legal, economic and political" (Haddad 1985a:287).

There are a number of obstacles to achieving this equality. One is society's "dangerous 'misandry,' a belief that masculinity itself is responsible for most of the world's woes" (Kimbrell 1995:xiv; Kipnis 1991:64; Farrell 1993:27). Closely connected to this is media male bashing: "Male-bashing has become a popular exercise. One can observe this daily on television or in print—in ads, cartoons, articles—and even in entire films . . . " (Kipnis 1991:68). A third obstacle is simply ignorance, the failure to understand the powerlessness of men (Farrell 1993:27). Finally, there is the "masculine mystique" to which many men subscribe and that prevents them "from protesting their victimization, and even led them to support a system that has meant a near-fatal undermining of their gender" (Kimbrell 1995:xiv).

The obvious answer to these obstacles is education and communication with men, women, and the media. Goldberg, Farrell, Kipnis, Kimbrell, and all men's rights publications are dedicated to telling the other half of the story that is missing from public discourse. A good example of this educational mind-set is the National Coalition of Men's campaign to get journalist Bill Moyers to profile Warren Farrell because Farrell is "practically ignored by the national media," which is afraid "to do a show on Men's issues out of fear of being politically incorrect" (*The Backlash!* 1994:13). The First National Meeting of the National Congress for Men in Houston, Texas, in June of 1981 passed a resolution calling "upon the news media to give balanced and equal coverage of male and female issues and to stop treating sexism as though it were solely a women's issue" (Men's Rights Incorporated, June 1981, "News Release").

Although men's rights organizations do target the media and the general public, there are special efforts made to win politicians to their cause. The American Fathers Coalition lobbies in Washington, D.C., for such items as (1) "the father should be the placement of first choice if the mother applies for AFDC," (2) "both parties should be held responsible for supporting the child according to their ability to earn," (3) preferential treatment in hiring for "any person who is the sole support of a family," and (4) "job training and skills enhancement programs should be provided to parents who are unable to meet their financial child support obligations" (American Fathers Coalition 1995). Above all, fathers' rights organizations have taken up the demand for "shared parenting" or "joint custody" in divorce cases (Price 1993).

The Gender Bias Reporter, a newsletter of the Committee on Gender Bias in the Courts for the National Coalition of Free Men reports on court actions taken on behalf of men and reputed bias against men. For example, in 1990 the Madison Men's Organization published "Report on Wisconsin's Equal Justice Task Force," in which it objected to several procedures and findings of Wisconsin's Equal Justice Task Force, which was conducted under the auspices of the Wisconsin Supreme Court. The group objected to the fact that the task force studied only bias against women, ignored anti-male bias, noted but failed to address the sexual harassment of men on the job, noted but failed to address the bias against men in sentencing and incarceration, and, in spite of objections from Wisconsin Fathers for Equal Justice, did not give sufficient attention to the ways in which anti-male bias endangers children (Madison Men's Organization 1991).

Some actions by men's rights organizations have had a legal impact:

1. Massachusetts was forced to drop its sex-based insurance premiums, which charged male drivers up to double the premiums for female drivers. Men's Rights Incorporated argued that young males drive much more than females as part of their gender role and that there is no evidence that, mile for mile, young males are worse drivers than young females (Men's Rights Incorporated, January 1987, "News Release").
2. Efforts have been made to elicit testimony before state and national committees on how sexism harms males. According to Men's Rights Incorporated ERA Project Director Robert Gray, men would benefit from the passage of the ERA in many areas: child custody, prison sentencing and conditions, school policies, and parental leave (Men's Rights Incorporated, October 1982, "News Release"; cf. Farrell 1993:367).
3. Men's Rights Incorporated stopped free basketball clinics for female fans by the Sacramento Kings professional basketball team.

In many states efforts are being made to establish state commissions on the status of men so that issues of discrimination against men can be discovered and corrected. According to Men's Rights Incorporated, "We cannot afford the price of not having a Commission. The cost of pretending that men don't have problems includes . . . the billions lost by male breadwinners killed off by destructive roles . . . [and] the money paid in welfare after robbing fathers of their motivation to care for children. . . . No agency yet has stopped to ask why all this is happening to men" (Men's Rights Incorporated, July 1985, "News Release"). There are also media-watch campaigns, sponsored by Men's Rights Incorporated, that seek to expose the bias that only mothers are capable of judging their children's best interests or of caring about those interests. The group also monitors greeting cards, news programs that focus only on violence against women, and talk shows that regularly practice male bashing (Men's Rights Incorporated, July 1984 and September 1985, "News Release[s]").

A relatively new cause for various men's rights groups is the anticircumcision campaign. Arising from Billy Ray Boyd's book, *Circumcision: What It Does,* this campaign seeks to outlaw all male circumcisions, which it compares to the rape and genital mutilation of women (Goodnow 1992). Many urologists, however, argue that medically there are still good reasons for male circumcision and that men's rights ideology is in conflict with sound medical practice (Goodnow 1992).

In addition to the group-based agenda, individual authors, especially Kipnis, Farrell, and Kimbrell, offer their own agendas and manifestos on behalf of men. Kipnis is a psychotherapist who follows a twelve-step program in his practice of therapy. His version of the revolution is psychological.

> We need a revolution in psychology today. Men need to shake themselves out of their slumber and begin looking at the many ways in which the field fails to respond to their needs. Any clinic not offering groups for men, any therapist who works with men without having been trained to understand them, any training program that overlooks men as a special category of client—are failing to meet our needs. . . .
>
> Through creating strong supportive male community we can create a field of masculine health that will circumvent the emergence of a multitude of pathological expressions. This is the real work ahead of us. (Kipnis 1991:276–277)

Farrell is a board member of NCMC, and with close ties to Men's Rights Incorporated, the National Coalition of Free Men, and associated fathers' rights groups sees the beginnings of a national political movement that will bring "an end to 'woman the protected' and 'man the protector'" (Farrell 1993:369).

Kimbrell is perhaps the most revolutionary of all, in part because he sees the wounds of masculinity as originating largely in failed economic structures.

> Men must fight for reduced work hours. The most important single step that men can take as part of the masculinist revolution—and the restoration of fatherhood—is to fight alongside labor leaders, feminists, parents' organizations, and others in the struggle to reduce work hours. Real liberation for men is only possible if they begin to reverse the enclosure into the workplace. . . . Only by having more time away from work, but still sufficient income, can men truly recover fatherhood and return as a real presence in their families and communities. (Kimbrell 1995:314)

Of course, the various strategies of men's rights can be combined. And there is some evidence of a coalescence of strategies. Men's rights groups, however, have between them some fundamental conflicts. Some of them are following the wing that endorses traditional fatherhood; others are steadfast in rejecting this as the foundation of their association. Some are adamantly opposed to affirmative action; others call for affirmative action for sole providers. Some can find no reconciliation with the feminist agenda; others seek to build a movement on that reconciliation. Perhaps more than any other perspective, the men's rights perspective accommodates many voices.

CRITIQUE: CRITICISMS AND RESPONSES

Criticism 1

The men's rights perspective, for all its talk about equality and destroying traditional roles, often seems to have taken an antifeminist and even misogynist-backlash stance. It frequently conflates "feminist" and "woman," and expresses hatred of both. Robert Brannon in *Brother* (December 1987) quotes Fred Hayward as having said that "I can identify more with males of other species than with American women!" and "Feminism is sexist itself. It is they who are the sexist pigs" (Brannon 1987:5). Woman hating is pervasive among men's rights advocates. For instance, Richard Doyle quotes Noel Coward's remark that "women should be beaten regularly, like gongs," and adds that "perhaps some should, but who would want them?" (Doyle 1976:210). Doyle also refers to feminists as "shrews aspiring to invade male sanctuaries" and speaks of "braying, foul-mouthed feminists [demanding] concessions and conditions ranging from the merely unfair and unnatural to the revolting (Doyle 1976:175,113). Doyle further notes that "if, for some masochistic reason, a man wants to keep a divorce-bound wife, the best method again is to attack strongly in court; to prove up a case that will take the house and kids away from her. Then, he may hire her back as housekeeper. . . . This modern-day, cave-man approach seems to have a psychological appeal to women" (Doyle 1976:223).

Response

The excessive rhetoric of Richard Doyle, Fred Hayward, and others has been a problem for the men's rights movement, but it should not be used to label the views of Goldberg, Haddad, and Farrell as misogynist. We can also point to the rhetoric of feminists who target and scapegoat men, but their rhetoric must be taken as indicative of their anger and should not be invoked as a condemnation of feminism. The men who use such rhetoric, however, are (to paraphrase Goldberg) acting like irresponsible children who attribute to others the failures and problems of life rather than focusing on their own part in these problems.

Furthermore, the men's rights movement can hardly be called a backlash movement, if by that term one means an attempt to completely reverse "everything the women's movement has stood for" (Williamson

1985b:315). On the contrary, men's rights advocates are clearly committed to equality—to the true equality of both sexes and to the liberation of both sexes from their traditional roles.

Criticism 2

The use by men's rights advocates of the new domestic-violence studies suggesting women's violence against men is misleading and only compounds the problem of violence against women. As Daniel Saunders points out,

> At first glance, surveys can indicate that men and women are equally victimized in marriage. More careful study, however, indicates that women's use of defensive violence, smaller physical size, and greater economic dependence explains why they are more victimized. McNeely and Robinson-Simpson's portrayal of domestic violence as "a two-way street" only adds insult to injury for the many women who literally are fighting for their lives. (Saunders 1988:182)

And, as Jack Straton argues (Straton 1994),

> Police and court records persistently indicate that women are 90 to 95 percent of the victims of reported assaults (Dobash et al., 1992). Promoters of the idea that women are just as abusive as men suggest that these results may be biased because the victims were self-reporting. But Schwartz's analysis of the 1973–1982 U.S. National Crime Surveys shows that men who are assaulted by their spouses (Schwartz, 1987). In any case, criminal victimization surveys using random national samples are free of any reporting bias. They give similar results:
>
>> The 1973–81 U.S. National Crime Survey, including over a million interviews, found that only 3 to 4% of marital assaults involved attacks on men by their female partners (Gaquin, 1977/78; Schwartz, 1987).
>>
>> The 1981 and 1987 Canadian surveys (Solicitor General of Canada, 1985; Sacco & Johnson, 1990) found that the number of assaults on males was too low to provide reliable estimates.
>>
>> The 1982 and 1984 British surveys found that women accounted for all of the victims of marital assaults (Worral & Pease, 1986).

Response

R. L. McNeely and Gloria Robinson-Simpson can be quoted by way of response:

> In our view, it is a gross error to conceptualize and classify spousal violence as a women's issue rather than a human issue. . . . "The Truth about Domes-

tic Violence" reviewed sufficient evidence to cause practitioners and others, at least, to question whether or not women are the sole victims of domestic violence, as is assumed popularly. That having been achieved, we feel the groundwork has been laid to broaden the scope of resources, human and otherwise, being deployed to solve the problem. (McNeely and Robinson-Simpson 1988:184)

Criticism 3

The men's rights movement is premised on the idea that male privilege and power are myths. One argument (used repeatedly by Goldberg, Haddad, Farrell, and Hayward) against the claim that men enjoy privilege and power is that men die sooner and are subject to more stress-related diseases. As Farrell puts it, "It is in the area of physical health and longevity that men's power . . . begins to fall considerably short of women's power. There can be no greater loss of power than loss of life" (Farrell 1987:12; cf. Goldberg 1976:181–182). But something seems to be missing in this counterargument. In the first place, by almost all accepted criteria of power (such as who owns and controls businesses, who holds public office, who is sanctified as spiritual leaders, who sits on the judiciary, who controls the military, who sits on the chief boards of directors, and who holds the management positions), it is the American white male who has the power (see Rix 1987). But power is not without costs and burdens. Specifically, those in power tend to work hard, are subject to stress, and may very well live shorter lives. But it is a strange twist to argue that men do not really have privilege and power because they suffer from the effects of privilege and power. It is rather like arguing that because a rich man subject to gout, he is not rich, when in fact it is his wealth and the diet it can afford him that have caused his affliction.

Response

We need to redefine power as "control over our own lives" (Farrell 1987:10). In doing so, we ensure that men have some power and women have some power—but that neither group has complete power. Farrell asks, "Does a company president who has never known how to be intimate have power? Does a thirteen-year-old Olympic gymnast who has never known whether she is loved for herself or for how she performs have power? Does a boy who must register for the draft at eighteen or who is shot through the face in Vietnam have power?" (Farrell 1987:10). When we are talking about the relationship between men and women, we need to use an appropriate notion of power. Of course, if one defines power in terms of the control wielded by men, men may have power. But in that case, male power would be the result of definition and not the result of an honest look at reality.

Criticism 4

Schenk, Hayward, and Farrell have repeatedly argued that men's lives are valued less than women's because men are drafted and killed in war (Schenk 1982:37; Farrell 1987:360–362). But this argument, too, greatly distorts reality. In the first place, most men do not even serve in the military, and for those who do it is often a vehicle for educational opportunity, preferential hiring, medical and insurance benefits, subsidized housing, and retirement opportunities. Moreover, the nearly exclusive hold men have had on the military has historically been, if anything, a source of power and privilege for them. Women have been denied military roles because they were considered weak and, therefore, unfit to serve. This is not to dispute the horrors of war or the fact that men, especially poor and minority men, are sometimes used as "cannon fodder." And it is not to minimize the unjust suffering of Vietnam veterans. But over the years, the military experience has been more a benefit to men than a cost, in times of both war and peace.

Response

One can concede the fact that men do benefit in some ways from military service and still argue that society at large devalues men's lives. As Farrell points out, television and films depict the dramatic killing of males more than 200 times more frequently than that of females. "We call male death heroism. Or villainism" (Farrell 1987:362). Some accept male death in war because it is said that men start wars. But the trouble with this argument is that the men who start those wars are not the ones who die in them. In any case, women, too, contribute to the war effort—by raising patriotic sons willing to fight and by admiring and making heroes out of men who fight and die. In the final analysis, both women and men must accept responsibility for war (Farrell 1987:360).

Criticism 5

Ultimately we just reject the parallels that underlie the liberal profeminist and men's rights perspectives. Granted, both boys and girls are socialized into gender roles and, as men and women, they are kept in these roles by a series of rewards and punishments. It is also true that these gender roles limit the possibilities for both men and women to develop well-rounded abilities or to pursue special individual talents. But there is an important difference. Whereas boys are told that certain roles are not worthy of them as future men, girls are told that certain roles are not available to them because they do not have the necessary capacities, talents, or abilities. Yet boys and men certainly pay a price for being regarded as more worthy, whereas women are excluded because they are often not seen as complete human beings. Sadly, much of the history of Western science is filled with theories about how women are mentally, emotionally, or physically defective compared to men. Thus, although both men and women are subjected to coercion, humiliation, and limitation in the socialization process, men are so treated because they are considered superior to women. That is the crucial dissimilarity between the socialization of males and that of females, and it certainly accounts for much of the power difference between men and women (Clatterbaugh 1992).

Response

Socialization severely limits both men and women—in equally dreadful ways. "When a woman is divorced, has two children, no alimony, no child support, and no job experience—that is her experience of powerlessness; when a man is in the hospital with a coronary bypass operation caused by the stress of working two jobs to support two children his former wife won't let him see, and he feels no other woman will get involved with him because of those very circumstances—that is his experience of powerlessness" (Farrell 1987:xvii; cf. Schenk 1982:47). The suffering of a woman denied admission to medical school because she is a woman can, indeed, be compared to the suffering of a man denied the intimacy of his family members because he must work overtime in order to support them. But the essential objective is to end the suffering caused by gender roles. The parallel between men and women is simply that both are socialized and both suffer for that socialization.

Criticism 6

There is a kind of silliness to the logic of men's rights thinking. These men want to talk about the evils of rape and the evils of being turned down for a date, but they do not want to talk about the difference between the two. Harry Brod, in his review of *The Myth of Male Power*, captures some of the silliness of Farrell's argument:

> One can go through every one of Farrell's points to show the same sort of misbegotten logic by which he arrives at his conclusions. To give just one more example here, he argues that men should not be charged with date rape when they have sex with a woman who has become so intoxicated she's

no longer capable of giving consent because (emphasis in original) "many men feel 'under the influence' the moment they see a beautiful woman" (p. 320). . . . Do we really need once again to unmask the fallacy here? What man who has been robbed or mugged has ever been accused of provoking the crime because their greater wealth made the criminal feel so weak that he fell "under the influence" of that greater financial power and just had to rob him? Now that the legal system has finally learned that we cannot blame a woman for provoking rape just by her appearance, Farrell wants us to return with him to those prefeminist days of yesteryear. (Brod 1994)

Response

Brod's analogy does not hold. Men are taught to come under the influence of women's beauty from the time they are boys. That is the message given to men (Farrell 1993:82–84). There is no comparable message about someone else's money. Although men are expected to have money and to be successful, these are things they must earn, not be lured into.

SUMMARY AND CONCLUSIONS

Men's rights advocates fall into two broad categories. The Goldberg-Farrell-Kimbrell-Kipnis wing denies that men are privileged and holds that men and women are equally afflicted by gender roles, although women have done a better job of removing their restrictions. This wing often argues that women have erotic power over men and that men are oppressed through that power, socialization, and negative stereotyping (see Clatterbaugh 1992). This wing generally favors gender reconciliation only if women will recognize the ways in which men are powerless and give up the claim that men hold all the power. This wing often thinks of itself as true to the early feminist movement and concurring with feminism in rejecting the traditional masculine role. The Richard Doyle-*The Backlash!-Liberator* wing believes that greater male power is in some sense natural and that women, especially feminists, have usurped that power. Being a traditional male is one mode of behavior this wing would endorse as a positive step for a man. Both wings agree with profeminists about the harms of being male, but most profeminists argue that the harms that come to men come from their privilege and power and the expectations that come with this first-class status. Men's rights advocates hold that the harms come from men's powerlessness and second-class status. Profeminists think women understand men all too well; men's rights advocates think women understand men not at all.

Much of the appeal of the men's rights perspective for both men and women has to do with its refusal to blame men, its recognition that both sexes are harmed by gender stereotypes, and its assertion that the provider role afflicts men both emotionally and physically. It also recognizes that masculine gender roles, ideals, and stereotypes are not internally consistent and that they often demand the impossible of men.

Many of the above issues are dealt with in detail by the other perspectives discussed in this book, but only within the men's rights perspective are they frequently merged with the conservative premise that women hold much of the power in society. And if it is conceded that women hold this power and that men are treated unjustly, then the women must be responsible for many of the terrible costs of masculinity. It is this analysis that accounts for much of the anger directed against women and feminism. According to the men's rights perspective, after all, feminists who claim that women need to be further empowered are only making a bad situation worse.

But this view is only as solid as its claim that men do not hold extensive power and privilege in society. To make this claim, men's rights advocates must confront and redescribe the facts that are usually taken to be indicative of male power and privilege. Accordingly, the fact that men make the money is transformed into the fact that men are burdened with the role of provider and women spend the money; the fact that men use pornography and visit prostitutes is transformed into the fact that men are humiliated by these experiences; the fact that men hold political office is transformed into the fact that women either control these men or are afraid to assume such a responsibility; the fact that men rape women is transformed into the fact that women reject men; and so on, to an absurd degree. Indeed, every feminist claim about the oppression of women becomes transformed into a claim of equal or greater oppression for men. The great weakness of the men's rights perspective, then, is not that it points to masculine burdens but that few are able to accept its elaborate caricature of reality.

SUGGESTED READING

Jed Diamond's *The Warrior's Journey Home* (1994) supersedes his earlier book *Inside Out: Becoming My Own Man* (1983). Like the earlier book it blends the men's rights perspective with the mythopoetic perspective discussed in Chapter 5. It is a much more personal account than any of the books used here as primary sources.

The reader may also wish to contact the following organizations for further material: The National Coalition of Free Men, Box 129, Manhassett, NY 11030; Men's Rights Incorporated, P.O. Box 163180, Sacramento, CA 95816; National Congress for Men and Children, P.O. Box 171675, Kansas City, KS 66117; MERGE, Suite #501, 10011–116 Street, Edmonton, AB T5K 1V4.

▪ FIVE ▪

The Mythopoetic Movement: Men in Search of Spiritual Growth

Since the Wild Man cannot stay in civilization, the boy has no choice at last but to go off with the Wild Man and overcome . . . his fear of irrationality, intuition, emotion, the bodily and primitive life.
—Robert Bly, *The Key and the Pillow*

The Horned God is all about change. He is the Lord of the Dance. . . . He brings personal change and social change. He shows us the madness in the tasks of the sane world of every day. He resents us with a sense of being at the edges, the borderlines, so that we can't tell whether he is mad or sane, bourgeois or revolutionary, poet or printer, wild or sober.
—John Rowan, *The Horned God*

HISTORICAL SKETCH AND PRIMARY SOURCES

Not every perspective aims at the creation of national organizations, legislative programs, or political-action task forces. The spiritual perspective on masculinity offers a quite different kind of agenda, indeed. From this perspective, masculinity depends on deep psychospiritual patterns that are best revealed through inherited stories, myths, and rituals. The traditional masculinity, defended by conservatives, is psychically and spiritually injurious. Until men descend into themselves and come to understand themselves, they will not be able to heal their psychic and spiritual wounds and achieve a better life. The profeminist and men's rights perspectives included personal change and growth as important parts of their agendas, but for the spiritual perspective personal growth assumes a centrality and urgency that is not found in any other perspective. Hence, the spiritual perspective is not overtly political. Its message is spread through an informal network of workshops, retreats, and counseling sessions—a message found not in ideologically pure newsletters but in a variety of interviews and short essays, many of which appear in "new-age" publications.

The spiritual perspective is primarily indebted to Carl Jung (1875–1961). Its adherents agree with Jung that men start life as whole persons but, through wounding, lose their unity and become fragmented. Eventually, if men probe the archetypes buried in their unconscious, they will be able to heal these wounds and restore themselves to a state of wholeness and psychospiritual health. Although practitioners of the spiritual perspective offer different paths to health, most accept the Jungian belief that these archetypes are best discovered through participation in rituals, myths, and story telling. Jungian psychology is essentialist; that is, it posits an intrinsic difference between men and women that is more than physical. Thus, the rituals and healing for each sex are also different. In short, this perspective interprets feminism as a psychospiritual movement in which women have created both a positive force for women and a model by which men can do the same.

The current practitioners of the spiritual perspective include Robert Bly, Keith Thompson, James Hillman, Jed Diamond, Michael Meade, Danaan Parry, Robert Moore, Douglas Gillette, and John Rowan. The registration form for a workshop with James Hillman and Michael Meade, both of whom also present workshops with Robert Bly, neatly summarizes some of the assumptions of this perspective:

> Teaching through the drum, story and mythology James Hillman and Michael Meade will trace the archetypal path of every man who must first separate from the mother and eventually find his exit from the house of his father.

> Myths reveal the archetypal relationships which are the foundations of dances between the gender groups of women and men. . . . This workshop will explore how an individual's psyche and daily life are shaped by the potent feminine and masculine archetypes. (West Hills Counseling Center 1989)

I consider Robert Bly and John Rowan to be the principal representatives of this perspective. Robert Bly's mythopoetic movement, the most widespread and influential of the spiritual approaches in the United States today, contrasts sharply with John Rowan's Wicca tradition, which is more humanistic, more political, more feminist, and less Freudian. As one primary source, I shall refer to Rowan's recent book *The Horned God* (1987).

The Jungian approach to masculinity has been practiced by psychotherapists and analysts for many years. However, it was Keith Thompson's interview with Robert Bly entitled "What Men Really Want" and published in *New Age Journal* in May 1982 that provided the first glimpse of Bly's best-selling book *Iron John,* which appeared in 1990. This book—portions of which were published in 1987 and 1988—quickly became the primary text for the mythopoetic men's movement. In the early 1990s Bly frequently appeared at men's gatherings, where he did the active work that is prescribed in *Iron John.* These gatherings, captured on cassette, serve here as primary sources: One is his keynote address, "Men and the Wound," delivered to the Midwest Regional Men's Conference in Minneapolis in 1985; another is "Men and the Life of the Soul, Grief, and Desire," from a gathering in Seattle in 1990 where Bly was a presenter along with Michael Meade. A second influential book for this movement is Robert Moore and Douglas Gillette's *King, Warrior, Magician, Lover* (1990). Moore is also a presenter with Bly at gatherings. Along with *Iron John* and Bly's presentations at gatherings, Moore and Gillette's book will also serve as a primary source.

As the spiritual perspective cannot be understood without some background in the psychological theory of Carl Jung, I have selected as an additional primary source Calvin S. Hall and Vernon J. Nordby's *A Primer of Jungian Psychology* (1973). Our last primary source, which complements Bly's more informal work, is Robert Johnson's lectures entitled *He!: Understanding Masculine Psychology, Based on the Legend of Parsifal and His Search for the Grail, and Using Jungian Psychological Concepts* (1988). This book has been endorsed by Ruth Tiffany Barnhouse, a psychiatrist at Harvard University, for its "clear expositions of Jungian tenets" (Barnhouse 1988).

As noted, the spiritual perspective is generally less political and more personal than other perspectives. It is also more symbolic than literal, and more therapeutic than theoretical. Bly's message to men is summed up as follows: "Instead of arguing about what masculinity is or about what macho is, try to cure your own wound" (Bly 1985). For Rowan, personal growth is a first step toward political struggle with patriarchal society: "Until we do better justice on a spiritual level to the female . . . sexism will flourish" (Rowan 1987:82). Yet, in spite of their emphasis on personal growth, these spiritual approaches also offer answers to the four framework questions listed in Chapter 1 and thereby qualify as parts of a contemporary perspective on masculinity.

DESCRIPTION AND EXPLANATION OF MALE REALITY

Masculinity

For Jung, masculinity is created and maintained through an interaction between society and patterns of behavior that originate in our collective unconscious. The idea of the collective unconscious is a source of Jung's break with Freud. In addition to the personal conscious (centered in the ego) and the personal unconscious (a repository of personal experiences), there is a vast unconscious set of patterns of behavior that served our ancestors and now serves us (Hall and Nordby 1973:38–40). Jung calls the patterns lodged in this unconscious "primordial images" or "archetypes." It is the possession of these patterns that makes us behave as humans. "Man [sic] has a certain pattern that makes him specifically human, and man is born unconscious of this fact only because we all live by our senses. . . . We are deeply of ourselves. If a man could look into himself he could discover it" (Jung 1977:295).

For example, one of the archetypes that resides in our collective unconscious is the Oedipal complex (Jung 1977:289). In the Freudian account, as a boy is raised by his mother, the two become very close; he identifies with her and she finds in him a way of fulfilling her own masculine needs and overcoming her lack of masculinity (Rochlin 1980:26–27). The mother wants her son to be a "nice boy" and to achieve great things. She "creates" his masculinity (Rochlin 1980:25). At the same time the mother fears this masculinity; it is something "superior" to her. She both wants it for her son and fears it in him (Rochlin 1980:32, 37). The boy, realizing that he has identified with his mother, comes to believe that she can never be what he considers masculine. Hence "these early anxieties of masculinity compel him to find a solution. It must be one that will be adequate to alleviate his hidden concern that his mother, the woman he so values, is also critically deficient" (Rochlin 1980:15). The boy will try to deal with these anxieties by becoming the "little man" who replaces his father, but he quickly realizes that his father will not tolerate this replacement. Eventually, the boy comes to fear "castration" by his father—a fear that constitutes the first major blow to his emerging masculinity and self-esteem (Rochlin 1980:63). The Jungian solution is that the boy, the mother, and the father already contain the "resistance against [Oedipal relationships]" in their collective unconscious. Freud, by contrast, held that society must impose constraints on individuals to block these incestuous tendencies (Jung 1977:290).

According to Jungian psychology, each male's collective unconscious contains an archetype called "the shadow." "The shadow contains more of a man's basic animal nature than any other archetype. . . . It is the source of all that is best and worst in man, especially in his relations with others of the same sex" (Hall and Nordby 1973:48). But in the boy there is also the *anima*, the archetype of the female, which encompasses the patterns of being feminine—what Jung calls the "eternal image of the woman" (Hall and Nordby 1973:47). The self, which is also an archetype, strives for self-realization. Self-realization can come only if the individual understands that these patterns will ultimately find expression (Hall and

Nordby 1973:52–53). The man who is in harmony knows both his shadow and his *anima,* and accepts them as parts of himself. That acceptance, in turn, is self-knowledge, and it restores the unity lost in childhood.

But how does one gain an understanding of these unconscious patterns? Jung held that the patterns within us are the same as those that unfold in ancient stories, myths, and legends. The language of these stories is often symbolic and antiquated; but, to the analysts trained to see their hidden aspects, they can reveal key dimensions of our behavior patterns.

> Yet it is quite certain man is born with a certain way of functioning, a certain pattern of behavior, and that is expressed in the form of archetypal images. . . . For instance, the way in which a man should behave is given by an archetype. . . . And that is always supported by mythological tales. Our ancestors have done so and so, and so shall you. Or such and such a hero has done so and so, and this is your model. . . . They show us what to do, they serve as models. [Christians] have their legends and that is Christian mythology. In Greece there was Theseus, there was Heracles, models of fine men, of gentlemen, you know, and they teach us how to behave. They are archetypes of behavior. (Jung 1977:292–293)

Both Bly and Rowan agree with Jung that a boy begins life as a unity, suffers fragmentation while growing up, and thereafter pursues the process of becoming whole again (Bly 1985; Rowan 1987:89–90; Johnson 1988:3, 11). They also make use of Jung's theory of archetypes, inasmuch as they both believe that within each man there are numerous archetypes that influence male behavior and attitudes, some in healthy ways and some in violent and unhealthy ways. "The great psychologist Carl Jung taught us long ago that these ideals—or archetypes, as he called them more precisely—needed to be studied in their own right. What happens at an archetypal level affects everything we do. If the archetypes are healthy, we are healthy; if the archetypes crumble, our civilisation crumbles too" (Rowan 1987:89). Rowan identifies present-day masculine archetypes as the Hairy Chested Macho Man, the All Wise Daddy, the Cheery Life and Soul of the Party, and the Horned God (Rowan 1987:90–91). Bly, too, offers a list of unconscious character archetypes:

> Below the surface man there is a psychic base, or soulstructure, that remains stable no matter what happens on the surface. We could imagine that sea bottom as a crystal-like formation created by the interlocking of inner figures thousands of years old: for example, the Wild Man, the King, the Trickster, the Lover, the Quester and the Warrior. (Bly 1988:11; Bly 1990:229–230).

Archetypes play the same role for the spiritual perspective as nature plays for conservatism. The number and kind of archetype depend upon the Jungian theorist; an archetype can be any "psychological realities of a biological, psycho-biological or image producing character that are typical, stereotypical, and universal" (Pascal 1992:79–80). Masculinity, then, is the product of these deep psychological scripts, which are selectively played out according to social structures that appear at different historical moments. Accordingly, Bly talks about the 1950s male, the 1960s male, and the 1970s male as quite distinct forms of masculinity. Furthermore, "each boy [in the course of his life] is actually living through the entire history of the human race" (Bly 1988:19).

Although Bly is inclined to speak metaphorically about archetypes, Moore and Gillette are more direct in talking about these structures—"instinctual patterns and energy configurations probably inherited genetically throughout the generations of our species" (Moore and Gillette 1990:9). The different archetypes are "hard-wired" into the psyche (Moore and Gillette 1990:9). And these Jungian theorists agree that at different developmental ages, different archetypes hold sway. But they also trace the individual's development as the coming to the fore of different archetypes, moving, it is hoped, from the immature to the mature archetypes. "Different archetypes come on line at different developmental stages. The first archetype of the immature masculine to 'power up' is the Divine Child. The Precocious Child and the Oedipal Child are next: the last stage of boyhood is governed by the Hero. Human development does not always proceed so neatly, of course; there are mixtures of the archetypal influences all along the way" (Moore and Gillette 1990:14).

Moore and Gillette tend to see the individual struggle as one of bringing to the fore the mature masculine archetypes—king, warrior, magician, lover. But the struggle for maturity is also a way to view political society; patriarchy is domination by immature masculine archetypes that are violent, deceiving, and careless of others and the environment. "Patriarchy is really 'puerarchy' (i.e., the rule of boys)" (Moore and Gillette 1990:143). Ultimately, however, greater political change must come about through individual transformations. "Our effectiveness in meeting these challenges [greed, environmental degradation] is directly related to how we as individual men meet the challenges of our own immaturity. How well we transform ourselves from men living our lives under the power of Boy psychology to real men guided by the archetypes of Man psychology will have a decisive effect on the outcome of our present world situation" (Moore and Gillette 1990:145).

For Rowan, too, these archetypes unfold historically and eventually become outdated: "Starting way back around the beginning of the nineteenth century, people have become more and more aware of a shift, a cracking, a slide in the underlying layers of the collective unconscious" (Rowan 1987:89). Both Bly and Rowan follow Jung in finding archetypical male patterns in the stories of Apollo, Heracles, Zeus, and Dionysius.

These tales offer glimpses of different patterns that have been historically important to men—patterns that still influence male behaviors and attitudes as well as female understandings of what it is to be male (Bly 1987:20–23; Rowan 1987:89).

Bly presents his account of the development of masculinity in his telling of the story "Iron Hans," which he retitled "Iron John" (Grimm 1975:612–620). In the mythopoetic movement the telling of such stories not only presents a perspective on masculinity but also initiates men into manhood.

In "Iron John," the Wild Man (the symbol of the shadow) is found in the bottom of a bog and becomes imprisoned in the courtyard of a king. The king's son loses a golden ball, which rolls into the Wild Man's cage. He recovers his golden ball (the symbol of his youthful unity) when he steals the key from under his mother's pillow. He then releases the Wild Man and goes away with him (Bly 1990:12; Bly 1985). His departure is symbolic of the need to separate from parental authority; it is part of the resolution of his Oedipal pattern. In opening the Wild Man's cage, he hurts his finger; he is "wounded." His injury symbolizes that there is no growth, no change, without pain; it also symbolizes the real hurts of life (Bly 1985). The boy lives with the Wild Man in the forest for a time and, while there, guards the spring, which turns to gold. These events symbolize the importance of a boy's initiation into manhood by a male other than his father. The boy's own hair and his wounded finger likewise turn to gold when he dips them into the magic spring; the gold symbolizes his healing into manhood. In short, he learns that a man can heal his wounds (Bly 1990:15; Bly 1985). Eventually, the boy is sent away by the Wild Man to live in, and learn about, poverty. He becomes a gardener, a caregiver (his feminine side), and a knight of great bravery (his masculine side) (Bly 1990:123–145). His identity is kept secret from the young princess he admires from afar. She loves him as a hero but does not know him as the gardener who works for her father. In Jungian terms she is projecting onto him her archetype of what a male should be. Ultimately, he reveals to her that he is *both* the gardener and the knight. Thus he has achieved unity (i.e., self-realization). They become engaged and the Wild Man emerges from the forest as a king, thus symbolizing the creative power of the shadow self.

Bly highlights parts of "Iron John" to illustrate the unfolding of the Oedipal struggle. A boy loves his mother deeply and is eager to please her; she "seduces" him and they are "psychically" incestful; the father sees this and says "Enough!" (Bly 1987:10; Bly 1985). It is the father's role to save the son from becoming a "momma's boy." But the boy's *anima* is already developed by his mother (Bly 1985; Johnson 1988:26). She wants the boy to remain under her control; hence he must *steal* the key (Bly

1987:10). The boy cannot discover a healthy masculinity from the father alone; he must separate from his parents' home (Bly 1985; Bly 1990:14; Johnson 1988:64). The boy learns that he can be nurtured by other men when he is initiated by them. Only men can initiate boys into manhood (Bly 1987:12–13; Bly 1985). For instance, it is the Godfather who initiates Parsifal into manhood by making him take off the clothes his mother made for him (Johnson 1988:27). In learning to be masculine, Parsifal goes on to fight many battles and suffers many wounds. For a time he even forgets his feminine side (Bly 1985; Johnson 1988:76–78). Eventually, he learns to be caring, passive, and accepting, but also assertive and vigorous (Bly 1987:22–23; Johnson 1988:61–62,77). He has again become a unity consisting of his shadow and his *anima*.

We have already seen that the boy in "Iron John" hurts his hand while releasing the Wild Man; he is later wounded in the leg. In the story of Parsifal, to which Bly also refers, the central character receives many wounds that symbolize the psychic hurt that fragments boys and young men (Bly 1985). When Bly talks about the kinds of wounds that men experience in their pursuit of self-knowledge, he is referring to the specific injustices and disappointments of life (Bly 1988:2–3; Bly 1985). A son sometimes wounds his father if he does not follow in his footsteps (Bly 1985); men are wounded by the unsuccessful resolution of their Oedipal feelings toward their mothers and fathers; and some parents have unresolved wounds that they pass on to their sons (Bly 1985; Bly 1990:19–20; Simpkinson 1986:1). Bly stresses that boys must find healing at the hands of other men who understand these wounds because they, too, have been wounded and healed.

Perhaps the most devastating wound of all happens when something separates a man from his shadow—the wild and primitive part of him from which his creativity and energy spring.

> Some Jungians suggest that it may be part of the projected shadow self that the child's parents don't like and wouldn't acknowledge. For men, this disowned side often contained the wild, hairy, creative male characteristics that didn't fit with what Alice Miller calls the parent's narcissistic agenda for diverting the child's energy to meet their own needs. To illustrate this, Bly cites the example of a mother who emotionally pressures her son to become a nice, rich, well-behaved doctor. The pain of this loss of self often leads children to construct a strong defensive barrier between themselves and their unique life force. (Simpkinson 1986:13; cf. Bly 1987:10–11)

Christianity, too, separates individuals from their shadow selves inasmuch as its goal (like that of parents, especially mothers) is moral goodness, not wholeness or self-realization (Bly 1985). Both Christianity and parents fear the shadow, who is not always "nice" (Johnson 1988:5; Bly 1985).

Rowan's account of becoming a man is less detailed than Bly's. He begins with the radical profeminist premise that being a man is a privilege and that "male ways of talking, thinking and acting are generally held to be better than female ways." (Rowan 1987:8). Men generally dominate women—at least the women within their group (Rowan 1987:7, 12–13). Rowan's spiritual understanding of "patriarchy" is that it allows only certain male archetypes to flourish—namely, oppressive ideals such as Hairy Chested Macho Man—while repressing "what is underneath, behind and below" (Rowan 1987:78, 88–90). Men are wounded by the patriarchal selection of archetypes because the archetypes are violent and insensitive; they cause men to wound other men, women, and themselves (Rowan 1987:9–11).

For both Bly and Rowan, "being a man" is a historically changing thing; masculinity varies along with social values that allow certain archetypes to prevail (Bly 1987:1–2; Rowan 1987:4). According to Bly, men are fragmented and wounded by the Oedipal struggle as well as by forces such as industrialization. The 1950s male was the organization man, the 1960s and early 1970s male was an angry macho warrior, the late 1970s and 1980s male was a soft, femininized man. According to Rowan, however, masculinity is the result of patriarchal privilege; because it is separated from what is gentle and feminine, macho archetypes (both intellectual and physical) prevail. In both Bly and Rowan there is the theme that masculinity is currently an unhealthy, spiritually limiting manifestation of ancestral archetypes.

Feminism

Jung himself was not optimistic about changing gender roles. As he pointed out in 1955:

> A man's foremost interest should be his work. But a woman—man is her work and her business. Yet, I know it sounds like a convenient philosophy of the selfish male when I say that. But marriage means a home. And home is like a nest—not enough room for both birds at once. One sits inside, the other perches on the edge and looks about and attends to all outside business. (Jung 1977:244)

Robert Johnson echoes these Jungian concerns in his lectures on Parsifal: "I've been reading a rash of articles lately on the new feminism that scares me out of my wits because so much of it is woman demanding to come out of her traditional feminine role of serving man" (Johnson 1988:48).

When Jung and Johnson express concern about attempts to change basic social roles, they are picking up a theme in Jungian psychology that is deeply antagonistic to feminism and comforting to moral conservatives. Males and females have existed in certain roles for many generations. Over this time the psyche has formed its archetypes on the basis of these roles, which in turn have become the "eternal male" and the "eternal female." Jung believed that the archetypes of the collective unconscious are simply patterns inherited because our ancestors practiced them over time. Simply stated, a "fear of snakes or of the dark learned by one generation or a sequence of generations can be inherited by succeeding generations" (Hall and Nordby 1973:40). A more sociobiological reading of Jung would see the collective unconscious as a metaphor for the inherited dispositions that allowed individuals to be biologically successful. In any case, Jung seems committed to the conservative view that masculinity is natural to men and femininity is natural to women. By *masculinity* and *femininity*, moreover, he means the traditional behaviors and attitudes of men and women.

Neither Bly nor Rowan follows Jung down the conservative path, although it is unclear as to how they would modify the theory of archetypes to escape this path.

Bly's view is that feminism is a mixed blessing. Feminism has been a positive force for women and, to some extent, has made men less violent and aggressive (Bly 1990:3–4). It has allowed women "to say what they want, to dance with skulls around their neck, to cut relationships when they need to" (Bly 1990:27). At the same time, Bly insists that feminism hurts men and holds them back from finding themselves (Bly 1987:2–3; Bly 1985). "Some feminists confuse fierceness with hostility," and separatist feminists have "labored to breed fierceness out of men" (Bly 1988:17–18). Moreover, feminists such as Susan Brownmiller and Phyllis Chestler have wounded men by asserting, for instance, that "all men are rapists" (Bly 1985).

According to Bly, feminism has contributed to an imbalance of "hard women" and "soft men." "Nonreceptive maleness was equated [by many feminists] with violence, and receptive maleness was rewarded. . . . Young men for various reasons wanted harder women, and women began to desire softer men. It seemed like a nice arrangement, but it isn't working out" (Bly 1987:3), because the women are energetic and the men lack vigor. In a passage reminiscent of Goldberg and other men's rights advocates, Bly notes: "We see more and more passivity in men, but also more and more naiveté. The naive man feels a pride in being attacked. If his wife or girlfriend, furious, shouts that he is 'chauvinist,' a 'sexist,' a 'man,' he doesn't fight back, but just takes it" (Bly 1990:63).

Part of the problem is that women, feminist or not, are sometimes called upon to serve as "initiators" of men—a role they cannot perform. Thus, in his talk entitled "Men and the Wound," Bly tells of his friend Keith Thompson who grew up with his mother and a distant father, was raised by a series of maids, made several best friends who were women, and came to be influenced by the "energy of the Women's Movement" (Thompson 1987:174). Feeling lonely for his father, he dreamed one night that "I was carried off into the woods by a pack of she-wolves who fed and nursed and raised me with love and wisdom and I became one of them. . . . One day after we had been running through the wood together in beautiful formation and with lightning speed, we came to a river and began to drink. When we put our faces to the water, I could see the reflection of all of them but I couldn't see my own! There was an empty space in the rippling water where I was supposed to be" (Thompson 1987:174–175). Bly concludes from this dream story that a man so constantly exposed to female energy will not only lack a masculine face but will have "no face at all" (Bly 1985; cf. Bly 1990:25).

In Jungian terms, most women, including feminist women, encourage the *anima* in men and discourage the shadow (i.e., the Wild Man who is integral to male vitality and fierceness). Accordingly, Bly describes the 1970s male as "soft"—that is, "life-preserving but not exactly life-giving . . . superior to his father, sympathetic to the whole harmony of the universe, yet he himself has no energy to offer" (Bly 1987:2–3).

Rowan's spiritual perspective is openly profeminist. As a struggle against patriarchal domination, feminism rejects the masculine archetypes that are currently flourishing. Initially, it was in the spiritual feminism of Starhawk that Rowan found the road to be followed by men:

> Starhawk . . . describes herself as a feminist witch, and not only studies the ancient archetypes, but actually lives them out in rituals and ceremonies. And in these observances, in mixed covens, there is a place for the male. . . . We are talking about . . . a Western tradition, usually called Wicca. This is a pagan form of worship, centering on a Goddess, who can take many forms, but at least the three persons known as the Maid, the Mother and the Hag. (Rowan 1987:73)

Sexism in the Wicca feminist tradition is a spiritual distortion (Rowan 1987:82). Hence the Horned God, which is the positive dynamic symbol of maleness in this tradition, must operate in the service of the Goddess in order to guarantee that patriarchy once banished will never return (Rowan 1987:86). Like the radical and liberal profeminists, Rowan finds in feminism both leadership and insight into maleness. Like the radical profeminists especially, he is attracted to the idea "that a male is most naturally and ideally initiated by a female" into this spiritual journey, unlike Bly who holds that "only men can initiate men, only women can initiate women" (Bly 1987:14; Bly 1985).

ASSESSMENT OF MALE REALITY
AND AGENDA FOR CHANGE

Both Bly and Rowan believe that men must descend into their spirits and make contact with an important archetype—the Wild Man (for Bly) and the Horned God (for Rowan). Yet their assessments and agendas for change are significantly different. According to Bly the Wild Man is not found through the "feminine"—through the mother, through women, or through Goddess worship. "We have to conceive the possibility that the deep nourishing and spiritually radiant energy in the male lies not in the feminine side, but in the deep masculine, and not in the shallow masculine, but in the deep masculine, the instinctive one who's underwater and who has been there we don't know how long" (Bly 1987:7). Rowan, by contrast, seems to reject the division into deeply male and deeply female: "The Horned God has complete freedom in this respect. . . . He can be male or female . . . he can go down into the collective unconscious and start to understand at a deep level what it is to menstruate, what it is to give birth" (Rowan 1987:92–93).

From Bly one gets the strong impression that it is because of contact with women and the feminine that men are separated from the vitality of the Wild Man—although certainly men, too, are to blame (Bly 1987:17). Specifically, Bly mentions three causes underlying men's failure to connect with this deep masculine archetype. First, "The Industrial Revolution in its need for office and factory workers has pulled boys away from their father[s] and from other men, and placed them in compulsory schools, where the teachers are mostly women" (Bly 1990:19). When women schoolteachers teach boys to despise the physical labor of their fathers, they drive a wedge between sons and fathers (Bly 1987:18). Second, the complex Oedipal relationship that ties boys to their mothers also separates them from their fathers. Bly cites Jung as follows:

> Jung said something disturbing about this complication. He said that when the son is brought up primarily by the mother's feeling, he will learn the female attitude toward masculinity and take a female view of his father, and his own masculinity. He will see his father through his mother's eyes. Since the father and the mother are in competition for the affection of the son, you're not going to get a straight picture of your father out of your mother. . . . Many instinctual male qualities will be seen as inadequacies, and she'll make sure you are aware of all of them. (Bly 1990:24)

Third, men have failed to provide opportunities for male initiation into manhood. Old men who could initiate boys are pushed away, and boys are given only partial or shallow initiations in sports and the military (Bly 1987:12–15). In such partial initiations they do not receive the deeply spiritual "religious life in the broadest sense" (Bly 1987:23). Such partially initiated boys may become what Bly calls "savage men" who refuse to look at their wounds and admit their vulnerability (Bly 1985; Bly 1987:23; Bly 1988:19). Such boys lack the self-knowledge that puts the individual in "harmony with his own nature" (Hall and Nordby 1973:53; cf. Bly 1987:23; Bly 1985; and Rowan 1987:94). Bly concludes that, "in our culture now, the young male, being parted from positive masculine values by the collapse of mythology, and separated physically from his father by the Industrial Revolution, is often in this new age full of feminine values. Many of these values are marvelous, but their presence in his psyche are not well balanced by positive male values" (Bly n.d.; cf. Bly 1988:15; Burant 1988:9; cf. Moore and Gillette 1990:xviii).

For Rowan, too, today's male is the product both of unhealthy archetypes and of his failure to recognize an important masculine ideal—the Horned God. But it is not so much the Oedipal struggle or the feminine point of view that separates men from this archetype as patriarchal culture, which allows the Macho Man to flourish. "All these images [current ideals for men], the feminists discovered painfully, are about oppressing women in some mode or other, and about restricting the female archetypes to just those acceptable to men as serving them in some fashion" (Rowan 1987:91). Whereas Bly considers men to be immersed in feminine energy and feminine perceptions of the masculine, Rowan believes that they are cut off from the feminine and in need of finding their positive archetypes through feminist spirituality. Rowan's Horned God *is* feminine, and the initiation to that God is through women, because the God serves the Great Goddess. Patriarchy works by preventing men from seeing the deep feminine side of their nature (Rowan 1987:78, 86, 93, 119; Moore and Gillette 1990:xvii). In Jungian language, whereas Bly sees men as confronted by the dominance of *anima* (female energy and feminine archetypes inappropriate to men's nature), Rowan sees men as separated from their *anima* and awash in strongly masculine ideals. Thus, although both Rowan and Bly find men resistant to admitting their vulnerability and unable to heal their psychospiritual wounds, it is for opposite reasons.

At the core of the mythopoetic agenda is the restoration of male initiations into manhood. Bly, Moore, and the leadership of this men's movement are clear that such initiations are either missing or inadequate in today's society.

The recovery of some form of initiation is essential to the culture. The United States has undergone an unmistakable decline since 1950, and I believe that if we do not find a third road. . . . We have the grandiose road, taken by junk-bond dealers, high rollers, and the owners of private jets; and we have the depressed road, taken by some long-term alcoholics, single mothers below the poverty line, crack addicts, and fatherless men. (Bly 1990:35)

Our own culture has pseudo-rituals instead. There are many pseudo-initiations for men in our culture. Conscription into the military is one. The fantasy is that the humiliation and forced nonidentity of boot camp will "make a man out of you." The gangs of our major cities are another manifestation of pseudo-initiation and so are the prison systems, which, in large measure, are run by gangs. (Moore and Gillette 1990:5)

Ultimately, in Moore's language boys must pass from the immature masculine archetypes into the masculine. This requires appropriate ritual, leadership, a willingness of elder men to share, and a self-awareness of the scripts written in the psyche (Moore 1990). Men must take responsibility both for "the destructiveness of immature forms of masculinity" and "stop accepting the blame for everything that is wrong in the world" (Moore and Gillette 1990:155–156).

Robert Arthur Carlson, who has worked as a Jungian counselor for more than twenty years, has noted four ways in which men's (initiation) needs are met through counseling with other men (Carlson 1987). First, "being in the company of other men is teaching us to stop projecting our needs for caring support onto women. . . . It is difficult to stop the projections when we're constantly in the company of women." Second, "the lover we men have been looking for is inside of us . . . and we keep looking for it in the form of a romanticized woman. . . . In the company of other men, we can learn ways to allow our inner woman [anima] to love us as we are and then we can love the women in our lives for who they are." Third, "facing our father issues is . . . one of the most important benefits of meeting with other men. . . . There are very few men in this culture who don't have some kind of unhealed father wound." And, fourth, "healing the inner man involves coming to terms with the little boy and the wildman/warrior inside of us. There is a playful, spontaneous and powerful force that flows through us as men. This is one reason why being a nice guy finally get to us."

Bly's ideas have also been applied both to men who wish to struggle against macho, heroic images and to men who are violent toward women. Jed Diamond, a therapist of twenty years' experience and director of the Center for Prospering Relationships, writes:

Yet, I believe strongly that the violence we experience in our lives is not the result of tapping this reservoir of primal emotion, but rather results from the

THE MYTHOPOETIC MOVEMENT ■ 109

suppression of this emotion. As Robert Bly says, getting in touch with the "Wildman Within" is different from returning to the old-style macho. In fact the two are incompatible. The Wife-beater and the Wimp are actually very closely related to each other and men most often alternate from wimp to wife-beater and back again. Both share a common fear of women along with an emotional dependency on them. (Diamond 1988:9; cf. Bly 1988:19)

The most significant part of the agenda of the mythopoetic men's movement, however, pertains to the hundreds of retreats supervised by practitioners. The goal of these retreats is to give men an initiation that makes them aware of their deep masculine archetypes, especially that of the Wild Man. The primary target is the "soft male" who is out of touch with his animal instincts and does not have a direction (Hillman 1987:182–186).

Virendra Hills offers a description of healthy masculinity and the self-realized male; it is a description that could have come from Bly or Hillman:

> The new hero will not be clad in armour, and he will flow around adversaries rather than stand and fight, but he must not be confused with the spuriously gentle man of our time, whose softness protects a core of anger. This man is simply in retreat from the father and from his own aggression and drive, whereas the hero can confront his shadow without flight. (Hills 1983:25–27)

Rowan, too, has constructed rituals around wounding and healing. In particular, he describes a five-part ritual for men working on the issues of feminism. In the first stage, *the wounding,* the focal man is reminded of the wounds he has inflicted on women. This state is accusatory and confrontational. In the second stage, *the silence,* the accusations "sink in" and the focal male is given the message that he is a good man and does not have to control everything. In the third stage, *the healing,* the man is welcomed into the group, where music or a change of clothes is used symbolically. The fourth stage is one of *application,* during which the man presents ideas of how he will deal with the accusations. If the group members are convinced, they may agree with him; if not, they will question the application. Finally, during the fifth stage, *the maintenance,* the group gathers around the focal man and focuses on the means by which he can maintain the new strategies. About this ritual Rowan writes:

> It is important to realise that this is not psychotherapy. It is working in archetypal forms: first the archetype of the accuser—here particularly the accusing female, the virago, the angry woman; then the archetype of despair . . . and then the archetype of initiation and acceptance, of entry into the bosom of the group. (Rowan 1987:125)

Initiations that deal with patriarchal thinking (such as this one) constitute the first step on the path to the Horned God, the positive male archetype (Rowan 1987:140). There are many paths to this archetype; some follow the rituals of the Wicca tradition (Rowan 1987:127). Once reached, the Horned God, who loves the Goddess, enables men to heal their own wounds and to stop wounding women. Contact with the Horned God also raises political consciousness. "We cannot experience the Earth as our Mother Goddess and let her be poisoned by plutonium" (Rowan 1987:95). "Equally political is the inability of those who love the Goddess to oppress women. . . . This is a real alternative to male chauvinism" (Rowan 1987:95).

The mythopoetic emphasis on initiation has also inspired other movements. The New Warrior Adventure Training founded by Ronald R. Hering involves weekends of drumming, dancing, shouting "ho" (as a release of masculine energy), making masks, cleansing rituals, talking, and rugged physical challenges as a way of reclaiming positive male energy (Donahue 1992). The idea that is central to New Warrior Training and the mythopoetic movement is that men need to come together, without women, in a place of nature to talk about fathers (Gross 1990). Such gatherings have common justifications, although the actual practices vary from group to group—usually dancing, drumming, and some degree of nudity is included (Daly 1991; Schuenemann 1990; Daly 1992). Bly, however, has distanced himself from these interpretations of his work: "A third possibility is for men to find a center inside themselves. And that's what the men's work is all about. It really has nothing to do with going out in the woods . . . and dancing around naked. I hate all that shit. That isn't it at all" (Bly and Tannen 1992).

CRITIQUE: CRITICISMS AND RESPONSES

Criticism 1

Bly's treatment of women has elicited some very real concern. Rowan, for instance, writes: "I am unhappy about the isolation of Iron John. There are no women in this story, except for the princess the young boy eventually marries. We have no hint at all of what this wildman thinks about women. And in fact fairy stories are usually very bad on the question of women. They usually show women as passive, opportunistic or cruel" (Rowan 1987:111).

Bly's discussion of women certainly does raise questions. In spite of his claim that "women in my experience do not try to block men's growth," he goes on to say that feminist women and mothers do not let men or boys contact their shadow selves, women school teachers teach values that demean the father, mothers find instinctual masculine traits to be faults and lie to their sons about their fathers, and mothers cannot raise sons because they have a feminine (i.e., limiting and negative) view of masculinity (Bly 1987:2, 3, 5, 7, 10, 14, 17–18, 21; Bly 1985).

Response

Bly is a long-time participant of "Great Mother" conferences; his feminist credentials are excellent. As he does not allow all the blame to fall on men, however, he is sometimes accused of blaming women. Bly clearly states that "a clean break from the mother is crucial, and it's not happening. This doesn't mean that women are doing something wrong: I think the problem is more that the older men are not really doing their job" (Bly 1987:17). For Bly, women do not play a central role in the initiation of men because *men* need to take more responsibility in this respect. He is talking to *men* and trying to initiate *men*.

Criticism 2

A stronger criticism is that "Bly is reacting against the demands of feminist and provoking a surge of anti-woman sentiment" (Burant 1988:7). Bly uses mythological images that are frightening to women, and he tells men that feminist values are harmful to the male psyche. "In some Wild Man—type workshops being offered to men across the country, what is being marketed as 'wildness' is often nothing more than thinly disguised anger at women, a militaristic attitude, and familiar patriarchal roles" (Burant 1988:7).

Bly uses his theory to excuse even male violence against women. In a *New Age* interview he told about a teenage boy who knocked his mother across the kitchen when she asked him to set the table. Of this Bly said, "The boy couldn't bring what he needed into consciousness, but his body knew it. And his body acted. The mother didn't take it personally either. . . . There was too much female energy in the house for him" (Bly 1987:16–17). At best, even if Bly is focusing on men who have become too soft and unassertive, his words and images may affect other men differently; "for unreconstructed male chauvinists, the Wildman is simply an invitation to be even more aggressive" (Rowan 1987:111).

Except for his spiritual language and reliance on mythology, Bly's approach is not significantly different from the men's rights view that stresses the power of women to harm men and then concludes that it is for this reason that men are violent toward women. Along with men's rights advocates, Bly is really saying that men need to get beyond the deceptive feminist perspective to see what is really going on.

Response

As Bly is very concerned about being misunderstood, he goes to great lengths in his talks to distinguish between the Wild Man and the Savage Man. The Savage Man has repressed his shadow, ignored his hurts, and is in many ways the antithesis of the Wild Man. Bly has drawn this distinction in talks such as "Men and the Wound" and throughout other writings (Bly 1987:23; Booth 1987). Some who follow Bly do not make this distinction, however (Diamond 1988:9; Lee 1984; Binder 1989:46–47). In a warrior society, the Wild Man is too frequently mistaken for the warrior.

Still, Bly's Wild Man is neither woman hating nor antifeminist. As Christopher Burant points out, "Robert Bly has fashioned a contemporary understanding of the nature of the Wild Man. In his view the Wild Man possesses spontaneity, the presence of a developed female side and the embodiment of a positive male sexuality" (Burant 1988:8).

Criticism 3

Bly and Rowan employ the principles of Jungian psychology, but they do not want to accept the corollaries of those principles. As noted, Jung was conservative in his ideas about the social roles of men and women; in particular, he believed that men are fickle and that women want to keep them at home. "A woman's best prey," he claimed, "is the man that no other woman has been able to catch. . . . Once she gets her man, woman holds him in a strong grip and makes sure that no other women are in the offing. That is natural and necessary, for it is man's nature to alight here and there and then take flight again—if he can" (Jung 1977:246). This view approaches the tenets of sociobiological conservatism, except that Jung talks about archetypal patterns instead of about genetic predispositions. Bly and Rowan maintain that men need to go down into their archetypes, but Jung suggests that what they will find are conservative patterns of behavior. If Bly and Rowan employ Jung's theory of archetypes, how do they escape Jung's conservatism?

Response

The spiritual perspective need not accept all of the conservative corollaries of Jungian psychology. One response to the above criticism is that new archetypes are still being created. The women's movement has recently changed the archetype of the feminine, and men are currently changing the archetype of the masculine. An understanding of the myths and stories about these archetypes is important because it helps men to comprehend their collective unconscious. But the spiritual perspective is not as deterministic as Jung's own psychology: If men want to change they will change. First, however, they must understand the patterns that are affecting them.

Criticism 4

Bly, Rowan, and Moore and Gillette fare no better than Gilder and the sociobiological approach in explaining how male nature, understood as a set of archetypes, interacts with social structures. Both Bly and Rowan claim that archetypal patterns are important. But they obviously do not see them as determining human behavior; if they did, they could not escape the conservative consequences of such a view. How these patterns work, how they influence us, how they change, and just what the intrinsic differences between men and women are remain mysteries. The Jungian theory of archetypes seems to have all the disadvantages of the conservative muddle about human nature and none of the scientific backing that is claimed by Edward O. Wilson and others. In fact, the way mythopoetics talk about archetypes makes their theories useless as explanations of various masculinities. What mythopoetic authors do is to find some trait they believe is widespread, posit a psychic entity as its source, name it, and then pretend it is real. It is like the old seventeenth-century game of explaining fermentation by means of ferments, or whatever it is that causes fermentation. Such circles explain nothing; to tell us that the trickster is whatever it is that makes us tricky, the king is whatever it is that makes us kingly, and the warrior is whatever it is that makes us brave is to play a silly game (Clatterbaugh 1995a:52).

Response

The existence of the archetypes is well documented by mountains of clinical evidence from the dreams and daydreams of patients, and from careful observation of entrenched patterns of human behavior. It is also documented by in-depth studies of mythology the world over. Again and again we see the same essential figures appearing in folklore and mythology. And these just happen to appear also in the dreams of people who have no knowledge of these fields. The dying-resurrecting young God, for example, is found in the myths of such diverse people as Christians, Moslems, Persians, ancient Sumerians, and modern Native Americans, as well as in the dreams of those undergoing psychotherapy. The evidence is great that there are underlying patterns that determine human cognitive and emotional life. (Moore and Gillette 1990:10)

Besides, Bly and Rowan are offering not a *scientific* theory of human behavior but, rather, a story that initiates men, helps them to understand themselves, and can motivate them to change in healthy ways. Rowan mixes his theory with Jungian psychology and humanistic psychology, whereas Bly borrows from Jung and Freud. The story that Bly and Rowan tells is a significant one; it moves men. It does not matter to them how archetypal patterns work. The important thing is that men respond to the spiritual perspective in positive ways.

Criticism 5

Bly claims that the story "Iron John" is maybe ten or twenty thousand years old. Yet some folklore scholars doubt that the Grimms' stories are actually folk stories as much as they are stories made up by the brothers to convey certain messages about gender (Ellis 1987:32). Boys should be active, warriors who receive the passive girl as a prize for their actions (Bottigheimer 1989). The gender messages of these stories were so strong that they were selected by Prussian and Nazi conservatives to illustrate proper roles for boys and girls (Kamenetsky 1984; Zipes 1989).

Response

It is irrelevant how the stories have been used or that particular cultures read in them specific gender roles. The stories still contain human archetypes that are far older than any particular made-up version of the story and that can be illustrated in other stories from many cultures (Moore and Gillette 1990:10).

Criticism 6

The best Bly seems to offer men now and in the future is second best . . . — hanging around older men—instead of the real thing, a caring, involved father. He focuses almost exclusively on male initiation rites as the healing path that will restore to fatherless men a sense of connection with men and a sense of their own masculinity. In support of this emphasis, he tells us that in most traditional cultures "old men simply go into the women's compounds with spears one day when the boys are between eight and twelve and take the boys away" . . . (Bly 1990:86). But Bly ignores anthropological research indicating that it is precisely those societies where little boys are deprived of fathering that have elaborate, often excruciatingly painful, male initiation rites . . . (Burton and Whiting 1961:90). In brief, the crisis in male identity is only a problem when the father is not involved in early child rearing, thus depriving his son of a male role model and emotional bond. (Miedzian 1992:128)

Response

". . . Only men can initiate men, as only women can initiate women. . . . Initiators say that boys need a second birth, this time a birth from men" (Bly 1990:16). But boys must be initiated by men other than their fathers. True, boys can be raised and initiated by fathers as they were in preindustrial society, where "fathers and sons [lived] in close—murderously close—proximity" (Bly 1990:19). The industrial revolution changed that by taking the fathers away, and that is why a nonparental initiation is required (Bly 1990:19–20).

SUMMARY AND CONCLUSIONS

The spiritual approaches of Robert Bly and John Rowan offer both an account of why men are the way they are and a hope of living better. They promise men a new strength, vitality, and freedom through their contact with their deeper selves. To an extent they echo Herb Goldberg's admonition that men must be nonaccommodating, spontaneous, and vigorous. Bly's Wild Man cannot live in civilization; he represents the "intuitive, the primitive," the source of male energy (Bly 1987:12). Similarly, the Horned God cannot be "compromised, diluted, made safe, moulded or tampered with" (Rowan 1987:140).

Many of Bly's ideas about current male reality appeal to adherents of the men's rights perspective. Included in this category are the notions that men are overwhelmed by femininity and cut off from healthy nurturing by males; that there is a Freudian tendency to blame women for male afflictions such as failure to know one's father; and that feminism wounds and limits men. At the same time, Bly's insistence that feminism has brought to women the creative energy that men need to find, as well as his insistence that men take responsibility for the initiation of other men into masculinity, appeals to liberal profeminist men. But Bly's approach is not feminist; he does not see women as initiators of men or as having an accurate picture of masculinity. By contrast, Rowan's point of view is a spiritual version of the radical profeminist movement. Women, he claims, have shown the way for men to combat patriarchy. Spiritual feminists have even presented men with a clear and positive image of the Horned God. Spiritual feminists have not distorted masculinity so much as uncovered its essence. They are the best and most appropriate initiators of men.

For those who are interested in a scientifically grounded theory of masculine development, these anachronistic Jungian theories are not the answer—nor do they claim to be. But so long as the spiritual perspective is kept at the level of a spiritual or religious quest (i.e., a story that tells sto-ries), and so long as it does not ask scientific questions, it can serve both as a therapeutic device and as a motivator for personal change. Although Jung's theory of archetypes has a conservative corollary, neither Bly nor Rowan is a pure enough Jungian to end up as a conservative.

SUGGESTED READING

Since Robert Bly is an important American poet I recommend his *The Man in the Black Coat Turns* (1981). The humanistic psychology underlying Rowan's ap-proach is pointed up in his *The Reality Game: A Guide to Humanistic Counseling and Therapy* (1983). James Hillman's *Facing the Gods* (1980) offers a detailed Jungian look at the stories of Gods and Goddesses. In particular, it tries to "present the psychological possibilities of particular myths and the workings of these figures in human lives" (Hillman 1980:Preface). A very readable psychoanalytic account of masculinity is Gregory Rochlin's *The Masculine Dilemma* (1980). Starhawk's *The Spiral Dance: A Rebirth of the Ancient Religion of the Great Goddess* (1979) gives a good account of the spiritual feminism that inspired Rowan's perspective. And, finally, Gerald Gardner's *The Meaning of Witchcraft* (1959) provides an account of the rituals used in the Wicca tradition.

Critics of the mythopoetic movement and its defenders will enjoy *Women Re-spond to the Men's Movement* (1992), edited by Kay Leigh Hagan, and *The Politics of Manhood: Profeminist Men Respond to the Mythopoetic Men's Movement (And the Mythopoetic Leaders Answer)* (1995), edited by Michael S. Kimmel. Rabinowitz and Cochran's *Man Alive: A Primer of Men's Issues* (1994) offers a men's studies curricu-lum that is definitely mythopoetic in its approach.

For a published list of conferences with Robert Bly, write to Ally Press, 524 Or-leans Street, St. Paul, MN 55107.

▪ SIX ▪

A Matter of Class: Socialist Men

[A fundamental] threat to the masculine identity is posed by the very structure of "work" in a capitalist society. There is a tragic irony in the fact that men themselves collude in supporting a capitalist culture of work which, as it expands, destroys its own human foundation. In essence, this is the observation pinpointed by the Marxist concept of "alienation."
—Andrew Tolson, *The Limits of Masculinity*

[Alienated labor] . . . estranges from man his own body as well as external nature and his spiritual essence, his human being.
—Karl Marx, "Estranged Labor"

HISTORICAL SKETCH AND PRIMARY SOURCES

Socialist approaches to masculinity build on three basic ideas: first, that masculinity is shaped and created primarily by the relations of production, which include the relations of power and the divisions of labor that are part of a class-structured capitalist society; second, that the costs of masculinity are alienations produced by these relations; and, third, that there can be no significant alteration of masculinity until the class structure, with its relations of power, is itself altered.

Although many men who joined the ranks of the radical profeminist men's movement came out of the New Left movement, explicitly socialist viewpoints are rare in the literature on men and masculinity. Conservatives, liberals, and men's rights advocates are openly hostile to socialism. And radical profeminists, while they may be interested in a socialist economic structure in the abstract, prefer an analysis that explains masculinity in terms of male sexual violence.

Karl Marx (1818–1883) did not invent socialism, but he is the single most influential theoretician of socialist thought. Therefore, when I talk about socialism I am referring to the ideas articulated by Marx. Marx offered a broad theory of history that tries to explain why periods of stability alternate with periods of change throughout history. He also explained what capitalism is, how it works, why it arose, and what its long-term consequences are likely to be. What is more important for our purposes is the fact that Marx offered suggestions as to how structures in capitalism help to create and maintain social roles such as masculinity and feminity.

For Marx, capitalism is a system in which a small minority of persons—owners—control most of the productive resources such as factories, raw materials, and technology. The owners enlist helpers to represent their interests. These helpers are the managers and overseers whose sole accountability is to the owners and whose responsibility is to facilitate production. Other professionals, usually self-employed individuals such as attorneys, contract directly with the owners and often act in their behalf. And there are politicians whose tenure in office depends on the backing of the owners. The vast majority of workers own nothing of these "productive forces" but are "free" to sell their "labor power" to the owners. The owners pay the workers a wage that varies with respect to economic prosperity and other factors. For this wage the workers produce a product that has greater value than the wage. The owners, sell this product, taking out of its price the workers' wage, capital costs, interest, taxes, and profit. Marx described this exchange between workers and owners as "exploitation" and termed the ratio of the value of the product to the value of the wage the "degree of exploitation." These relations of production give the owners control over the workers' labor; that is, the owners control who works, what they work at, how they work, and the disposition of the products of that work.

The lower the workers' wage, the more profit the owners have to reinvest and compete with other capitalists. In such a system, owners must continually press for lower pay and benefits and / or more productivity for the existing wages. And the workers, in their efforts to survive inflation and periods of unemployment, must continually try to raise their wages. Thus, the workers and the owners have antagonistic interests; the owners want greater exploitation and a surplus of workers willing to work for less; the workers want less exploitation and greater job security. Socialist theory predicts that, in the long run, worker and owner interests will become increasingly antagonistic as profits fall and workers' wages, benefits, and security are reduced. Ultimately, the workers will take the productive forces away from the capitalist in a socialist revolution because they can no longer subsist on the wages they receive, given the prices they have to pay. This revolution may be violent or nonviolent depending on the historical circumstances.

Marx's collaborator, Friedrich Engels (1820–1895), advanced the theory that the situations of men and women were more equal before the advent of capitalism. In *The Origin of the Family, Private Property, and the State,* Engels argued that with the development of wealth, men found it important to ensure an heir and, hence, there emerged the patriarchal family headed by a man. Some Marxists have found in Engels's theory a satisfactory explanation of the oppression of women. Angela Davis, for instance, considers the oppression of women to be a historically recent development: "Sexual inequality as we know it today did not exist before the advent of private property. During early eras of human history the sexual division of labor within the system of economic production was complementary as opposed to hierarchical" (Davis 1981:234).

Socialists who locate the oppression of women and the dominance of men in the class structure of capitalist society are often labeled "classical Marxists," "traditional Marxists," or "Marxist feminists" (Tong 1989: 39–69). I shall use the first of these labels—not because I think it accurately represents Marx's view but simply because it has become standard.

Classical Marxists are committed to the view that sexism benefits capitalism and is so intrinsically tied to the class structure that, if capitalism were to end, the oppression of women would virtually disappear. By contrast, "socialist feminists" do not believe that the oppression of women is fully explained by Engels's theory. They claim that sexism and the oppression of women existed prior to capitalism. They also argue that sexism does not benefit just capitalism; it also benefits men collectively and individually. Capitalism has merely built on the prior oppression of women and given it a specific form. Socialist feminists do not believe that a socialist revolution will end the oppression of women. But they do share with classical Marxists the idea that an end to class structures is *necessary* to produce an end to sexism (Tong 1989:173–193). The resolution on women written in 1968 by the Students for a Democratic Society provides a clear statement of the separateness of capitalism and sexism:

> Male supremacy in the movement mirrors male supremacy in capitalist society. The fact that male supremacy persists in the movement today raises the issue that although no people's liberation can happen without a socialist revolution in this country, a socialist revolution could take place which maintains the secondary position of women in society. Therefore the liberation of women must become a conscious part of our struggle for people's liberation. (Roszak and Roszak 1969:255; cf. Morgan 1978:4)

Classical Marxists claim that socialist feminists are seeking to change something that does not exist—namely, a specific oppression of women apart from class structure. They also believe that the socialist feminist agenda diverts energy and resources from the "real" struggle against capitalism. To classical Marxists, certain feminisms (including liberal feminism and socialist feminism) are actually an impediment to socialist revolution (Davis 1988). Socialist feminists, on the other hand, are likely to claim that classical Marxism overlooks the oppression of women precisely because of its exclusive focus on class struggle. "Traditional marxism takes class as its central category of analysis. Feminists have rightly claimed that this category does not aid the analysis of women's specific oppression, or even its identification" (Young 1981:50).

To socialists interested in developing a perspective on men and masculinity, the power and privilege of men is the other side of the oppression of women. Thus, the socialist perspective on masculinity is divided between those who lean toward classical Marxism and those who lean toward socialist feminism. The classical Marxist, who locates the oppression of women entirely in capitalist structures, holds that masculinity is shaped by the same structures. The socialist feminist, for whom the oppression of women is something distinct from capitalism, maintains that masculinity is shaped by patriarchal structures over and above the class structure of capitalism.

I have chosen Tony Cliff's *Class Struggle and Women's Liberation: 1640 to the Present Day* (1984) to represent the classical Marxist analysis of masculinity and critique of feminism. My second primary source is Andrew Tolson's *The Limits of Masculinity* (1977). Tolson represents a widely held socialist feminist viewpoint. He sees patriarchal domination as the result of ideological structures, including stereotypes and ideals, that give greater power to men than to women (Tolson 1977:19). According to Tolson, masculinity is historical and class relative (Tolson 1977:13), and in a capitalist society the cost of masculinity is alienation (Tolson 1977:58). Socialist feminism is the perspective I favor as well. In this chapter I shall defend a version of socialist feminism that is slightly different from Tolson's. My main point in this connection is that masculinity and patriarchy are maintained by the relations of production, by which I mean the relations of control over people, their labor, the products of their labor, and the productive resources (Miller 1984:202). What makes the current form of capitalism a patriarchy is that men of any class have great control over at least the labor of the women of that class.

The concept of *work* is prominent in any socialist school of thought. Accordingly, my third and fourth primary sources are Ian Harris's "Media Myths and the Reality of Men's Work" (1986) and Studs Terkel's *Working* (1984). Harris's insights into men and work, as well as Terkel's interviews with men and women about work, give us concrete examples of the ways in which the relations of production structure masculinity.

DESCRIPTION AND EXPLANATION OF MALE REALITY

Masculinity

Socialism in the Marxist tradition is a form of economic materialism. The economic structure under which people live greatly influences other social aspects of their lives. Among the most significant economic conditions are the ways in which materials are produced—that is, the relations of production. These relations have primacy simply because they determine how most people spend their time and energy—in short, how they subsist. Similarly, the organization of society depends on production, and those people who control work or the products of work are the most powerful in that society. To assert the primacy of production is not to deny the importance of other conditions such as race, education, religion, or sexual orientation. But each of these factors is in itself imbedded in work, and central to each is the question of how that group is included in the relations of production and how this inclusion either impedes or facilitates the conditions of work for society.

Most socialist discussions of the relations of production begin with Marx's broad division of the working class from the owning class. Here, "owning class" is short for the owning/managerial/professional class. (There are important distinctions to be made within each of these classes, of course, but in this brief chapter I must omit references to such subclasses.) Since we are interested in a socialist understanding of working-class and owning-class masculinity, we shall focus initially on the effects of wage labor on working-class men. (Needless to say, women are affected by wage labor as well.) Next, we shall address the issue of how the oppression of women affects the development of working-class masculinity. Finally, we shall explore the ways in which the relations of production affect owning-class men and create their masculinity.

For working-class men, wage labor is typically exhausting; it consumes most if not all of their energy. Indeed, an owner who buys a worker's labor also buys his creativity, his time, and his dedication. Studs Terkel provides the following example: "This plant runs seven days a week, twenty-four hours a day. They have a scheduled five-day week. But many of them work six days and some of them seven days. Sometimes ten hours a day, sometimes twelve hours a day. In some instances, the overtime is compulsory" (Terkel 1984:112). Because of this work schedule, the worker needs assistance at home; without it, he cannot spend so much time on the job. If the worker cannot allocate that time because of other commitments such as children, a second job, or job-training needs, then he simply cannot remain available to that work.

As the worker has nothing but labor power to sell, he must constantly worry about not being able to sell it because of surplus labor, automation, injury, or old age. One worker claimed, for instance, that "I've known them to have six hundred people here. Now they're down to less than three hundred due to automation.... (Terkel 1984:112). But as Terkel points out, "You just don't walk from job to job" (Terkel 1984:105).

The insecurity of the working man also derives from the constant challenges to his wages, work opportunities, and benefits. These economic pressures are not the exclusive domain of the past; indeed, the last two decades have seen a dramatic erosion in the opportunities for work and the wages from work. "The real wage of the American worker is falling. Between 1973 and 1979, the average real wage of non-agricultural production workers in the private sector fell by 4.4%. Between 1979 and 1984, real wages fell even more—by 5.7%" (Center for Popular Economics 1986:32). And as the economist Lester Thurow has observed: "From 1976 through 1985 male incomes (after correcting for inflation) [fell] 8.4 percent and female incomes [rose] 6.9 percent. Male incomes are still far above female incomes ... [but] the [chief] reason for the closing of the gap is reductions in male incomes. The most entrenched workers have lost the most" (Thurow 1987:32). In the 1980s there was also a marked decline in the percentage of new jobs that paid well and an increase in low- and mid-wage work that, moreover, was often part time and without benefits (Thurow 1987:32). "Although female-headed families have always made up a disproportionate number of the poor, their rate of poverty increased only 10% from 1978 to 1983. In male-headed households, the rate of poverty rose 50%" (Center for Popular Economics 1986:31).

The insecurity of many working men is aggravated by the factor of race. Black and Latino men face more uncertainty than white males in finding jobs, keeping them, and being promoted. At work, they must deal with racial harassment and find it more difficult to build solidarity with workers of a different race. Thus, although all working-class men suffer from the decline in male earning power, the gap between white males on the one hand and black and Latino males on the other has widened in recent years (Center for Popular Economics 1986:31, 48–49; "Recovery Fails Latinos" 1989). Of the many men who have *no* realistic expectation of being able to work, 70 percent belong to minority groups (Harris 1986:10). They are also most likely to be homeless: About 80 percent of homeless people are male. These men constitute the underclass of the male working class.

Wage laborers are rarely considered successful compared to the standard of being owners, managers, or professionals (Cliff 1984:214). These men often talk about their inability to feel a sense of dignity and security—an inability that affects even skilled workers who have some resources and a chance of upward mobility (Harris 1986:9; Weissman 1977:201; Terkel 1984:162). Blue-collar workers, especially, are assaulted by oppressive stereotypes that portray them as strong, durable, sexually potent, unintelligent, and insensitive to pain (Gray 1987:226; Shostak and Gomberg 1965:57, 60). The physically exhausting tedium of work only underscores these stereotypes. It also prevents wage laborers from being able to learn new skills that might open the way to less restrictive work (Terkel 1984:159; Gray 1987:225).

The working man must be submissive to the powers that control him— namely, his boss, his foreman, efficiency experts, or other managers and professionals who represent the owner. In his chapter on the nature of work Marc Feigen Fasteau quotes the Special Task Force on Work in America:

> [Corporations] . . . typically organize work in such a way as to minimize the independence of workers and maximize control . . . for the organization. Characterologically, the hierarchical organization requires workers to follow orders, which calls for submissive traits, while the selection of managers calls for authoritarian traits. (Fasteau 1974a:127)

At the same time that the worker is expected to be submissive to man-agement, he must try to find strategies that allow him to resist authority. And he can engage in resistance only as part of a network of peers (Tolson 1977:59). Tolson argues that it is the shared masculinity of the working man that has traditionally enabled him to feel solidarity with other work-ers and to resist the authority of owning-class men and women (Tolson 1977:63; Gray 1987:219).

Under the usual conditions of work, the worker's home becomes a refuge of peace and quiet, a place distinct from work where he has the leisure and authority to air complaints and exercise a responsibility he does not feel at work (Tolson 1977:70–71). "I'm not responsible for my work. I'm not responsible for the job I've got. I was led into that by cir-cumstances, shall we say, as everybody is you know. But I am responsible for my family, since I am the prime source of their well-being on earth. . . . I mean, if one of my children were ill or anything like that, that child would come before anything. That's got to be, well that's just got to be a fact of life" (Tolson 1977:80–81). Home remains particularly important even to the migrant worker, who has limited opportunity to spend time there (Shostak and Gomberg 1965:275). A common statement made by male workers is that, in the absence of family, they would not put up with the work.

Up to this point our discussion has focused on male wage labor. Wage labor constitutes a substantial part of a man's life, and it is important to the formation and maintenance of the attitudes and behaviors that consti-tute his masculinity. Classical Marxists are inclined to find in the condi-tions of wage labor a satisfactory explanation of working-class masculinity (Cliff 1984:220–221). But socialist feminists in recent years have argued that masculinity is formed by other crucial factors—even though they do not agree as to what those factors are (Tong 1989:179–181). In Tolson's view, for example, masculinity centers around work—hence the worker's concern with a set of sexist values that are needed to maintain a long-term commitment to an alienating work situation (Tolson 1977:48).

But the relations of production are not limited to wage labor. Working-class men also spend many hours doing socially necessary but *unpaid* labor: They maintain their vehicles of transportation, for themselves and others; they maintain their dwellings, either for the property owner or for themselves; and they produce goods or services for barter (Hartsock 1983:236).

Masculinity is grounded in the patriarchal aspect of the relations of production. Heidi Hartmann locates this aspect as follows: "The material base upon which patriarchy rests lies most fundamentally in men's control over women's labor power" (Hartmann 1981:15). Of course, capitalism did not create this power; it was built on previously patriarchal feudal structures in which men controlled women's labor (Hartmann 1981:18).

The use of a preexisting system of male domination to meet its own ends has served capitalism extremely well. Men probably could not work the hours they do at the wages they earn without the domestic labor of women. Moreover, it is unlikely that the work force could be reproduced without women's labor; and given the insecurity of work, the injury rate, and need for care after retirement, it is unlikely that men could live their lives without women's labor. Patriarchal capitalism has been quick to involve women in wage labor during times of labor shortages, as in war, or to help keep male wage demands under control. And as men's real wages continue to decline, families will be increasingly less able to survive without the products and wages that accrue from women's labor.

Throughout most of its history, capitalism has augmented the fact that women (and children) have been the "property" of men (Rowbotham 1973:64; Gray 1987:227–228). When men have had access to the labor power of women, they have traditionally controlled (1) the reproductive work of women, (2) the products of that work (i.e., children), (3) the domestic labor of women and children in the home, apart from reproduction, (4) the products that result from this labor in the home, and (5) the wages of women and children who work outside the home (Hartsock 1983:234–240). This control, the essence of traditional male power over women, is what the socialists understand to be "patriarchy."

The subservient and vulnerable position of working-class men on the job, their control over women's labor in the home, and their production outside of wage labor are interconnected. Given the overtime demanded by many jobs and the amount of outside work required just to get by, many men have felt compelled to increase their demands on women to do the work at home *and* to work outside. These demands only add to the oppression of women and increase the responsibilities and costs of masculinity for men.

Finally, as the home is principally the place of female labor, masculinity is fully attained only "by escaping from contact with the female world of the household" (Hartsock 1983:241). Thus the exclusion of women from the masculine workplace—an additional control over women's labor—is further rationalized (Gray 1987:221–223). It follows that among the relations of production that shape working-class masculinity one must include male control over women's wage labor—that is, their exclusion from the masculine workplace, male domination of unions, and women's segregation into specific divisions of wage labor such as clerical work, teaching, and nursing.

Most of the literature on masculinity focuses on men who are owners, managers, and professionals. As the lives of these men are taken as representative, masculinity becomes identified with competitiveness, not solidarity; making ever more money, not getting-by; promotion, not fear of being laid off; learning to live in healthy ways, not being maimed at work; how to spend leisure time, not the exhaustion of compulsory overtime. Thus *Men and Masculinity,* in its section on work, deals with highly paid athletes, stockbrokers, and doctors, and features one chapter entitled "Executives as Human Beings" (Gould 1974:96; Bartolome, 1974:100). Moreover, virtually every man discussed in Goldberg's *The Hazards of Being Male* and *The New Male* is a professional, manager, or owner (Goldberg 1976:61–85; Goldberg 1979:20–28). In actual numbers, however, the owning/professional/managerial class is relatively small. In 1981 it constituted only about 15 percent of all employed men, whereas 45 percent were blue-collar workers, 27 percent were nonprofessional technical workers, and 13 percent were service and farm workers. In other words, the working class totaled a substantial 85 percent of all men (Harris 1986:8).

The owner, manager, or professional "does not do a 'job', he pursues a 'career'; he is paid not a 'wage' but a 'salary'; he works not by the 'clock' but by 'appointment'. His career is a long-term investment, a ladder of individual achievement" (Tolson 1977:81). A large part of his training taken up with his learning both how to manage other people and to value efficiency and profit over human well-being. Terkel quoted one man as saying, "You have control over people's lives and livelihood. [Managing] is good for a person who enjoys that kind of work, who can dominate somebody else's life. I'm not too wrapped up in seeing a woman fifty years old get thrown off her job because she can't cut it like the younger ones. . . .

That's the thing you get in any business. They never talk about personal feelings. They let you know that people are of no consequence" (Terkel 1984:398–399). Moreover, "to the board of directors, the dollars are as important as human lives" (Terkel 1984:409).

The life of corporate managers and executives is not easy. There are frequent crises or mergers that can mean insecurity through reorganization. "They put on a front: 'Oh, it can't happen to me. I'm too important.' But deep down, they're scared stiff. The fear is there. You can smell it" (Terkel 1984:407). The man who intends to advance must regard everyone with suspicion and do everything right, or at least cover up his mistakes. "You're always on guard. Did you ever see a jungle animal that wasn't on guard? You're always looking over your shoulder. You don't know who's following you" (Terkel 1984:409; cf. Tolson 1977:88).

Men at the level of management put in long hours. Their compulsiveness is necessary given the intense competition for such "high" positions and the need to keep ahead of competitors. Fasteau gives the example of "an executive from the company [who] took a vacation for the first time in two and a half years. After the first day, he couldn't take just being with his family" (Fasteau 1974a:137). Terkel quotes another executive: "My day starts between four-thirty and five in the morning, at home in Winnetka. I dictate in my library until about seven thirty. Then I have breakfast. The driver gets there about eight o'clock and oftentimes I continue dictating in the car on the way to the office. . . . I get home around six-thirty, seven at night. After dinner with the family I spend a minimum of two and a half hours each night going over the mail and dictating" (Terkel 1984:390–391).

These comments on work by owning-class men reveal a life that is highly competitive, intense, and oriented toward promotion, money, and status. These men do not have the sense of home as haven that working-class men do. Their fears of job security are certainly present, but absent is any talk about noise, danger, injury to oneself, or the trauma of seeing someone else suffer an injury. Also absent is worker solidarity. Managers occasionally express remorse at having to make decisions that adversely affect their employees; but they are the agents, not the recipients, of these injuries.

Men of the owning class have even greater control over women's labor power. In many instances they control it directly through wage labor; they hire women and fire women (Hartmann 1981:15). Thus, not only do they have control over the women's labor power, but their power to sexually harass women is increased (Tolson 1977:89). And in the home, owning-class men (like those of the working class) rely on women's labor power as they either work directly in the home or manage the labor of other women in that home. At the same time, owning-class men seem more accepting of egalitarian marriage; perhaps because they have some-what more control over their lives and the lives of others, they are more willing and able to give up some control at home (Kimball 1983:233).

This book is not an empirical study of the differences between worker masculinity and that of owner-managers. But we have seen enough indicators of these differences to understand why socialists do not want to assume that owner masculinity is the only masculinity that "afflicts" the American male. For socialists, the conditions, behaviors, and attitudes of the masculine social role, together with its associated stereotypes and ideals, are class specific; and within each class there are further divisions of control by sex and race. Stated another way, "achievement," "success," "home," "work," "security," "competition," and even "control of women's labor power"—the concepts that are used to describe masculinity—take on different meanings as we move from class to class (Tolson 1977:92–95; Cliff 1984:210–211).

For socialists it is also important to note the interlocking structures that hold the different masculinities together. As many economists have noted, the United States and Canada are undergoing a rapid transfer of wealth from the lower and middle classes to the upper classes (Thurow 1987:37; Center for Popular Economics 1986:24–29). Crudely stated, this transfer of wealth translates into more opportunities to become successful for owners, managers, and professional males, and fewer work opportunities and more unemployment or underemployment for workers. The leisure, purchasing opportunities, and career opportunities of one class are gained by squeezing the same resources out of other classes. There is even some antagonism between the classes over the aspects of women's labor that they control; the owning-class men want to lower the wages that women take home, whereas the working-class husbands, who often appropriate these wages, would like them to be higher.

Feminism

As noted, socialists are divided between those who are inclined toward classical Marxist theory and those who accept socialist feminism. In the former camp are socialists like Tony Cliff, who rejects as counterproductive any feminist theories that attribute the oppression of women to men and male control rather than to capitalism.

> But, many feminists argue, the actual oppression of women is carried out by men. Men are rapists, pornographers, wife-beaters and so on, they say. . . . These are the actions of individuals and are small compared to the way the capitalist system structures and perpetuates women's oppression through its institutions. Low pay, sections of the economy effectively barred to women, lack of childcare provision, and the institution of the family itself are the

means by which reproduction remains privatised and whereby women are ensured a double burden. (Cliff 1984:229)

Cliff is inclined to see American feminism as creating "escapism and division" of women from men and, ultimately, women from women (Cliff 1984:156, 162–164). The women's movement, he claims, not only prevents the natural alliance between working men and women but also allows the bourgeois agenda of liberalism to lead it into the Democratic party, resulting in a loss of political influence. The practice of consciousness raising assumes that "personal relationships are moulded merely by the ideas which we carry in our heads"; it also encourages women to turn away from political activity (Cliff 1984:163–164). Socialist feminist efforts to identify the oppression outside of class have resulted in what Cliff calls a "mushrooming of 'oppressions'" (Cliff 1984:164). Thus for classical Marxists, feminism has had the largely negative effect of separating men from women and directing energies to areas that have no impact on the central oppressive structure of capitalism.

But whereas classical Marxists accuse socialist feminists of marginalizing the working class, socialist feminists worry that the focus of classical Marxism ignores the specific oppression of women. For example, Cliff's discussion does not deal with the control that men have over women's labor power. "In the hierarchy of patriarchy, all men, whatever their rank in the patriarchy, are bought off by being able to control at least some women" (Hartmann 1981:15).

For socialists (such as myself and Tolson) who are not persuaded by the classical Marxist position, the diversity of socialist feminisms presents a difficult challenge: How does one choose among competing socialist feminist theories? Tolson is drawn to theories that see patriarchy as an "ideological imposition" on the class structure of capitalism (Tolson 1977:142). For him, masculinity "comprises a structure of inter-related conventions" (Tolson 1977:8). He believes strongly that socialist men, working in "the male dominated socialist tradition," must begin to understand their own sexism through consciousness raising (Tolson 1977:18–19, 145). "The challenge to socialist men is to understand masculinity as a social problem— and thus to work together for a nonsexist socialist society" (Tolson 1977:146). Although I accept Tolson's construction of masculinity by class, and although I agree that patriarchy is ideologically reinforced, I am more inclined to stress the relations of production in which men control women's labor power as the material condition that renders this ideology effective. Given Tolson's own emphasis on work, I suspect that he would partially agree. After all, he has pointed out that "patriarchy operates by giving men a family-based image of work which is then reaffirmed by a work-based masculine culture" (Tolson 1977:141–142).

ASSESSMENT OF MALE REALITY AND
AGENDA FOR CHANGE

One of the striking commonalities throughout much of the literature on men and masculinity is agreement about the cost of being masculine. Even if men themselves are not oppressed, those who assume a traditional masculine role tend to pay a price. The socialist analysis of masculinity does not deny this cost. For the socialist this cost comes down to the fact that men's lives, too, are controlled by the relations of production. Equally striking is the fact that none of the other perspectives take advantage of the long tradition, beginning with Marx, that discusses this very cost (which in the socialist tradition is known as "alienation"). Socialist feminists are described by Alison Jaggar as feminists who "characterize women's oppression in terms of a revised version of the Marxist theory of alienation" (Jaggar 1983:353). Accordingly, when women are controlled by men in their reproductive work, their domestic work, and in the work world, they become alienated from their bodies, their motherhood, their homes, and their jobs (Tong 1989:187). They relate to men according to many of the same dynamics by which workers relate to owners. Socialist feminism has taught that femininity is a kind of alienation; the socialist perspective on masculinity teaches the same: Masculinity, too, is a form of alienation largely produced by the relations of production in which men control and are controlled (Harris 1986:10; cf. Cliff 1984:205–206).

The classic discussion of alienation is taken up in two essays by Karl Marx: "Estranged Labor" and "The Meaning of Human Requirements." These essays are parts of a work usually published as *The Economic and Philosophic Manuscripts of 1844* (Marx 1964a).

Marx gives more than one characterization of the state of alienation, but the account that fits the situation of men is that alienation occurs when one's activity or products are controlled by an alien will or power (Marx 1964b:115; Marx 1964c:147, 150). I understand Marx to be saying that alienation is the opposite of autonomy. The more one's life is limited by other people, the greater the degree of alienation. In a capitalist economic structure a male worker has only his labor to sell, but he is forced to sell it in order to make a living (Marx 1964b:111). When he does sell his labor, he comes under the working conditions set by the owner and, regardless of his preferences, must make what the owner demands. Even after he has made the product, it is appropriated from him by the owner.

As noted, the lives of working-class men are filled with monotony and danger culminating in an exhaustion that greatly circumscribes their lives. What is alienation in this context? It is "the fact that labor is external to the worker. . . . He does not affirm himself but denies himself, does not feel contented but unhappy, does not develop freely his physical and mental energy but mortifies his body and ruins his mind" (Marx 1964b:110). Indeed, as Ian Harris points out, "A man's work (or lack of work) is at odds with fulfilling personal goals and becoming the sort of person he wishes to be" (Harris 1986:10). The exhausted worker has little time or energy to devote to himself, but his talent makes the world richer and his constant labor makes him poorer—physically, intellectually, and often in terms of purchasing power as well. The worker who is part of the reserve army of labor, who irregularly or rarely receives a wage, is even more controlled by alien powers. As wealth accumulates and his debt increases, he is confronted by a world that is ever more powerful, alien, and independent of his will (Harris 1986:10).

As noted, working-class masculinity is divided between the powerlessness of male wage labor and the privilege and power of men over women of the same class. In other words, male workers have the dual roles of submission to owners and authority over women's labor.

In wage labor a worker has little control over his activity or its products. He is little more than a means to an end, a profit for the owners. He is interchangeable with machines and easily discarded. The owners do not relate to him as a full human being; he has little opportunity to choose which talents he will pursue. When masculinity is developed in an authoritarian atmosphere where men see other men as rivals who might replace them, perceive women workers as a threat, or are divided by race, what is undermined is the very solidarity that might otherwise enable them to counter the alienations of work. As Tolson observes, work under capitalism "destroys its own human foundation" (Tolson 1977:49; Gray 1987:218–221).

A man's power over women, too, often means that he does not relate to them as persons but only as a means of achieving sexual satisfaction, having children, and continuing his work. In other words, women are easily dismissed. This dehumanization of women only produces further alienations in the male worker. He becomes isolated and unable to care for himself; he is separated from his children and becomes fearful of losing control and descending into violence against those he cares about. In short, a man may lose the very benefits for which he presumably labors in the first place (Cliff 1984:212). At the same time, he creates in women alienations analogous to those he has experienced in wage labor—loss of control over their bodies, their activities, and the products of their labor. Under these conditions, women, too, can neither grow nor develop their talents, and they come to feel dehumanized and expendable.

Although Marx's essay "Estranged Labor" was left unfinished, he did suggest that the worker is not the only one confronted with an alienated life (Marx 1964b:119). The owner is alienated as well. He, too, must put in long hours away from his family. He, too, is forced to treat his workers not as men or women but as machines. He, too, tries to establish control over his world by controlling women and other men. He is subject to the power of the market, which may make him either richer or poorer. If he is sufficiently careless or unlucky, he could end up experiencing the alienations of the worker. He is neither oppressed nor exploited (unlike the worker) but he is alienated by his power and the need to maintain it. Controlling the lives of others does, indeed, place severe restrictions on the lives of those in power.

Given this assessment of masculinity as a condition of alienation, the socialist goal is to change the material conditions that produce alienation. And, like radical profeminists who eschew the use of patriarchal institutions, socialists spurn the use of capitalist institutions. Thus electoral politics, legal reforms, court rulings, and even improvements in the educational system are not promising strategies for change. Thus is not to say that socialists—given a choice between doing nothing for progressive reform and lending support to that reform—will do nothing. My point is simply that the socialists are skeptical about working through organizations or institutions that they believe are ultimately committed to the interests of the owning class.

Socialists are also unlikely to support the contemporary men's movement. The current effort of this movement is to built a politically viable momentum around the costs of the male gender role. But for socialists, working- and owning-class males have antagonistic interests; the leisure, freedom, and wealth that owning-class males enjoy derives from the forced labor, lack of leisure, and relative poverty of working-class males. Thus a movement made up only of men is unlikely to be politically viable. And until the men's movement abandons its professional managerial class orientation and aligns itself with "the struggles of working-class men, minority men and underclass men," it will not even begin to take up the issues that are important in the socialist agenda (Harris 1986:44).

So the question remains: What is the socialist agenda, and where should it be implemented? For socialists, worker control over the workplace is a first significant step toward ending the alienations of masculinity. At the least, worker control means greater accountability of managers to workers and more control over working conditions. These are the issues of labor disputes, whether they pertain to miners in Virginia striking against a large corporation or to miners in Siberia striking against a bureaucratic state.

The long-term goal of socialism is to eradicate the owning class through implementation of worker control. As a consequence, workers would not only democratically control their working conditions but would also have time for themselves and others in their lives. Owning- and managing-class men would no longer experience the alienations of owning and managing because they would no longer exist as a class;

managers, to the extent they are needed at all, would be workers themselves, democratically accountable to the collectivity of workers.

Similarly, according to the socialist feminist analysis, the oppression of women can end only when women gain control over their own labor. For socialists, the oppression of women can be fought to some extent in the workplace, where inequality between the sexes has given rise to a lengthy agenda: Female workers not only face the same problems confronting male workers, but they are also the last to be hired, the first to be fired, sexually harassed, sexually assaulted, punished for their traditional involvement with children, deprived of childcare and maternity leave, underemployed, and underpaid (Gray 1987:234). An antisexist workplace supportive of strong solidarity between men and women would indeed go a long way toward undercutting male owning-class control over women's labor.

In the final analysis, progress against the costs of masculinity and the oppression of women must occur together through a substantial restructuring of the relations of production. But the socialist agenda faces difficulties similar to those of other perspectives. If the deeper causes of alienation and oppression are the relations of production, how should socialists respond to reforms that do not affect these deeper causes? To what extent can socialists depend on the state to implement such changes as affirmative action, individual rights, and bargaining rights? How can socialists get working-class men to see the connection between their sexism and their working conditions? How can working-class men build solidarity with working-class women, given the history of sexism in labor unions and among workers? These questions point to formidable problems that will not be easily or quickly solved.

CRITIQUE: CRITICISMS AND RESPONSES

Criticism 1

Richard Haddad voices our first criticism.

The men's movement must not be aligned with any particular political party or philosophy. I feel that I have to say this because it looks more and more like the women's movement has aligned solidly with the left-of-center Democratic politics, and because most male feminist groups have a very silly habit of mixing leftist politics and an anti-corporate attitude with men's issues.

The men's movement can no more be Marxist in its orientation than it can be capitalistic; no more liberal than conservative; no more Democratic than Republican. Men of all political persuasions, of all income levels, of all classes, the black and the WASP and the Catholic and the Jew; the laborer and the corporation executive . . . all suffer . . . the same provider burden. (Haddad 1985a:288)

Response

If this is a prescription, it looks like a prescription for a movement with no identity. Social movements usually assume a political orientation and generally unite people who share a common history or set of problems. The political orientation of the group will affect its understanding of its problems and their solutions. As our previous examinations of masculinity have demonstrated, what one thinks of masculinity, how one evaluates it, and which agenda is proposed depend on a particular political orientation. That orientation is what gives a movement its identity.

An important question is thus implied: Is there a universal provider role around which men could unite? Workers and owners are not providers in the same way. And the conditions that make the workers good providers will often make the owners poor ones. For many men of the underclass, levels of unemployment are so high and opportunities for work so few that they experience little chance of being providers.

Criticism 2

Jack Nichols provides our second criticism.

Neither the economic system nor the advance of technology can bear primary blame for social chaos. They add to the chaos, they give it strength, but they are only symptoms of maladies, not causes. The causes are more fundamental. They are rooted in the values to which men subscribe, and since men control most businesses, these values are reflected through the economic and technological structures they create. . . . A saner society will flower when men liberate themselves from contrived, socially fabricated prohibitions, cultural straitjackets, and mental stereotypes that control and inhibit behavior through arbitrary definitions of what it means to be a man. (Nichols 1975:317)

Response

Capitalism may be harsh, immoral, sexist, and insensitive to the needs of workers, but it is hardly chaotic. It is a system of ruthless competition and efficiency. Nor is the definition of what it means to be a man entirely "arbitrary." The power relations that teach men to be masculine make for good workers and authoritarian managers. And sexism survives in part because it benefits men and facilitates capitalist production.

This objection also raises the old question of whether material change results when people begin thinking differently about it or whether they begin thinking differently about it as a result of material change. Most socialists are inclined to agree with Marx and Engels, who stated in *The Ger-*

man Ideology that "life is not determined by consciousness, but consciousness by life" (Marx and Engels 1984:47). In other words, if the object is to get men to seriously think differently about masculinity, it is more important to change their power relations than to try to reeducate them. Or to put it another way: Reeducation (changing the stereotypes and ideals of masculinity) will work only if it goes along with changes in the relations of production.

Criticism 3

Capitalism, not socialism, has the best chance of achieving the goal of increasing autonomy (i.e., by reducing alienation). As David Conway puts it:

> By way of defence of capitalism, it has to be said that the fact that capitalism permits intrinsically unfulfilling forms of employment to exist does not in itself show that, in capitalism, anyone's autonomy is thereby reduced. If capitalism divides up the way work is distributed amongst members of society in a way that makes work unfulfilling for many, it does so because such a division of labour has been found to be more productive than a distribution that offers more fulfilling work. . . . If workers elect to opt for unfulfilling work plus higher wages, this is their decision. Indeed, capitalism can claim to augment the autonomy of workers by offering them the choice between meaningful work or higher income. (Conway 1987:47–48)

Response

Most workers would respond by asking, "What choice?" Theoretically, it is true that workers are "free" to sell their labor to any employer whatsoever. In practice, however, this freedom is constrained by surplus workers, owner conspiracies to keep workers from being paid more, a lack of fulfilling jobs that pay a living wage, and legal as well as financial barriers that prevent workers from "going into business" for themselves. The idea that workers freely choose unfulfilling work is a classic case of blaming the victim who has few resources, limited prospects, and immediate needs. It is, indeed, a myth to say that capitalism maximizes choices for workers who have only themselves to blame for making poor ones.

Criticism 4

Socialist feminists who sharply separate the oppression of women from the struggle against capitalism may end up marginalizing that oppression to the same extent as do classical Marxists who deny that there is any separate oppression. Suppose a socialist feminist were to locate the oppression of women and the development of masculinity within the feminine stereotypes and ideals that prevail in society. Suppose also that these stereotypes and ideals are treated as virtually independent of the relations of production. It would follow, then, that those who hope to eradicate the oppression of women and the current form of masculinity should struggle against these stereotypes, and that those who hope for greater worker control should aim at the relations of production. Such a view segregates women's issues and men's issues from the struggle to change the conditions of work. As a result, these issues are often marginalized by socialists whose efforts are directed primarily against capitalism (cf. Young 1981:64).

Response

Concerns such as those of Young arise out of the historical fact that women's issues have been marginalized within the socialist movement. If a socialist theory is to avoid this problem, it must show that the struggle for a socialist society is intrinsically linked to the struggle against the oppression of women. In this chapter I have attributed the major features of masculinity to the nature of work under capitalism. I have argued that work gives rise not only to the costs of masculinity but also to many of its undesirable characteristics—the very characteristics (such as authoritarianism, absence from the home, and emotional distance) that contribute to the oppression of women. Furthermore, the direct control that men exercise over women's labor power—a control that is required by the current relations of production—is at the core of women's oppression and is partially responsible for the alienations of masculinity. Thus, although the oppression of women is distinct from the capitalist class structure, it is also intrinsically tied to it.

SUMMARY AND CONCLUSIONS

A basic tenet of socialist theory is that men are divided by class interests. Indeed, socialists believe that masculinity is very much a product of the power relations that exist among men and between men and women in the relations of production. The cost of masculinity is alienation—that is, restricted human potential. But because this restricted potential derives from the conditions under which men labor and control women's work, attempts to educate men into a new masculinity or to unlearn the old masculinity are unlikely to be successful until these conditions are changed.

For socialists, the other perspectives fall far short of advancing the necessary changes in relations of production. The liberal vision of a society in which there is equality between men and women owners at one level and equality between the men and women working for them at another level is hardly an attractive prospect for socialists; such a society promises only to distribute some of the alienations of current masculinity to both men and women equally.

In favoring stereotypes and ideals as the causes of masculinity, liberalism offers an incorrect causal analysis. And the radical profeminist analysis, though revolutionary in the changes it requires, is too focused on issues of sexual power to the exclusion of work conditions; it, too, offers an incorrect causal analysis. Furthermore, it tends to ignore differences among men in terms of their degree of sexual power. The men's rights perspective, meanwhile, advances a universal and an ahistorical view of masculinity that no socialist could accept. The spiritual perspective, although it points up the alienation that is created by the structure of work, stops short of suggesting a restructuring of the relations of production.

Against the classical Marxists, socialist feminists argue that a mere end to male owner control in the workplace will remove neither the oppressions aimed at women nor the many alienations of masculinity that derive from the control of women's labor. Thus, the socialists who wish to address the alienations of men must simultaneously address the oppression of women: They must also be feminists.

SUGGESTED READING

One classic socialist feminist text is Sheila Rowbotham's *Woman's Consciousness, Man's World* (1973). More recent works in this tradition are Ann Foreman's *Femininity as Alienation: Women and the Family in Marxism and Psychoanalysis* (1977) and Nancy C. M. Hartsock's *Money, Sex, and Power: Toward a Feminist Historical Materialism* (1983). A book by a socialist feminist who looks at the ideological side of masculinity is Barbara Ehrenreich's *The Hearts of Men* (1983).

Friedrich Engels's *Origins of the Family, Private Property, and the State* does not say a great deal about masculinity, but it contains the original Marxist statement about the origins of male dominance. Eli Zaretsky's *Capitalism, the Family, and Personal Life* (1976) is another classic work that, although it follows Engels, also tries to integrate feminist ideas about the oppression of women into socialist theory.

Victor J. Seidler's *The Achilles Heel Reader: Men, Sexual Politics, and Socialism* (1991) is the only book I know of that details the struggles of men who are both socialist and profeminist.

Two excellent books that demonstrate how socialists see the relationship between racism and capitalism are Cedric J. Robinson's *Black Marxism* (1983) and Manning Marable's *How Capitalism Underdeveloped Black America* (1983). The first presents the history of the relationship between Marxism and black radicalism; the second looks at the impact of capitalism on black men and women, and offers a socialist feminist perspective of black masculinity. (See also Chapter 7 of this volume.)

SEVEN

Gay Men: The Challenge of Homophobia

The limits of "acceptable" masculinity are in part defined by comments like "What are you, a fag?" As boys and men we have heard such expressions and the words "queer," "faggot," and "sissy" all our lives. These word encourage certain types of male behavior and serve to define, regulate, and limit our lives, whether we consider ourselves straight or gay.
— Gary Kinsman, "Men Loving Men"

Straight men, while your dignity is not at stake in establishing justice for gays, your freedom is. As long as you define yourself in terms of some type and find your worth in putting down those of another type, then you will be trapped by the expectations and requirements of your type and you will always be subject to social blackmail for perceived failures to live up to type. If you use anti-gay attitudes and behaviors to prop up your perception of your gender, and hold your gender, rather than your accomplishments, as what defines you as good, then you will never be able just to be yourself, your will never realize the distinctive human potential for freedom—the ability to develop your own capacities in your own way.
— Richard D. Mohr, *A More Perfect Union*

HISTORICAL SKETCH AND PRIMARY SOURCES

The relationship of gay men to the men's movement is unique in several respects. First, along with black men, gay men are one of the two most reviled groups of men in North America. Gay men's struggles, like the struggles of black men, are intimately connected to a struggle for liberation and security from oppression. Thus, gay men have often been the main challengers of perspectives ranging from those held by religious and moral conservatives to those held by socialists. Second, gay masculinities present perhaps the greatest single challenge to dominant forms of masculinity. This challenge in part stems from the widely held belief that "gay masculinity" is an oxymoron, because to be gay is to fail to be masculine (Connell 1995:143; Doyle 1995:231). Third, gay men have been a part of each of the major perspectives from their various beginnings. In the profeminist men's movement, gay men have had a significant role in shaping both the critique of masculinity and the movement's agenda.

The contemporary gay liberation movement began with the four-day Stonewall (Inn) Rebellion in Greenwich Village on the night of June 27–28, 1969. Raids on gay bars were commonplace in the 1960s; Los Angeles had had a near confrontation in the previous year over police harassment of gay men and lesbian women (Adam 1995:81–82). Out of this rebellion came a politically active set of loosely affiliated gay liberation fronts such as the Mattachine Action Committee, the Gay Liberation Front, the Gay Activist Alliance, and in the 1990s Queer Nation and ACT-UP. Every year since Stonewall tens of thousands of gay men and lesbians have marched in Gay Pride marches across the nation.

Gay political struggles with conservative organizations might be expected, but on the Left many gay men had to create their own radical vision because they were marginalized within North American leftist organizations (Fernbach 1981:61–63). The Socialist Worker's Party, for example, banned openly gay men from membership in the 1970s, and the Communist Party was hostile to the issues of gay liberation. Indeed "gay socialists spend most of their time trying to reconcile the contradiction between their gayness and a predominantly anti-gay movement" (Kennedy 1977:167).

From the outset, gay men have sought to change traditional gender roles and to pursue alternative masculinities. In the early 1970s gay liberationists in Ann Arbor, Michigan, taught that "being gay means not relating to people on the basis of gender. Gayness means being open to the full range of relationships with people regardless of sex" (Ellis 1982:12). Dennis Altman, in *Homosexual: Oppression and Liberation*, states: "In many ways we represent the most blatant challenge of all to the mores of a society organized around belief in the nuclear family and sharply differentiated gender differences" (Altman 1972:56). Gay men often do not have the need or the opportunity to practice dominant forms of masculinity; they must live together and thereby nurture one another and support themselves. If they are parents, they must be the primary caregivers. In short, they must take on the multiple roles of both genders in maintaining their families and communities.

The so-called effeminists were among the first gay men to adopt a distinctive feminist vision within the gay movement. Of their publication, *Double F: A Magazine of Effeminism,* Jon Snodgrass writes:

> [T]his publication of the Revolutionary Effeminists . . . began . . . in response to sexism within the gay male liberation movement. In 1970, the three men [Steven Dansky, John Knoebel, and Kenneth Pitchford] formulated their concept of "flaming faggots," effeminate men fighting patriarchy with revolutionary means. (Snodgrass 1977a:111)

The effeminists rejected the use of the term *gay* and criticized the left, the gay liberation movement, and the emerging men's liberation movement as different versions of patriarchal domination because they all lacked sufficient commitment to radical feminist politics.

RFD: A Country Journal for Gay Men Everywhere originated in Iowa in 1974. This journal came to represent a later vision of gay liberation—namely, that of the Radical Fairies, who advocated a gay spirituality and a separate gay culture (Thompson 1987b:260–269). The Radical Fairies took pride in the word *gay* and advocated nonmonogamous collective living with nonhierarchical social structures and community spaces apart from heterosexist institutions and women. The strong spirituality of this viewpoint brings to mind the spiritual perspective of John Rowan, particularly given its adherents' belief in the value of pagan traditions and witchcraft. At the same time their idea that they are prevented by heterosexist stereotypes and ideals from achieving full self-realization gives this viewpoint a decidedly liberal tone.

The emerging profeminist men's movement of the mid- to late 1970s appealed to many of these gay men. The early writings of the profeminist perspective, such as *For Men Against Sexism, Men and Masculinity,* and *The Forty-Nine Percent Majority,* include essays describing the gay masculine experience and identifying homophobia among heterosexual men as a prejudice to be confronted and overcome. However, as seen from the gay perspective of the 1980s, these efforts to amend standard profeminist theory were not satisfactory. "None of the 1970s books-about-men made a serious attempt to get to grips with gay liberation arguments, or to reckon with the fact that mainstream masculinity is heterosexual masculinity" (Carrigan, Connell, and Lee 1987:171). Joe Interrante further notes that, "as a gay man, I also had suspicions about the heterocentrist bias of this work [the early profeminist writing]. It told me that my gayness existed 'in addition to' my masculinity, whereas I had found that it colored my entire experience of manhood. I distrusted a literature which claimed that gay men were just like heterosexual men, except for what they did in bed" (Interrante 1983:4).

In spite of its heterosexual bias, however, many gay men stayed in the profeminist men's movement and participated in the M&M conferences. In one survey at the 1984 California Men's Gathering, 20 percent of the respondents to a questionnaire indicated that they were gay or bisexual, whereas only 2 percent said they were black, Asian, Hispanic, or Native American (Shiffman 1987:301). Anthony Astrachan estimates that 30 percent of the men who attend the national M&M conferences are gay (Astrachan 1986:297). Thus it is not surprising that the gay viewpoint on masculinity is well represented in the literature.

There are three probable reasons for this ongoing participation. First, the political agenda of NOCM/NOMAS is partially defined by the gay liberation agenda. Fear of homosexuality is clearly identified as a major issue for men. Among NOMAS's principles is the following:

> One of the strongest and deepest anxieties of most American men is their fear of homosexuality. This homophobia contributes directly to the many injustices experienced by gay, lesbian and bisexual persons, and is a debilitating restriction for heterosexual men. We call for an end to all forms of discrimination based on sexual-affectional orientation, and the creation of a gay-affirmative society. (National Organization for Changing Men n.d.)

NOMAS also maintains a Homophobia Task Group that is active in projects aimed at lessening homophobia ("National Conference on Homophobia" 1988).

Second, gay men themselves are struggling with many of the same issues such as violence against women and male privilege in the economic and social spheres. Gay men who are divorced fathers are also concerned about being good fathers and about their rights as fathers.

Third, the gay viewpoint in the men's movement gives gay men an opportunity to guide heterosexual men in their fight against homophobia and in their understanding of their own masculinity. There is more than one gay point of view on masculinity. But the gay viewpoint discussed in this chapter is widely held among profeminist men, both gay and straight. Their basic premise is that the dominant form of masculinity is substantially shaped and maintained by homophobia, a generalized fear of homosexuality embedded in the masculine gender role, stereotype, and ideal.

Gay men also have an ongoing involvement with the men's rights perspective; yet the gay liberation agenda has not gained a foothold within this perspective. The men's rights perspective does acknowledge homophobia as a problem that keeps heterosexual men from bonding (Logan 1985:19–20; Treadwell 1985:302–303). But the national organization reflects Richard Haddad's view that gay liberation is not a "men's issue." Rather, he claims, it is a "civil rights issue," and "waving the gay flag" loses nine out of ten prospective converts (Astrachan 1986:311). Astrachan also quotes Peter Cyr, the chair of the National Congress for Men's planning committee, as having said: "We will make no gesture toward gay rights. A lot of the support for divorce reform comes from men on the conservative right. . . . These men are homophobic; they don't want to deal with gay rights" (Astrachan 1986:311–312).

In the preface to *Iron John,* Bly notes:

> Most of the language in this book speaks to heterosexual men but does not exclude homosexual men. It wasn't until the eighteenth century that people ever used the term homosexual; before that time gay men were understood simply as a part of the large community of men. The mythology as I see it does not make a big distinction between homosexual and heterosexual men. (Bly 1990:x)

Dan Gawthrop, a gay man who attended a mythopoetic wisdom council meeting in the late 1980s, takes several exceptions to Bly's remarks. The term "homosexual" was actually coined in the nineteenth century (see Halperin 1990). And "gays could only have been considered 'part of the large community of men' by pretending they were straight. Even in some parts of the Western world in the last 20 years, attempts to lead openly gay lives have been met with public humiliation, lengthy imprisonment, or death" (Gawthrop 1992). At the mythopoetic gathering of men Gawthrop was taunted with "faggot," "queer," and "wimp." Thus, the place of gay men within the mythopoetic movement remains ambiguous; it would seem that at best gays are invisible members of the community of men, at worst they are unwelcome.

The gay viewpoints examined in this chapter are well represented in some of the sources already cited: specifically, Snodgrass, Kimmel and Messner, and Kaufman. To these sources I would add *Gay Spirit: Myth and Meaning* (1987a), edited by Mark Thompson; R. W. Connell's *Masculinities* (1995), which explores in depth the relationship between dominant (hegemonic) masculinities and gay masculinities; and Barry D. Adam's *The Rise of a Gay and Lesbian Movement* (1995), which provides a general and up-to-date account of the gay liberation struggle.

Following Thompson and other gay social theorists, I shall try to maintain a distinction between the terms *gay* and *homosexual:*

> The word *gay* should not be confused with *homosexual,* as by definition they mean quite different things. Gay implies a social identity and consciousness actively chosen, while homosexual refers to a specific form of sexuality. A person may be homosexual, but that does not necessarily imply that he or she would be gay. (Thompson 1987a:xi)

David Fernbach also draws a distinction: Gayness involves "above all our refusal to repress the maternal culture and to cultivate masculine violence" (Fernbach 1981:85). But because this distinction is not consistently maintained in the literature, I cannot always maintain it either (cf. Kilhefner 1987:124). Finally, in presenting the gay viewpoint I have tried to avoid taking sides with either the gay essentialists or the gay constructivists; I assume neither that gay people have existed throughout history nor that gay culture is the product of contemporary society (Thompson 1987a:xv). The themes of the gay viewpoint discussed here can be maintained within either paradigm.

DESCRIPTION AND EXPLANATION OF MALE REALITY

Masculinity

Boys who become gay men receive standard socialization. Connell notes:

> All the men in the group grew up in families with a conventional division of labour and a conventional power structure. . . . Nor was there much gender nonconformity for the boys. These conventional family settings were the sites of masculinizing practices exactly parallel to those in the heterosexual life-histories. Their mothers put them in pants, rather than skirts, their fathers taught them football, they learned sexual differences. Moving out of the family they were inducted into the usual sex-typed peer groups, received the usual sexist informal sex education, and were subjected to the gender dichotomies that pervade school life. (Connell 1995:145–146)

Similarly, in his review of the literature, Pleck found little scientific support for deficient male identity among homosexual males (Pleck 1981; Doyle 1995:231).

Yet when boys become gay men, they immediately face a specific set of problems that do not enter into the realities of men who have heterosexual masculinities. In the first place, there is the threat and the actuality of institutional and personal violence. In the 1970s, being homosexual was treated as a pathology by the American Psychiatric Association and the American Psychological Association. There were many "cures" for gay men, including aversion therapy shock treatments. Gay bashing—the beating and killing of gay men, especially by young heterosexual males—has been an ongoing and growing concern for the gay community (Adam 1995:143–144). Police violence either in the form of physical abuse or harassment is commonplace worldwide (Adam 1995:142–143). Thus, fear of revealing one's sexual identity becomes a focus in the life of a gay man; violence keeps gay men in the closet.

Discrimination because of sexual orientation is a second aspect of gay male reality. Gay men are often discouraged from pursuing certain traditionally masculine careers because of the fear of harassment: Gay men may choose "acceptable" work for gay men, thereby contributing to gay stereotypes, as hairdressers or nurses (Levine 1992). Even if gay men do accept traditionally masculine work, they are vulnerable to job loss, denial of promotions, or working well below their capabilities (Levine 1992:264). In the military it is official government policy in the 1990s for gay men and lesbians to stay in the closet; that is, the military will not seek them out, as in the past, but if they openly acknowledge their sexual identity they will be discharged (Shilts 1993).

In their domestic relations gay men cannot marry or, in most cases, receive spousal benefits. They must pioneer new ways of taking care of one another and their families, which often include children (Horn 1992; MacDonald 1995). The right to marry is a hotly contested issue in the 1990s as more and more gay men and lesbians seek that right and "the additional empowerment that derives from legal recognition" (Kaplan 1994).

In light of this reality it is small wonder that most gay viewpoints see heterosexual masculinities as privileged and as created and maintained by homophobia. And gay theorists are quick to point out that with respect to domination of women by men, gay men are in a very different situation. Indeed, gay men may share with women fears of discrimination and violence. Thus, many gay theorists begin with the radical feminist premise that through sexual violence and the threat of violence, heterosexual men dominate women. An important difference between gay and heterosexual men is implied here. "The problem lies in the fact that a primary means of expressing identity with other men remains the sexual domination of women. . . . But when this link drops out . . . there is an intense alienation of straight men from gay men" (Nierenberg 1987:132). And "while we share with straight men the economic benefits of being men . . . we do not participate as regularly in the everyday interpersonal subordination of women in the realms of sexuality and violence" (Kinsman 1987:104–105). From this domination of women heterosexual men derive the benefits enumerated by radical profeminists: lack of competition from women at work, caretakers at home, and sexual objects to be exploited and enjoyed.

But this critique amounts to more than the claim that gay and straight men are different. It also challenges the radical profeminist assumption that *all* masculinity is created and maintained by male sexual power over women. Gay men who do not exercise that sexual power can be masculine; their masculinity is often formed without it. At this point, one can argue that gay men really do have a derivative sexual power over women or that gay men are not masculine in the same sense. But, as stated, the radical profeminist account is inadequate. Similarly, the liberal account, which argues that masculinity is shaped by images of men who are macho and virile toward women, simply fails to explain gay masculinity. And, finally, although socialism may find differences among gay men based on class differences, the division between heterosexual masculinity and gay masculinity is not easily explained in terms of class.

A second part of the gay critique of other viewpoints is that privilege and power over women or women's labor are not enough to socialize men and keep them in the masculine role. Gay men argue convincingly that homophobia is the club that is used to keep men in their gender role. According to Gregory Lehne, "homophobia is a threat used by homosexist individuals to enforce social conformity in the male role, and maintain social control." As he argues in his classic essay, "Homophobia Among Men," the taunt "What are you, a fag?" is often used to encourage certain types of male behavior and to define the limits of "acceptable" masculinity (Lehne 1976:78; cf. Kinsman 1987:103). "Homophobia" is variously defined by different authors; others prefer to avoid the term entirely, preferring "fear of homosexuality," "the oppression of gay people," "heterosexism," or "heterosexual chauvinism" instead (Carrigan, Connell, and Lee 1987:171; Kinsman 1987:106). Following Lehne, however, I shall continue to use *homophobia* to refer to this generalized socially instilled fear of homosexuality.

Many writers within the gay viewpoint try to demonstrate the special relevance of homosexual men's experiences to an understanding of heterosexual masculinity. As homosexual masculinity is not the norm, "gay men have had to question the institution of masculinity—which associates masculinity with heterosexuality—in our daily lives. We have experimented with and developed new ways of organizing our sexual lives and our love and support relations" (Kinsman 1987:105; Connell 1995:143–163). Furthermore, homosexual men suffer oppressions similar to those inflicted on women by heterosexual men; they are raped by straight men, battered and killed by heterosexual gangs, and mocked for their "effeminacy" (Fernbach 1981:85; Kinsman 1987:106; Carrigan, Connell, and Lee 1987:174; Connell 1995:154–155). It is these facts that lead gay men to conclude that heterosexual masculinity is strongly molded by homophobia. Because homosexual men are oppressed and because their lives are beyond the limits of accepted heterosexual masculinity, some theorists argue that the history of homosexual masculinity is "the most valuable starting point we have for constructing a historical perspective on masculinity at large. . . . The history of homosexuality obliges us to think of masculinity not as a single object with its own history, but as being constantly constructed within the history of an evolving social structure, a structure of sexual power relations" (Carrigan, Connell, and Lee 1987:176).

Lehne's early essay reveals many of the ways in which heterosexual masculinity is created and maintained by homophobia. Citing studies done in the early 1970s, Lehne points out that homophobia correlates strongly with people who "support traditional sex roles and the double standard [for men and women], and [are] authoritarian and conservative in their social attitudes" (Lehne 1976:76). Even certain areas of work are defined with respect to heterosexuality. "The areas of employment where most Americans feel homosexuals should not be allowed to work (medicine, law, politics and the judiciary, higher education, the ministry) are the same fields which have generally excluded blacks and women. In most states homosexuals are excluded by law from obtaining state certificates necessary to practice medicine or law or to teach" (Lehne 1976:77). Men who are actors, artists, nurses, musicians, florists, and beauticians are suspected of being homosexual, and these professions are deemed "appropriate" jobs for homosexual men (Lehne 1976:69). Men who do not participate in pursuing, talking about, and objectifying women are also suspected of being homosexuals. If a man does not marry and support a woman, he is suspect. The same is true of men who do not enjoy contact sports. Everywhere heterosexual men turn, they are confronted with the challenge of proving they are not homosexual: "The proof of 'manhood' must be continuous" (Lehne 1976:79).

Homophobia is also responsible for many of the costs of traditional masculinity. According to Lehne, "The pain which heterosexual males bear as a consequence of homophobia . . . is so chronic and pervasive that they probably do not notice that they are in pain" (Lehne 1976:82). Homophobia leads men to be destructively competitive, to limit their love and close friendships with men. "The spectre of homosexuality seems to be the dragon at the gateway to self-awareness, understanding, and acceptance of male-male needs" (Keith 1974:92). The fear of being identified as homosexual leads men to behave in a hypermasculine (aggressive) way and to close up emotionally, thereby weakening their ability to have open and equal relationships with women (Lehne 1976:82; Dansky, Knoebel, and Pitchford 1977:118). Even the lack of affection between fathers and sons has been attributed to the phobic fear of being seen as homosexual males. Thus the gay viewpoint is able to offer an alternative account of what produces masculine behaviors and attitudes and accounts for the costs of masculinity.

But homophobia is not the only or even the primary force that creates and maintains masculinities. Many other factors are involved as well. Lehne, for example, asserts that "economic sanctions" are probably a greater socializing force; at the same time, however, he holds "that homophobia must be eliminated before a change in sex roles can be brought about" (Lehne 1976:79–80). At the very least, such arguments show that a necessary condition for understanding and changing masculinity is to understand the role of homophobia (Carrigan, Connell, and Lee 1987:174).

Feminism

The relationship of gay men and gay male organizations to feminism is difficult to determine. Many authors find a significant influence of feminist ideas, especially from radical and lesbian feminism, in gay organizations while at the same noting that gay male organizations often remain stubbornly patriarchal (Adam 1995:96–104). In the early days of the gay liberation movement, many women tried to become activists but found themselves withdrawing in the early 1970s in favor of their own organizations (Adam 1995:99). Marilyn Frye captures some of the reservations felt by lesbian feminists in the following summary:

> Far from there being a natural affinity between feminist lesbians and the gay civil rights movement, I see their politics as being, in most respects, directly antithetical to each other. The general direction of gay male politics is to claim maleness and male privilege for gay men and to promote the enlargement of the range of presumption for phallic access to the point where it is, in fact, absolutely unlimited. The general direction of lesbian feminist politics is the dismantling of male privilege, the erasure of masculinity, and the reversal of the rule of phallic access, replacing the rule that access is permitted unless specifically forbidden with the rule that it is forbidden unless specifically permitted. (Frye 1983:145)

Thus, Frye argues that gay men tend to see liberation in terms of the liberation of the male, which feeds a contempt for women, and in many ways seek an androcentric culture that is as hostile to women as is the traditional patriarchal society.

At the same time, Frye notes that there could be a basis for an alliance between gay men and women out of their common experience of "marginalization and victimization" (Frye 1983:145). It is precisely this commonality that leads profeminist gay men to argue for a natural empathy between women and gay men. According to Seymour Kleinberg, for instance:

> "Feminist" is a term that increasing numbers of gay men apply to themselves as they come to recognize the common oppression of homosexuals and women. The empathy of gay men in the past is the foundation for this new understanding, and it is heartening to discover that a mutual sense of victimization need not always lead to self-denigration. . . . As more gays come to realize the bankruptcy of conventional ideas of masculinity, it is easier for them to forego the sexism they shared with heterosexual men. (Kleinberg 1987:127)

Apart from such claims to a special empathy with women, however, the gay viewpoints cover the complete range from conservatism to socialism in their understanding of feminism. For example, the effeminists, who assume a radical feminist stance, believe absolutely in the leadership of women in the struggle against patriarchy. Accordingly, the fourth paragraph of "The Effeminist Manifesto" reads as follows:

> 4. WOMEN'S LEADERSHIP. Exactly how women will go about seizing power is no business of ours, being men. But as effeminate men oppressed by masculinist standards, we ourselves have a stake in the destruction of the patriarchy, and thus we must struggle with the dilemma of being partisans—as effeminists—of a revolution opposed to us—as men. (Dansky, Knoebel, and Pitchford 1977:117)

This manifesto makes clear the fact that, although gay men are oppressed, they are still men and, hence, must make decisions that can draw them into either protecting their privilege (conservatism) or opposing patriarchy (profeminism). As fathers, still other gay men are drawn to the fathers' rights movement. Other gay men show a surprising indifference, or even hostility, to feminism (Connell 1995:159). And there is a strong showing of conservative, Republican, or Reform Party gay men whose only quarrel with conservative ideology is that homosexual relations between men are condemned (Adam 1995:123). In short, the complexity of the gay community has produced a set of attitudes toward feminism at least as rich as the several views already considered (Lehne 1976:68; Nierenberg 1987:130–133).

ASSESSMENT OF MALE REALITY AND AGENDA FOR CHANGE

Because it emphasizes the mechanisms that produce and maintain the dominant masculinity, the gay viewpoint directs much of its assessment toward correcting the causal inadequacies of heterosexual analyses of masculinity. As Gary Kinsman points out, "Heterosexual men interested in seriously transforming the fabric of their lives have to stop seeing gay liberation as simply a separate issue for some men that has nothing to say to them" (Kinsman 1987:105). Moreover, "the gay movement's theoretical work, by comparison with the 'sex role' literature and 'men's movement' writings, had a much clearer understanding of the reality of men's power over women, and it had direct implications for any consideration of the hierarchy of power among men. Pleck was one of the few writers outside gay liberation to observe that the homosexual/heterosexual dichotomy acts as a central symbol in *all* rankings of masculinity" (Carrigan, Connell, and Key 1987:174). Although these criticisms are aimed at the profeminist men's movement, none of the four other perspectives can easily escape them. The socialist and spiritual perspectives do not give a significant role to homophobia. The men's rights perspective acknowledges homophobia as a problem for heterosexual men but fails to encourage the informed correction of homophobia by gay men who understand that phenomenon better than anyone else. And, finally, the conservative perspective simply denies that homophobia is a problem, suggesting instead that it is healthy and should be encouraged by the community. Thus, there exists a monumental task for men who seek to lead or guide the heterosexual male "beyond liberal tolerance of gays and lesbians" into a deeper understanding of how "'queer baiting' and the social taboo against pleasure, sex, and love between men serves to keep all men in line, defining what proper masculinity is for us" (Kinsman 1987:105).

In working out specific strategies to combat homophobia, gay men are often faced with the charge that they are effeminate, that in some sense they are women in men's bodies. Effeminacy is the description of homosexual males offered especially by moral conservatives (cf. Gilder 1973:237–244).

The effeminists argue that the charge of effeminacy that is so much a part of heterosexual culture should be accepted and used to expose the rigid, insensitive, and inexpressive heterosexual masculine social role. (Recall the Gay Liberation Front slogan, "Free the sister in ourselves" [Keith 1974:87–88].) But as "The Effeminist Manifesto" asserts, accepting effeminacy has political implications to the effect that effeminate men must not parody women.

> We effeminate men are given an option by the patriarchy: to become collaborators in the task of keeping women in their place. Faggots, especially, are offered a subculture . . . which is designed to keep us oppressed and also increase the oppression of women. This subculture includes a combination of anti-woman mimicry and self-mockery known as camp. (Dansky, Knoebel, and Pitchford 1977:117–118)

Sado-masochism and male transvestitism are seen by some as "heterosexual perversions" that "are particularly an insult to women since they overtly parody female oppression and pose as object lessons in servility" (Dansky, Knoebel, and Pitchford 1977:118–119). Effeminate men argue that, through their effeminacy, they can reveal heterosexual masculinity's "preference for thinking as opposed to feeling," "inflicting pain on people and animals," and "a lust for power-dominance" (Dansky, Knoebel, and Pitchford 1977:118). They also claim that even thinking in dichotomies such as subject/object, dominant/submissive, master/slave, and butch/femme is a heterosexual way of dividing the world that is alien to truly effeminate men (Dansky, Knoebel, and Pitchford 1977:118).

Radical Fairies do not accept the ascription of effeminacy. The concept of fairie was first introduced in 1970 by Harry Hay, who used the word *faerie* to connote a separate gay consciousness (Thompson 1987b:265). The man-woman category (effeminacy), he claims, is a false dichotomy imported from heterosexual culture. "How often do we allow ourselves—through fuzzy thinking—to accept, or to identify with Hetero-originating definitions or misinterpretations of ourselves? The Hetero-male . . . [is] . . . incapable of . . . perceiving that we Gay People might not fit in either of his Man-Woman categories. . . . Yet we fairies allow Bully-boy to persuade us to search out the 'feminine' in ourselves." (Hay 1987a:199). Like effeminists, Radical Fairies seek a subject-subject culture in which human "relations [are] superimposed over the now-obsolete Hetero subject-OBJECT traditions—*and the Heteros begin to perceive the value of that super-imposition*" (Hay 1987a:201; original emphasis). The Radical Fairies see themselves as "other" and argue that their inclusion in society would require a new "philosophy, science, religion, mythology, political system, [and] language" that are devoid of "their binary subject-OBJECT base" (Hay 1987a:200; Thompson 1987c:182; Hay 1987b:280). Thus, a first step in the struggle against homophobia is to get beyond the categories in use by the dominant culture.

Recent gay advocates, such as those represented in *Beyond Patriarchy* or *New Men, New Minds*, focus much of their assessment on the profeminists' analyses of masculinity. They argue that these analyses, especially the liberal ones, tend to assume that heterosexuality is natural and that men are subjects and women are objects. Most important, they ignore the power and privilege that heterosexual men have over gay men (Kinsman 1987:103–104; Carrigan, Connell, and Lee 1987:174–175). As gay liberationists they challenge all of these premises; they also point to the Kinsey Institute's homosexual-heterosexual study, which indicates that almost everyone is bisexual to some degree. Finally, they emphasize the role of heterosexual privilege in maintaining homophobia: "What makes heterosexuality work is heterosexual privilege—and if you don't have a sense of what privilege is, I suggest that you go home and announce to everybody that you know . . . that you're queer. Try being a queer for a week" (Charlotte Bunch, cited by Kinsman 1987:105).

Gay profeminists have always been clear about the oppressions brought to bear on gay men—oppressions such as their exclusion from many activities and institutions, and their treatment as sick, immoral, and indecent people by the media and a large section of the medical community. According to one gay man, "On city streets we are often violently attacked by gangs of 'queerbashers.' Most countries deny lesbians and gay men the basic civil and human rights, leaving us open to arbitrary firings and evictions" (Kinsman 1987:106).

Among the accomplishments of gay liberation organizations in the early 1970s was a successful effort to move professional organizations like the American Psychiatric Association, the American Psychological Association, and the American Medical Association away from their official views that homosexuality was a pathology. Gay activists also succeeded in getting many organizations, such as the National Association for Mental Health and the American Sociological Association, to call for the decriminalization of homosexuality, which several states have done (Adam 1995:88). In pursuing these changes, gay liberation had science on its side; literature reviews reveal that there is no basis for the classification of homosexuals as deviant, unhealthy, or suffering from any more pathologies than any other cross section of society (Doyle 1995:227–229). Thus, at least officially, certain grounds for discrimination and denial of opportunity have been removed.

Contemporary gay activists are still seeking to transform society, but the vision of recent activists has changed from the focus on gender roles of the effeminists, Radical Fairies, and the profeminist gay men. New and more ominous issues have come to the fore. These issues are: (1) the newfound political muscle of Christian religious conservatives, (2) the spread of AIDS/HIV and the identification of that disease as a "gay" disease, and (3) a renewal of the nature/nurture debate with respect to homosexuality.

The growing strength of Christian conservative political clout in the 1980s and 1990s has produced a series of propositions and initiatives in many states, including Arizona, Oregon, Colorado, Washington, and Florida, that would deny gay men or lesbians protection from discrimination in housing, insurance, and employment (Adam 1995:109–127). These same forces also oppose hate-crime bills that attach extra penalties for acts of violence motivated by hate and prejudice, even though gay bashing has become a growing problem for the gay community and the police, whose mandate is to protect all citizens (Speyer 1994). Montana, for example, adopted and then rescinded a law requiring gay men convicted of homosexual acts to register as sex offenders (Montana 1994).

Measure 9, voted down in Oregon in 1992, is typical of these statutes and initiatives. This proposed amendment to the Oregon Constitution was written by the Oregon Citizen's Alliance and backed by the Christian Coalition. It states:

> This state shall not recognize any categorical provision such as "sexual orientation," "sexual preference," and similar phrases that include homosexuality, pedophilia, sadism or masochism. . . . Government and their properties and monies shall not be used to promote, encourage or facilitate homosexuality, pedophilia, sadism or masochism. . . . Higher education and the public schools shall assist in setting a standard for Oregon's youth that recognizes homosexuality, pedophilia, sadism and masochism as abnormal, wrong, unnatural and perverse. (Hands Off Washington n.d.)

Other initiatives currently being considered deny the right of adoption to gay men or lesbians or the right of being a custodial parent. The argument for these legal restrictions is simple. The Bible says that homosexuality is a sin (1 Corinthians 6:9–10). If it is a sin, then homosexuality is a lifestyle choice. Lifestyle choices, unlike disabilities or skin color, should not be protected against discrimination. Indeed, as Sara Diamond observes: "It is safe to say that the leadership of the Christian Right will not be satisfied until homosexuality is banned in the United States" (Diamond 1989:101).

Complicating the whole issue of gay rights is the national fear of AIDS/HIV and the tendency to think of this disease as a gay disease. Some religious conservatives see this disease not only as divine punishment of gay men for their homosexuality but also as punishment of Christians for tolerating homosexuality in their midst (Diamond 1989:103). In the early 1980s the spread of this disease was ignored by U.S. government agencies responsible for tracking epidemics (Altman 1986; Shilts 1987). Today many Christian conservatives oppose AIDS education and prevention programs as part of their general opposition to sex education (Diamond 1989). Similar conservative opposition to gay and lesbian clubs in high schools limits the places where young gay men can get information and show films about the prevention of sexually transmitted diseases. The Salt Lake City school board in early 1996 banned all extracurricular clubs and activities rather than allow the formation of a club for gay youth.

Finally, a vigorous debate is being pursued as to whether homosexuality is a biologically determined behavior or a socially induced behavior. Dean Hamer, a researcher, and his colleagues at the National Institutes of Health claim to have found a particular DNA segment, or "marker," in two-thirds of gay men (LeVay and Hamer 1994; Bereano 1996). Simon LeVay, studying the brains of gay men who had died of AIDS, showed a reduced medial preoptic area in gay men. Hamer also found homosexuality clustering in families, which was seemingly strongest among more closely related males. Thus, in identical twins when one twin is homosexual, there is a greater likelihood that both twins will be homosexual than there is a likelihood that two nontwin siblings will be homosexual if one is (LeVay and Hamer 1994; Bereano 1996).

Other scientists find considerable fault with these studies. For example, Hamer did not check to see if straight men in the families of gay men also had the "marker." LeVay's work used only the brains of men who died from a disease that affects brain structure. The fact that brothers of gay men are also more likely to be gay than are men without gay brothers is no more evidence of biological determination than is the fact that men with Republican or Catholic brothers are more likely to be Republican or Catholic than are men whose brothers are not Republican or Catholic (Byne 1994; Bereano 1996).

Thus, the agenda for gay men (as well as for lesbians and bisexuals) has been set to a large extent by other groups within the larger society. The National Gay and Lesbian Task Force favors the idea that homosexuality is biologically determined: "Homosexuality is a naturally occurring and common variation among humans" (cited in Bereano 1996). This claim is similar to that made by sociobiologist E. O. Wilson. The advantage of this position is that it undercuts the religious conservative argument that being gay is a lifestyle *choice*. It puts being gay more on a par with being black or being white and hence enters a claim for civil rights protection. Also, if homosexuality is biologically determined, then homosexual teachers or curricula can no longer be blamed for youths becoming homosexual. This view has one obvious disadvantage, however: It invites a genetic solution, which was tried in Nazi Germany (Adam 1995:49–59). It does not prevent those who believe that homosexuality is a genetic defect from arguing for DNA testing and alteration of or even sterilization of individuals with the "wrong" DNA. In this way, deciding the nature/nurture debate in favor of nature is viewed by some gay and lesbian activists as a way to defeat the rash of antihomosexual initiatives and laws being proposed by religious conservatives.

AIDS education is an ongoing program that is controlled neither by religious conservatives nor gay activists. Condom distribution programs, clean needle programs, and units in sex education programs are driven by the growing number of heterosexual youth who are affected by AIDS/HIV, the visibility of heterosexual personalities who are HIV positive, and the failure of "just say no" campaigns to control sexual behavior.

On April 25, 1993, hundreds of thousands of gay men, lesbians, bisexuals, and other sexual minorities participated in a March on Washington for Lesbian, Gay, and Bi Equal Rights and Liberation. The march demands succinctly summarize the concerns of gay, lesbian, and bisexual people in the 1990s:

1. We demand passage of a Lesbian, Gay, Bisexual, and Transgender civil rights bill and an end to discrimination by state and federal governments including the military; repeal of all sodomy laws and other laws that criminalize private sexual expression between consenting adults.
2. We demand massive increase in funding for AIDS education, research, and patient care; universal access to health care including alternative therapies; and an end to sexism in medical research and health care.
3. We demand legislation to prevent discrimination against Lesbians, Gays, Bisexuals and Transgendered people in the areas of family diversity, custody, adoption and foster care and that the definition of family includes the full diversity of all family structures.
4. We demand full and equal inclusion of Lesbians, Gays, Bisexuals and Transgendered people in the educational system, and inclusion of Lesbian, Gay, Bisexual and Transgender studies in multicultural curricula.
5. We demand the right to reproductive freedom and choice, to control our own bodies, and an end to sexist discrimination.
6. We demand an end to racial and ethnic discrimination in all forms.
7. We demand an end to discrimination and violent oppression based on actual or perceived sexual orientation/identification, race, religion, identity, sex

and gender expression, disability, age, class AIDS/HIV infection. (A Simple Matter of Justice, *Program Guide*:16)

The clash of these demands with the demands of religious conservatives could not be greater. In Chapter 9 we shall explore this conflict in greater detail.

Clearly, the list of demands from the 1993 march reflects a concern of this movement to ally itself with other liberation movements concerned with racism, class, and disability. The demands also include a recognition that there are many sexual minorities other than gay men and lesbians; transsexuals, transvestites, and transgendered people all suffer from injustice and oppression at the hands of heterosexual society. This emphasis on coalition building is a significant change in the politics of the 1990s as contrasted with the politics of the 1970s. As Carrigan, Connell, and Lee note:

> The moment of opportunity, as it appeared in the early 1970s, is past. There is no easy path to a major reconstruction of masculinity. Yet the initiative in sexual politics is not entirely in the hands of reaction, and the underlying tensions that produced the initiatives of ten years ago have not vanished. There are potentials for a more liberating politics . . . not in the form of grand schemes . . . but . . . in the form of coalitions among feminists, gay men, and progressive heterosexual men. (1987:187)

CRITIQUE: CRITICISMS AND RESPONSES

Criticism 1

It is simply not true that gay men embrace significantly different forms of masculinity. As Frye argues, the guiding force in gay male politics is to secure male privilege for gay men (Frye 1983:145). And as Connell shows in his chapter "A Very Straight Gay," gay masculinities are formed by a complex of factors that certainly include male privilege, and many gay men simply adapt dominant or hegemonic masculinity in such a way as to accommodate sexual difference even though it is a contradictory experience (Connell 1995:143–163).

Response

The challenge to dominant forms of masculinity is not that gay men are not sexist or that gay men do not share in male privilege or even that gay men are not in many ways like heterosexual men. But there is a notable difference: Gay men experience a kind of sexual equality that is simply not available yet for heterosexual couples. As Connell argues: "Sexuality is the point of rupture in this project, and sexual relations are where it takes a potentially radical turn. Relative to the mainstream in heterosexual relations, gay men's sexual relations show a notable degree of reciprocity. There are exceptions, but reciprocity is emphasized as an ideal and is to a large extent practised" (Connell 1995:162).

Criticism 2

The whole discussion between gay activists and religious conservatives is confused. Too often it is assumed by both sides that if it can be shown that sexual orientation is produced by cultural factors, then it is *chosen*. This assumption is unwarranted: There are many culturally induced beliefs and preferences that are *not* chosen, such as one's religious preference. It may well be that sexual preferences are produced by cultural and environmental situations so subtle that we are unaware of how they affect us. Thus, the nature/nurture debate is irrelevant to whether or not sexual preference is voluntary (compare Halperin 1992:41–53).

Response

Perhaps the problem needs to be redefined. It is a necessary but not a sufficient condition for sexual preference to be a product of cultural and environmental factors. And that is why it is important to establish that sexual preference is a matter of nurture and not nature.

Criticism 3

It is a further mistake to argue that if homosexuality is a matter of nature and not of choice then there is a case for protecting gays and lesbians under some form of civil rights. Every citizen has a set of rights, and where there are systematic violations of those rights, as there clearly are in the case of gay men, then the duty of government is to protect those who are violated. It is irrelevant whether one chooses to be part of a group whose rights are systematically violated or not. People choose to marry and they choose to have children, and in many cases they choose a particular religion, yet the rights of these groups are protected just as much as are the rights of those who do not choose to belong to a group— for example, people who are Latino or African American. Thus, both sides make too much of whether it is or is not a matter of choice.

Response

Choice is an important issue to gay activists. If there is no real element of choice, then concerns about gay teachers and gay-positive curricula are weakened, because neither instruction nor curriculum are contributing factors to the homosexuality of students. Furthermore, if there is no real element of choice, then being gay cannot be a sin because gay men are therefore simply the way God made them. For the same reason, choice is an important issue for Christian conservatives. If homosexuality is not a matter of choice, then the Bible is wrong to condemn homosexual behavior, and some reading other than the literal of particular passages is required. And if either the Bible is in error or it cannot be read literally, then the underlying premises of the Christian fundamentalist attack on homosexuality are wrong.

Criticism 4

The importance of studying gay masculinities is often exaggerated by profeminists. Brod claims that "both methodologically and substantively, men's studies has a crucial relationship to gay studies. In a trend analogous to that in women's studies . . . gay studies has moved from simply supplying supplemental information about gay men to questioning the nature of the categorizations 'heterosexual' and 'homosexual.' It is therefore becoming increasingly difficult to draw a clear line between gay and men's studies" (1987c:61). The suggestion that gay and men's studies are collapsing into each other underestimates the roles of racism, class, and religion in the formation of masculinities. It would be just as unbelievable to claim that it is increasingly difficult to draw a clear line between black studies and men's studies.

Response

Gay men do occupy a special place in the study of masculinity. Gay men are the paradigms of the feminized male, the man who is not a real man. Thus, the best way to get at the social construction of masculinity is to look at how gay men have been treated both historically and in contemporary society.

SUMMARY AND CONCLUSIONS

The ways in which gay men challenge the other perspectives are numerous indeed. Gay activists have long challenged the moral religious conservative idea that homosexual men are unhappy, unsuccessful, and unnatural. In this regard many gay thinkers are drawn to a biological conservative position that makes sexual orientation a matter of biology. Socialists have been challenged in their belief that homosexuality is a bourgeois affliction. And gay men have asked profeminist heterosexual men to consider a masculinity that is not premised on the sexual domination or conquest of women. In profeminist, men's rights, and mythopoetic organizations, gay men have demanded that heterosexual men consider both their privileges and their homophobia as key ingredients of their own masculinity. Even father-son relationships and male friendships often fail because of fear of male intimacy. Homophobia is a common ingredient in almost all masculinities, including those that are formed by particular races, religions, and abilities.

Gay men, because they are among the most oppressed of men, also bring a certain critical skepticism to the organizations of which they are part. Richard Mohr's warning to gay people is widely accepted within the gay community: "Gay people, the landscape is littered with phony friends. Be wary of politicians and leaders, gay or not, who promise you happiness tomorrow if only you are just good enough today by the standards of those who have traditionally oppressed you. You can never be that good, for they judge you by what you are, not what you do" (Mohr 1994:123). This skepticism helps to keep the organizations honest in confronting their homophobia.

Gay men are caught in a crosscurrent of forces. On the one hand there is a growing movement for stability in relationships, gay marriage, and gay fathering. These desires require a community of support, some degree of acceptance by the greater society, and protection of basic rights. On the other hand, the assault on gay rights by Christian conservatives, violence directed against gay men by young heterosexual males, and efforts to criminalize homosexuality and to identify HIV / AIDS as a gay male disease create a climate in which the stability of gay communities is threatened.

SUGGESTED READING

David Fernbach's *The Spiral Path* (1981) and Dennis Altman's *The Homosexualization of America, the Americanization of the Homosexual* (1982), along with K. White's *The First Sexual Revolution: The Emergence of Male Heterosexuality in Modern America* (1992), offer many interesting historical insights into gay and straight masculinities. David Mohr's *Gay Ideas: Outing and Other Controversies* (1992) offers a lively cultural critique of issues in gay liberation, and his *A More Perfect Union: Why Straight America Must Stand Up for Gay Rights* (1994) is a highly persuasive case for straight men working for the protection of gay rights. Randy Shilts's *Conduct Unbecoming: Gays and Lesbians in the U.S. Military, Vietnam to the Persian Gulf* (1993) is indispensable in understanding the controversy of the 1990s.

EIGHT

African American Men: The Challenge of Racism

*As a starting point, I see the black male as being in conflict with the norma-
tive definition of masculinity. This is a status which few, if any, black males
have been able to achieve. Masculinity, as defined in this culture, has always
implied a certain autonomy and mastery of one's environment.*
—Robert Staples, "Black Male Sexuality"

*Black males start life with serious disadvantages. They are, for instance,
more likely to be born to unwed teenage mothers who are poorly educated
and more likely to neglect or abuse their children; the children of these mothers are also more likely to be born underweight and to experience injuries or
neurological defects that require long-term care. Moreover, such children are
more likely to be labeled "slow learners" or "educable mentally retarded," to
have learning difficulties in school, to lag behind their peers in basic educational competencies or skills, and to drop out of school at an early age. Black
boys are also more likely to be institutionalized or placed in foster care.*
—Ronald L. Taylor, "Black Males and Social Policy:
Breaking the Cycle of Disadvantage"

HISTORICAL SKETCH AND PRIMARY SOURCES

We have already noted that being masculine does not require that a
man be white, middle class, Anglo-Saxon, Protestant, or heterosexual; in
fact, the men who possess all these qualities constitute a minority. But because of the emphasis on dominant or hegemonic masculinities, men who
are outside of these boundaries, when they read the literature on men and
masculinity, feel left out (Franklin 1994b). They see that others who do not
share their experiences are speaking for them. Indeed, men who are

black, Jewish, gay, or physically unique may question whether they, like gay men, are being defined as "not measuring up" to the "masculine norm." As Michael Kimmel has noted, "Historically, the Jewish man has been seen as less than masculine, often as a direct outgrowth of his emotional 'respond-ability.' The historical consequences of centuries of laws against Jews, of anti-Semitic oppression, are a cultural identity and even a self-perception as 'less than men,' who are too weak, too fragile, too frightened to care for our own" (Kimmel 1987d:15). In a similar vein, Franklin speaks of the black male experience: "Understanding Black men means recognizing that in America adult Black males have been Black 'men' for only about twenty years. In addition, even during this time Black males have not been recognized as 'societally approved' men" (Franklin 1994b:275).

No group of men has received more attention in the late 1980s and 1990s than black men. (In this chapter, "black man," "African American man," and "Black man" are all conventions adopted by different authors or even the same author at different times; I shall use these terms interchangeably.) There are many reasons for this public scrutiny.

First, an increasing number of scholars, many of whom are black males, study and write on the social reality for black males. For example, the National Council of African American Men (NCAAM) was founded in 1990 by Richard Majors and Jacob Gordon (Majors 1994:302). This umbrella organization also publishes the new *Journal of African American Male Studies* and the *Annual State of Black Male America*. Programs such as the Albany State Center for the Study of the Black Male and the Morehouse Institute for Research add to the growing scholarship about the status of Black males in American society. Even prior to the Million Man March in Washington, D. C., on October 16, 1995, there was ongoing concern in the mass media about the situation of black males in America (Freeman 1990; Herbert, Price, Marshall, Day, and Singleton 1994). Much of the recent interest derives from books like Jewelle Taylor Gibbs's *Young, Black, and Male in America: An Endangered Species* and popular films like *Hoop Dreams* (1994), which seek to capture the dreams and difficulties of young black males.

Second, men's studies and the men's movements, which have always been dominated by white males, have continually struggled publicly with how to address issues of black masculinities. How much of the middle-class white male experience is applicable to the black experience? And how can black men become more involved in both academic programs and political movements? Black scholars, in return, have argued that in spite of efforts to counter academic racism and exclusion, men's studies and the men's movements remain tarnished by antiblack racism (Franklin 1994b; Segal 1990:169–204).

Third, conservatives and neoconservatives have launched a series of ideological and political attacks on social policies and programs that were intended to help groups, such as black Americans, who are subject to discrimination. These attacks, although they do not focus exclusively on the black population, often draw attention to the lives of African Americans. And books like *The Bell Curve*, for example, do target black Americans as intellectually inferior. The argument in *The Bell Curve* is that the lower average IQ among black Americans is mostly determined by genes and that IQ differences in a population determine whether that population is disadvantaged relative to other populations or whether programs that enhance opportunities are cost-effective (Herrnstein and Murray 1994; cf. Gould 1994; Reed 1994).

Fourth, closely connected to the conservative attacks on black Americans has been a national preoccupation with crime and the black criminal (Stewart 1994). Although black males remain a minority in the criminal class, they are a highly visible minority. Almost one in four black males between the ages of twenty and twenty-nine is either in prison, in jail, on probation, or on parole (Mauer 1994:82). Forty-four percent of the prisoners in the United States are black males (Mauer 1944:82; DiMascio 1995:13). Much of black male involvement with the prison system is due to differential sentencing for crack offenses (more likely to affect black men) and powder cocaine offenses (more likely to affect white men). Thus, "the U.S. Sentencing Commission reported in 1995 that 88 percent of offenders sentenced for crack offenses are African-Americans and 4.1 percent, white. Sentences for selling a certain amount of crack are equal in length to sentences for selling 100 times that amount of powder cocaine. If crack and powder cocaine were treated similarly, the average sentence for convicted crack traffickers would be 47 months, as opposed to 141 months" (DiMascio 1995:14). More black men go to prison for crack use in spite of studies like the *Oakland Tribune* study, which concluded that the typical crack addict is "a middle-class, white male in his forties" (Coontz 1992:24). In short, arrest, prosecution, and sentencing practices are biased in favor of putting the black male in prison, which only adds fuel to the national preoccupation with the black man as criminal.

A fifth reason for the sociological and political attention paid to black men is that being a African American male in the United States has always been a sociopolitical issue. Since being brought to the United States as slaves, black men and women have been resistant to the social reality in which they find themselves (Aptheker 1978:48–67; Turner, Singleton, and Musick 1984:11–41). When black men struggle, whether it is through the Congressional Black Caucus, the NAACP, or the Million Man March, their struggle becomes the focus of attention in the media, among racist vigilante groups, and among the general population (Lawrence 1994).

There are many voices among black writers who discuss the African American male's reality. Much of the black liberation movement is tied to a Christian Protestant tradition represented by the Reverends Martin Luther King Jr., Ralph Abernathy, and Jesse Jackson. But there are evangelical Christians as well, such as Tony Evans and Crawford Loritts, spokespersons for the Promise Keepers. These movements are generally moralistic and integrationist in nature. In contrast, the Black Panther Party for Self Defense, founded in 1967 by Huey P. Newton and Bobby Seale; the Congress for Racial Equality (CORE); and the National of Islam, founded in the 1930s, generally embrace separatist strategies calling for a "nation within a nation" (Marable 1983:139). There are also black socialists such as W.E.B. DuBois, Richard Wright, and Manning Marable, who are a crucial part of the history of U.S. radical politics (Robinson 1983). Thomas Sowell, Clarence Thomas, and J. C. Watts are prominent conservative thinkers who generally reject explanations in terms of slavery, racism, or poverty in favor of explanations that blame liberal government programs and the decline of family values (Sowell 1985; Alterman 1996). Clyde W. Franklin II, who coedited *Changing Men's* special issue on black men (Winter 1986) represents a profeminist men's studies perspective. Michael Meade, working with Malidoma Some, frequently does mythopoetic work on black-white relations in his gatherings under The Mosaic Multicultural Foundation. And Earl Ofari Hutchinson offers a men's rights perspective of black masculinity in *The Assassination of the Black Male* (1994).

In spite of the variety of viewpoints on black masculinities, there is remarkable agreement about the nature of black male reality. Richard G. Majors and Jacob U. Gordon's *The American Black Male: His Present Status and His Future* (1994) serves as our first primary source. This comprehensive collection offers history as well as descriptions and explanations of the present social reality for black males. Our second primary source is Manning Marable's *How Capitalism Underdeveloped Black America* (1983). Marable, a widely read social theorist, writes from a standpoint that is best described as black socialist feminism. His work emphasizes the impact of black oppression and its ongoing political struggle on black masculinities. The writings of Clyde W. Franklin II in the Majors and Gordon book as well as in *The Making of Masculinities* constitute a third primary source (Franklin 1987, 1994a, 1994b). Franklin is a profeminist concerned with the messages being given to young black men. In order to bring out the diversity of voices, we shall use a variety of materials, such as Louis Farrakhan's speech at the Million Man March, articles from the *Journal of African American Male Studies* and *emerge,* and essays by Sowell and Hutchinson.

DESCRIPTION AND EXPLANATION OF MALE REALITY

Masculinity

Almost any approach to black masculinity begins with a dismal set of figures descriptive of black male reality. Richard Majors summarizes some of the most dramatic statistics:

- Over 30 percent of black males (but only about 15 percent of white males) were not in the work force because they were unemployed or unaccounted for.
- Although 54 percent of the Black men are married, for every 100 unmarried Black women, there are only 63 marriageable Black men.
- Homicide is the leading cause of death of Black males between the ages of fifteen and thirty-four.
- A young Black male has a 1 in 21 chance of being a victim of homicide. . . .
- African-American males are the only segment of the U.S. population with a decreasing life expectancy. . . .
- One-third of all Blacks live in poverty.
- One-half of all Black children live in poverty. (Majors 1994:300–301)

For black men there is an acute shortage of work opportunities (Coontz 1992:245). "In 1978 only 1.8 million out of 18.1 million Black persons over 14 years of age could find employment" (Marable 1983:62; Franklin 1987:166). Sociologist Robert Staples estimates that 46 percent of black men between the ages of sixteen and sixty-two are not in the labor force (Muwakkil 1988:7). And "literally millions of Black Americans . . . have absolutely no meaningful prospects for future work" (Marable 1983:63). There are many reasons for the exclusion of black Americans from the work force (Taylor 1994:158–160). Technological replacement is certainly the cause of a decline of work opportunities in fields such as agriculture. Forty years ago, two out of five black men worked on farms; in 1960 only 5 percent of black men worked in agriculture. By the early 1980s the number declined to less than 130,000 men (Marable 1994:76). However, according to the U.S. Commission on Civil Rights, the exclusion of black Americans from the work force is due primarily to the racist structuring of work rather than to lack of skill or education (Marable 1983:270).

As a result of their exclusion from employment, "black men do not expect to assume a traditional male sex role" (Franklin 1987:163; Majors and Billson 1992:1). Young black men often turn to illegal work and gang activity to make a living. Marable states that "in Chicago, over one-fourth of all Black youth between the ages of 14 to 25 belong to gangs, which often deal in small robberies, drugs and prostitution" (Marable 1983:65). And Michael Dyson notes that gang membership in Los Angeles "has risen from 15,000 to almost 60,000 . . . as gang warfare claims one life per day"

(Dyson 1989:54). (Of course, black men do not have a monopoly on illegal activities. As noted, white males commit the majority of crimes in the United States, are convicted less frequently, and use most of the drugs, while black men are scapegoated (Mauer 1994; Taylor 1994:160–161).

Throughout U.S. history, antiblack racism has been particularly violent: "Between 1884 and 1900 more than 2,500 black men were lynched, the majority of whom were [falsely] accused of sexual interest in white women" (Staples 1986:4; Marable 1994:71). Some black men were lynched simply for being "too successful" as farmers or tradespeople (McMillen 1989). Such figures do not include the thousands of black men who have been harassed daily by police and other institutions and convicted by a racist judicial system that too often cannot even distinguish one black man from another (Marable 1983:246–253).

Violence against black men is often thought of as a thing of the past or something that happens to low-income uneducated black men. But racism is contemporary and pervasive; daily harassment and denials of opportunity continue in the 1990s, affecting all African American men, including middle-class and upper-class black males. Michael Dyson tells of trying to get a cash advance on his credit card while traveling. Because he was black, the teller (who was white) immediately confiscated his card, and the bank manager cut it in half, assuming it was stolen (Dyson 1989:56). The *Atlanta Journal/Constitution* tracked home-loan applications in the nation's banks from 1983 to 1988. Black Americans were rejected for loans at a much higher rate than were white Americans. Coontz notes:

> In many areas, rejection rates for high-income blacks were higher than for low-income whites. An Asian or Hispanic who finished only the third grade or who earns less than $2,500 a year has a higher chance of living in an integrated neighborhood than does a black person who has a Ph.D. or earns more than $50,000. College educated black men now make 75 percent as much as their white counterparts when employed, but their unemployment rate is four times higher. (Coontz 1992:234)

This pervasive antiblack racism carries over into many masculinities that are embraced by white males. White men simply behave differently, both verbally and in their body language, in the presence of black men, and many of these behaviors indicate a level of distrust or fear (Pierce and Profit 1994:169). Just as deeply ingrained patterns of sexism are included in most masculinities, so, too, do deeply entrenched patterns built around race infect these masculinities, especially North American hegemonic masculinities, which invariably include being white as a component. Kimmel cites Goffman's observation that "in America, there is only one complete, unblushing male" who is white, heterosexual, Protestant, a married father, attractive, and with a recent record in sports (Kimmel

1994:125). This racism is not simply a racism that sees white males as superior and as the normative men, but it is a racism that thrives on negative stereotypes of black males as violent, hypersexual, unintelligent, and insensitive. These attitudes since the time of slavery have resulted in a continuous series of violent and hateful acts aimed at black men (Staples 1986:3; Marable 1994; Hutchinson 1994; Turner, Singleton, and Musick 1984; Lawrence 1994; Farrakhan 1995).

Confronted with a seemingly endless series of oppressive structures that strip black men of much control over their lives, those men respond in a variety of ways, each of which tends to create a particular form of black masculinity. One form of masculinity is achieved by being "cool." Majors and Billson identify "cool pose" as a "ritualized form of masculinity that entails behaviors, scripts, physical posturing, impression management, and carefully crafted performances that deliver a single, critical message: pride, strength, and control" (1992:4). The purpose of this stance is clear: "As a performance, cool pose is designed to render the black male visible and to empower him; it eases the worry and pain of blocked opportunities. Being cool is an ego booster for black males comparable to the kind white males more easily find through attending good schools, landing prestigious jobs, and bringing home decent wages" (Majors and Billson 1992:5).

Cool pose is hardly the only kind of black masculinity to which black men turn. Franklin identifies at least five distinct masculinities: conforming black masculinity, ritualistic black masculinity, innovative black masculinity, retreatist black masculinity, and rebellious black masculinity (Franklin 1994b:280–281). *Conforming* masculinity is familiar to anyone who knows hegemonic masculinity: the acceptance "of mainstream society's prescriptions and proscriptions for heterosexual males" (Franklin 1994b:280). Franklin notes, "They [black males] do so despite the fact that, when society teaches men to work hard, set high goals, and strive for success, it does not teach Black men simultaneously that their probability of failure is high because blocked opportunities for Black males are endemic to American society" (Franklin 1994b:280; cf. MacLeod 1987). *Ritualistic* black masculinity resembles conforming black masculinity except that its practitioners do not believe in the rules and the institutions they obey—it is "'playing the game' without purpose or commitment" (Franklin 180–81). *Innovative* black masculinity is a form of masculinity that has abandoned conformity or even ritualistic conformity. Often in this masculinity traits of hegemonic masculinity are exaggerated, as in 2 Live Crew's "As Nasty As They Wanna Be," which "debases women" while making the group wealthy (Franklin 1994b:281). In other forms of innovative masculinity the pursuit of material success leads to black-on-black homicide, drug dealing, and theft. *Retreatist* black masculinity gives up any hope of success, and members of this group slip into drug addictions, alcoholism, and homelessness. These men give up looking for work or meaningful existence (Franklin 1994b:281–282). *Rebellious* black masculinity was symbolized by the Black Panther movement of the 1960s, but it can be found among black activists who work in many organizations committed to black liberation.

There are many other forms of black masculinity that combine many features of Franklin's categories; for example, Louis Farrakhan's vision of a black man is someone who is rebellious and angry—yet cool—a black separatist who espouses the values of traditional male-headed families, Christianized Islamic faith, and free enterprise (Farrakhan 1995). Thus, in spite of the many forms of oppression, or perhaps because of them, African American masculinities are at least as diverse as the masculinities exhibited by any other group of men in modern society.

In light of its ongoing struggle for liberation and equality, it is not surprising that the black liberation movement itself identifies black liberation with the assertion of black manhood (Marable 1983:76–78). This conception of black liberation is prominent in the writings of such leaders as Malcolm X, Stokely Carmichael, and Louis Farrakhan (Marable 1983:90–93; Cliff 1984:157–158). "Even Frederick Douglass, the leading male proponent of women's rights in the nineteenth century, asserted in 1855 that the struggle for racial liberation meant that blacks 'must develop their manhood'" (Marable 1983:77). The black movement recognizes the fact that black male power was severely restricted under slavery—not just in terms of personal freedom but also in terms of exclusion from the power relations of white patriarchy (Marable 1983:76). By the same token, if black men are to achieve equality with white men, they need to adopt a patriarchal structure—which, in the United States, would entail acceptance of the norms of white masculinity (Franklin 1987:162–163). This identification of black liberation with male liberation has been reinforced by the fact that the churches, the press, the business establishment, and the black liberation movement itself are male dominated.

How black masculinities are explained varies greatly among social theorists. Socialists tend to emphasize the material conditions of work that keep black men in poverty (Marable 1983). Coontz writes:

> The experience of black families has been qualitatively different from that of white, or even other minorities, all along the line. . . .
> More than other minorities, blacks encountered periodic increases in discrimination and segregation, first as democratic politicians tried to justify the continuation of slavery, then as blacks were pushed not up but off the job ladder by successive waves of immigrants.
> No other minority got so few payoffs for sending its children to school, and no other immigrants ran into such a low job ceiling that college gradu-

ates had to become Pullman porters. No other minority was saddled with such unfavorable demographics during early migration . . . or was so completely excluded from industrial work during the main heyday of its expansion. (Coontz 1992:237–238)

Black profeminists tend to stress that the patriarchal norms of masculinity set standards that are impossible for black men to achieve, thereby generating alternative but marginalized forms of manhood (Franklin 1987; 1994a). Many black sociologists point to the abandonment of the war on poverty—a war that was being waged successfully in the 1960s—as a cause of the 1970s decline in the well-being of black males (Gibbs 1988; Taylor 1994). During the 1960s, black family income doubled as federal spending on antipoverty programs went from $1 billion to $10 billion from 1964–1968. Poverty dropped among black Americans from 58 percent to 30 percent during these years, a decrease of 28 percent (Taylor 1994:149–150).

Conservatives such as Thomas Sowell, George Gilder, and David Blankenhorn paint a very different picture: They argue that these same programs were a failure, creating the very conditions that now plague young black males—fatherlessness, crime, and poverty (Sowell 1985; Sowell 1993:173–175; Blankenhorn 1995). Among conservatives it is fashionable to blame not racism or poverty but a failure of values, a lack of responsibility: "Robert Rector of the Heritage Foundation, writing in the *Wall Street Journal*, asserts that 'the primary cause of black poverty' is neither economic nor racial inequality but 'disintegration of the family'" (Coontz 1992:235). The disintegration of the family is laid squarely on the shoulders of antipoverty programs that "destroy the father's key role and authority" (Gilder 1981:114; cf. Blankenhorn 1995).

Still other theorists look to the history of slavery, Jim Crow segregation, and their accompanying racism (Gibbs 1988:17; Farrakhan 1995). Black authors such as Earl Ofari Hutchinson focus on negative images in the media and in popular literature (Hutchinson 1994). Of course, there are multiple causes for the fact that black males are considerably worse off today than they were twenty years ago. The preceding causal factors are not all mutually exclusive, but different thinkers tend to give weight to different explanations.

However, for all their differences, most writings about black men clearly implicate the role of racism in the development of white masculinities, especially hegemonic masculinities. This racism is further causally implicated in the decimation and degradation of the black male. White men learn a stereotype of blacks; it is a stereotype that attributes to blacks the traits that whites do not want to attribute to themselves. For example, in 1933 there was a zero percent overlap between white and black traits as determined by whites; by 1982 that overlap had increased to only 22 percent (Dovidia and Gaertner 1986:6). If antiblack racism is so important to the way in which whites think about themselves, it is safe to assume that other forms of racism and prejudice also help to form white behaviors and attitudes. In short, the earlier perspectives simply do not capture the role of prejudice in the formation of the dominant white masculinities.

Feminism

In many ways, the black liberation movements in North America contributed to the rise of various feminist movements. Within many civil rights organizations and many leftist organizations women were relegated to such menial tasks as mimeographing and making coffee; they were also confronted with a "gross sexism" that denied them opportunities to express their views in public (Cliff 1984:157–158; Jaggar 1983:230). Thus, a women's movement demanding that women be treated equally under the law, that women be heard, that violence and objectification be stopped, was bound to arise. Many leftist and civil rights organizations simply did not live up to their own rhetoric. At the same time, the emerging women's movement adopted much of the demands and language of the black liberation movements. Gayle Rubin's "Woman as Nigger" is a prime example (Rubin 1969:230–240). Rubin's essay is clearly an effort to merge the notions of sexism and racism, thus:

> The basic premise of women's liberation is that women are an exploited class, like black people, but that unlike blacks, they are not marginal to our technocratic society. So that one might expect that social control of women is less slipshod and more subtle than that of black people. In other words, women suffer from some form of racism, as that word is currently used. Racism has come to refer ... to something enormously more complex than what it meant in the days of the first sit-ins. It refers to any dynamic system of social, political, economic, and psychological pressures that tend to suppress a group. . . . (Rubin 1969:231)

Yet for all feminism's indebtedness to the language and ideas of the black liberation movements, feminism was met with considerable skepticism by many black Americans. "At the outset, the majority of Blacks who wrote on feminism were decidedly hostile. In one widely read 1971 essay published in *Ebony* magazine, Helen King denounced 'women's lib' as a white petty bourgeois fad that had little to nothing to do with the interests of Black women" (Marable 1983:95). Other arguments from the black community included the charge that the women's movement in the past had been racist and white dominated (Hooks 1981:124), and that it projected the domination by white males over white women onto the black community. This projection was seen by some black feminists as totally inappropriate. As Gloria Joseph put it, "Historically, Black men were definitely not afforded supremacy over any females. . . . During slavery the Black male was disallowed a superior position in relation to the Black female and there is really no question about Black men having control over white women" (Joseph 1981:99). In other words, given the authoritarian structure of slavery and the continued impoverishment of blacks, black men have never dominated women (including black women) in the same way that white men have. This is not to suggest that there is no violence between black men and black women or between black men and white women (Gary 1987:232–243). Joseph's claim is simply that black men have never been able to *control* women, either sexually or in terms of labor power, because such control has been preempted by white males (Joseph 1981:100–101). Some black feminists reject this claim, however. They argue that black women have always been subject to sexism and control by black men. Even under slavery, black men "regarded tasks like cooking, sewing, nursing, and even minor farm labor as woman's work" (Hooks 1981:44–45). Moreover, "women in black communities have been reluctant to publicly discuss sexist oppression but they have always known it exists. We too have been socialized to accept sexist ideology and many black women feel that black male abuse of women is a reflection of frustrated masculinity" (Hooks 1984:74).

Whatever the final arbitration of this dispute, it is clear that black and white men differ in terms of their power relations with women. In the first place, because of racism black men lack many of the privileges and powers over white women that white men have. In the second place, because of their tenuous place in the relations of production, black men wield less power over black women than white men wield over white women. Under these conditions, what becomes of the profeminist claim that masculinity manifests itself as power over women or the socialist claim that men control women's labor power? Indeed, these two perspectives fail to account for the differences among men based on racial privilege or disadvantage.

Black feminists such as Bell Hooks remain critical of the white feminist movement. "Despite the current focus on eliminating racism in the feminist movement, there has been little change in the direction of theory and praxis" (Hooks 1984:53). "Women will know that feminist activists have begun to confront racism in a serious and revolutionary manner when they are not simply acknowledging racism in the feminist movement or calling attention to personal prejudice, but are actively struggling to resist racist oppression in our society" (Hooks 1984:55).

Hooks's skepticism toward the white feminist movement is mirrored in the observations of black men who have worked in the profeminist men's movement. Tony Bell, for instance, indicates that, "while I have not regretted any of my involvement over the past three and a half years, I have had my share of worries and fears about the 'men's movement.' I continue to be discouraged that we have not attracted more men of color. I fear that we will become just another well-meaning liberal group that 'talks a good game'" (Bell 1986:12).

As of the 1990s black feminism is an established fact (Collins 1991). The contributions of black feminists to feminist theory and practice are undeniable and indispensable, yet still considered marginal. As black feminism moves more to the center of feminist theory, black men may yet respond by adopting a profeminist perspective or by moving into socialist organizations. If this is to happen, however, the marginalization of racial issues, the suspicion of white-led organizations, and the tradition of alternative black-focused movements that *do* put antiracism at the center of their agendas must be honestly confronted. Only then will the men's movement earn the trust of black men.

ASSESSMENT OF MALE REALITY AND AGENDA FOR CHANGE

Of all the assessments of male reality, the assessments of black male reality are the most discouraging and the most pessimistic. Because there is such an obvious need to address the problems facing black males of every age, there are probably more "solutions" for these problems than apply to any other group. For many writers, black men in America are facing nothing less than a literal, or at least a social, extinction. According to these writers, black men face "genocide" and "decimation"; they are an "endangered species" (Franklin 1987:155–156; Muwakkil 1988:7; Dyson 1989:51; Gibbs 1988; Majors 1994; Gilmore 1996).

> Staples characterizes the crisis as "genocidal" because he believes it is being fueled by economic necessities. . . . Staples cited these statistics to bolster his grim assessment: while black men are only 6 percent of the U.S. population they compose half its male prisoners in local, state and federal jails; more than 18 percent of black males drop out of high school; more than 50 percent of black men under age of 21 are unemployed;. . . approximately 32 percent of black men have incomes below the poverty level. . . . By the year 2000 it is estimated that 70 percent of all black men will be in jail, dead or on drugs or in the throes of alcoholism. (Muwakkil 1988:7)

Some black writers consider *genocide* too strong a word, but decimation is occurring. It is also a practice that serves racist society in distinctive ways (Marable 1983:251; cf. Franklin 1987:156). The pattern of decimation is such that, by the age of 45, there are 10 percent fewer black males than white (adjusted to their relative proportions); by the age of 65, 20 percent fewer; and by the age of 75, 30 percent fewer (Franklin 1987:156). As noted earlier, black males are the only group in North America for whom life expectancy is declining (Majors 1994:300–301).

The agendas to end this "decimation" vary according to the viewpoint. The black men who write about themselves and their communities tend to focus on the issues they can actually influence. Profeminists such as Clyde W. Franklin want to see a change in the "socialization message" for black youth as well as a black male community effort toward "a return to more peaceful and productive relations between black men, and between black men and black women" (Franklin 1987:168). Robert Staples calls for educational programs that sensitize black males to the need for responsibility in family planning, sex education for both sexes, opportunities for meaningful employment, and better communication between men and women (Staples 1986:47).

Ronald Taylor's solution is liberal, although it shares much with Marable's. Taylor argues that black males (and females) experience an "ecology of deprivation," which includes malnutrition, ill health, poverty, poor schools, family discord, and prejudicial treatment, throughout their lives. But one does not have to eradicate each of these negative factors in order to give black boys a chance to compete. Their natural resilience will compensate for many factors if a few disadvantages can be eliminated or small amounts of help can be given at the right times. Thus, programs like Head Start can help children enormously throughout their lives, even though the program helps only modestly with basic academic skills (Taylor 1994:165). Taylor also calls for a renewal of many of the training programs launched in the 1960s that do improve "the long-term employment prospects and life chances of disadvantaged Black males" (Taylor 1994:166). Sowell and other conservatives of course disagree. Sowell would dismantle all the 1960s programs and let the market and personal responsibility decide who survives and who does not, although Sowell's "facts" that prove the failure of antipoverty programs have been seriously challenged by Boston's *Race, Class and Conservatism* (1988).

Probably no single event has so focused the nation's attention on the struggle of black men than the October 16, 1995 Million Man March in Washington, D.C. This march, conceived by Louis Farrakhan and organized by Faye Williams, drew approximately a million black men from various communities in North America. Politically, the marchers were diverse: 31 percent claimed liberal ideology, 21 percent moderate, 13 percent conservative, 11 percent nationalist, 4 percent socialist, and 21 percent something else (Curry 1996:41). About one-third came from families with yearly incomes below $35,000 (Curry 1996:47).

Although the audience was addressed by a long list of black leader, male and female, the featured speaker was Louis Farrakhan, head of the

Nation of Islam. Farrakhan's speech was a blend of religious conservative capitalism. His focus was on the moral crisis facing the black community, which he blamed on the degradation of slavery, the attitude of white supremacy, and the fractured status of the black community. His solutions were essentially separatist and psychological. Black communities must come together and change the way they think, which means they must recognize individual and collective wrongs and take action to change these wrongs ("atonement") (Farrakhan 1995). The undeserved "furnace of affliction" of the black community is allowed by God because suffering is redemptive. Men are to be the leaders in this renewal because "in the beginning God made man" and a new beginning requires a new man (Farrakhan 1995). The new man is captured by a pledge recited by the marchers:

> I pledge that from this day forward I will strive to love my brother as I love myself. I, from this day forward, will strive to improve myself spiritually, morally, mentally, socially, politically and economically for the benefit of myself, my family and my people. I pledge that I will strive to build business, build houses, build hospitals, build factories and enter into international trade for the good of myself, my family and my people.

> I pledge that from this day forward I will never raise my hand with a knife or a gun to beat, cut, or shoot any member of my family or any human being, except in self-defense.

> I pledge from this day forward I will never abuse my wife by striking her, disrespecting her, for she is the mother of my children and the producer of my future. I pledge that from this day forward I will never engage in the abuse of children, little boys or little girls, for sexual gratification. For I will let them grow in peace to be strong men and women for the future of our people.

> I will never again use the "B word" to describe any female, but particularly my own Black sister. I pledge from this day forward that I will not poison my body with drugs or that which is destructive to my health and my well-being.

> I pledge from this day forward I will support Black newspapers, Black radio, Black television. I will support Black artists who clean up their acts to show respect for themselves and respect for their people and respect for the ears of the human family. I will do all this, so help me God. (Farrakhan 1995; *emerge* February 1996:67)

In short, Farrakhan's message stresses moral responsibility and black capitalism; in this he agrees with conservatives. But he also identifies social structures that are harmful to the black community, and he urges black voters to support programs that help the poor and vulnerable. Other speakers identified these programs; they include liberal programs such as affirmative action and Aid to Families with Dependent Children (AFDC). And in what was clearly a profeminist message, Farrakhan denounced lack of respect for women. Of note to religious conservatives is that Farrakhan believes that it is *man* and not *woman* who is made in God's image and on whom falls the task of righting what is wrong with the black community. It is small wonder that the march had widespread appeal to African American men of diverse political persuasions.

Manning Marable's socialist solution challenges both the liberalism of Taylor and the religious conservatism of Farrakhan. Marable connects contemporary racism with the current needs of capitalism and rejects the idea that any strategy "limited to Black Americans and their conditions" can succeed (Marable 1983:256). In the language of the socialist perspective covered in Chapter 6, the decimation of black men and the alienations of black masculinity can be addressed conclusively only within a system of meaningful work in which black men have greater control over their own labor. Teaching responsibility when there is little opportunity to exercise that responsibility and creating meaningful work when capitalism by design maintains black men primarily as surplus labor are liberal strategies doomed to fail. Marable concludes that "the road to Black liberation must also be a road to socialist revolution" (Marable 1983:256). Staples, too, seems to support this conclusion when he attributes the crisis facing black men to "the ravages of an unbridled and dying American capitalism" (Muwakkil 1988:7). A chilling corollary of this socialist assessment is that the decimation of black men and black male alienation will continue so long as capitalism refuses to use fairly black male labor.

Criticism 1

The danger of a focus on antiblack racism is always a risk. First, there is the risk of oversimplification. For example, many black men have lost jobs due to technology rather than to racism. And although racism is certainly common among white males who adopt hegemonic masculinities, it is not common in all such masculinities and therefore is hardly a necessary component. Hence, to build an analysis of dominant masculinities out of its common but unnecessary component—antiblack racism—distorts what creates and maintains these masculinities. Second, there is the risk of victimization. It is true that black men and women have been victims of racism, but so have Native Americans, gay men, Latinos, Asian groups, and many others. To see only one's own victimization may itself lead to racist attitudes toward other groups. Generally, black perspectives put too much emphasis upon racism (cf. Sowell 1993:169–170). By itself, racism explains very little.

Response

The black American experience is unique in many ways. Blacks in the United States are the only group deprived of its national and local heritage, the only group whose name and religion was taken away, the only group to be enslaved, and the group that suffers the greatest economic privation and denial of opportunity in modern society (Coontz 1992:237–238). And black men have carried the brunt of these afflictions. Thus, black Americans must focus on the antiblack racism, institutional and personal, that they face. Their oppression is unique in the history of the United States.

Criticism 2

Regarding the Million Man March: "There are friends of mine who would have absolutely nothing to do with the conservative fundamentalism of this platform under any other circumstance who find this call for a coming together irresistible—and they will not argue about it; they do not care to see beyond that Great Coming of togetherness. . . . I also worry about a 'personal responsibility' march, as some of the organizers have called it, on the site of the civil rights marches of the past" (Williams 1995:494).

Response

It is obvious from the breakdown of political opinions that most of the marchers did not share the conservative political opinions of Farrakhan that are referred to above; most of the march speakers did not share his views. But sometimes a gathering can transcend the political rhetoric of a particular speaker. Black men who were interviewed came together for the greater purpose of a show of strength and support for one another (Curry 1996:47; Smolowe 1995). Commentators like Williams underestimate the independence of black men and overestimate the impact of the words of religious conservatives like Farrakhan.

Criticism 3

Adolph Reed, a professor of political science at Northwestern University, noted that the march reflected the desperation of the black community, which fears a return to the days of even fewer opportunities. "People are feeling pinched and threatened, and a lot of political leaders don't seem to have any answers. . . . People like Farrakhan feed on that sort of desperation. The substance of his message and agenda meshes well with right-wing Republicans" (Terry 1995).

Response

"Professor Reed's concerns seemed far removed from the black men who had listened to Mr. Farrakhan for more than two hours. After the minister had finished, they hugged and shook hands with friends and strangers. Then they headed home past dozens of vendors selling T-shirts, videos, books and candy bars. Most of the items had a picture of a smiling Louis Farrakhan" (Terry 1995).

Criticism 4

The view that liberal programs were working in the 1960s and would so continue if only we had kept at it is simply wrong.

> For example, the employment situation of young Black males, eighteen to nineteen, continued to deteriorate in the 1970s, even as federal employment and training programs and related efforts became better organized and more extensive. . . . Moreover, the labor force participation rate of Black males continued its downward trend in the early 1970s, particularly among teenagers, despite a tight labor market. Similarly, the percentage of Black husband-wife households declined between 1968 and 1973 from 72 to 63 percent of all Black families, a precipitous decline in just five years. (Taylor 1994:153)

Response

To single out government programs as the cause of such troubles in the black community is irresponsible. The 1970s were a period of double-digit inflation, and a severe economic recession that set in in 1974 undid most of the post–World War II gains by black men (Coontz 1992:243–246; Taylor 1994:153). What the destruction of social programs in the late 1970s and 1980s did was to amplify the devastating effects of the economic downturn of the 1970s.

SUMMARY AND CONCLUSIONS

The issues raised by black men are instructive for all the perspectives already discussed. Let us begin with the perspective of gay men. Black men who are gay often find that gay perspectives are racist. And gay black men may feel that they have no place in either community because of homophobia in the black community.

Larry Icard, who studies how gay black men seek their identities, notes:

The black community . . . holds negative attitudes about homosexuality and the gay community. This negative attitude is influenced by the black community's emphasis on group survival, survival against social pressures from a white-oriented society. For many blacks, homosexuality is a culture phenomenon of whites—a white problem inimical to the interest of blacks.

As a member of the gay community, black gays are viewed as inferior members. This negative image limits their receiving the same kinds of positive psychological benefits that mixing in the gay community offers their white counterpart. Black gay men are frequently greeted with subjugation in bars, clubs, and other gay social gatherings. Often there are signs in the gay community which state, "No Blacks, Fems, or Faggots." These signs convey the restriction that blacks and other ethnic minority groups experience along with effeminate gays. (Icard 1986:86, 89)

What these attitudes reveal is that sensitivity to one kind of oppression does not translate into sensitivity to another kind. When one happens to fall into two oppressed groups—as gay black men do—there is a good chance that one will suffer from the prejudices of both groups rather than benefit from dual membership.

Profeminists—liberal, radical, or socialist—must also face questions that are raised by the black male experience. How has male domination been affected by the history of slavery and the domination of black men and women by white men? Do black men dominate black women in the same way that white men dominate white women? Is the socialist claim that men control women's labor power true for black men? Or is it largely white women and men who control black men's labor? If feminism marginalizes racism, why should black men join the profeminist men's movement? Indeed, writers like Hutchinson argue that feminist black women such as Bell Hooks or Alice Walker continue to contribute to the assassination of the black male image (Hutchinson 1994:84–87). Is there a case, given the very different experiences of white men and black men, for a separate black men's movement? Given the different behaviors of white men around black men, is there even a chance that a combined movement will work?

Conservatives also must continually struggle with the experience of black men. Black men have not done well in the unbridled marketplace. White men who are already advantaged seem simply to increase their advantages at the expense of black men. The best years for black men were in the 1960s, when the government programs that most conservatives now would like to dismantle took effect. It seems to be an undeniable fact that as antipoverty programs are discontinued, black men have greater difficulty in achieving the American dream.

Andrew Kimbrell, in *The Masculine Mystique*, suggests that the plight of black men should be moved to the forefront of men's issues. Such a strategy would "roll back the Social Darwinist 'competition man' dogma of winner and losers" (Kimbrell 1995:327). But Kimbrell hints at more: that the social reality of black men may well be the indicator of the future of white men. The economic enclosure of black men has been the most severe of all groups of men, but if such an enclosure can be allowed to succeed for one group of men, surely it can succeed for other groups. Unless all men support these causes, no group of men will be secure. Kimbrell's view probably underestimates the differences between groups—how the enclosure of some groups of men by other men means a lessening of their own enclosure. And Kimbrell tends to see the black male experience as just a special case, though perhaps the most dramatic, of how men are victimized in North American society.

Certainly there is no "quick fix" for the serious social problems that beset a racist society. But for all the identified ugliness in the lives of many black men, one must never forget the millions of black men who do overcome obstacles to live with dignity. Reflecting on the brutal murder of his best friend, Brian Gilmore writes:

> But regardless of any political or sociological analysis, the struggle for any black man is simply not to be next. This is the legacy that my friend Chico has left me. In D.C. and everywhere in America where black men feel hunted by their own and hunted by the system, thousands, even millions, of young black men are trying to avoid the destructiveness of other black men and not be next. The black man may be marked wherever he goes and whatever he does, but he must overcome these incredible obstacles placed in his path and live a life of dignity and beauty. It is not simply the violence alone that is an obstacle, but also this society's growing distaste for his continued presence. This might sound like an exaggeration. . . . But the daily body count that is currently a central part of that oppressive truth is too real to suggest even for a second that what is going on is not really happening. (Gilmore 1996:23–24)

SUGGESTED READING

Excellent sources for historical accounts of antiblack racism in the United States are Herbert Aptheker's *The Negro in the Civil War* (1938) and W.E.B. DuBois's *Black Reconstruction in America* (1935). And the powerful novel by Ralph Ellison, *Invisible Man* (1952), is probably the best account of antiblack racism in the early and mid-1900s. A more recent source that echoes many of the black viewpoints in this chapter is *Young, Black and Male in America: An Endangered Species,* edited by Jewelle T. Gibbs (1988). Richard Majors and Janet Mancini Billson's *Cool Pose: The Dilemmas of Black Manhood in America* (1992) and Jay MacLeod's *Ain't No Makin' It* (1987) both give a vivid picture of the difficulties facing young black males in America.

A look at the lives of men in other racial groups is important, too. David Suzuki's autobiography *Metamorphosis* (1988) is a rich personal account of a Japanese Canadian's struggle with racism, feminism, and cultural heritage. A more general history that discusses the role of republicanism in encouraging anti-Indian, anti-Asian, and antiblack racism is Ronald T. Takaki's *Iron Cages: Race and Culture in 19th Century America* (1979). In addition, Carlos Munoz, Jr., has written a powerful account of the liberation struggles of Chicanos in *Youth, Identity and Power* (1989), which begins with the 1960s and covers a dimension of the civil rights movements that is seldom presented. And Alfredo Mirandé's "Qué gacho es ser macho: It's a Drag to Be a Macho Man" (1988) not only offers a good discussion of *machismo* in Latino culture but also provides a good bibliography for further work.

The National Council of African American Men, Incorporated is located at 1028 Dole Development Center, Kansas University, Lawrence, KS 66045. The same address will serve as a subscription address for *The Journal of African American Male Studies.*

■ NINE ■

Promise Keepers: An Evangelical Christian Men's Movement

If masculine independence lends the cornerstone of health to a marriage, then the steadiness of credibility and credentials—and the appropriate self-confidence that results, is the capstone. . . . A healthy self-confidence will in turn transfer over to your wife and help her feel a similar self-confidence. In turn, it also gives her the security to allow her husband to lead the family.
—Gary Smalley and John Trent,
"The Promises You Make to Your Wife"

Seven Promises of the Promise Keepers

1. Honor Jesus Christ through worship, prayer, and obedience to His Word in the power of the Holy Spirit.
2. Pursue vital relationships with a few other men, understanding that I need brothers to help me keep my promises.
3. Spiritual, moral, ethical, and sexual purity.
4. Build strong marriages and families through love, protection, and biblical values.
5. Support the mission of my church by honoring and praying for my pastor and by actively giving my time and resources.
6. Reach beyond any racial and denominational barriers to demonstrate the power of biblical unity.
7. Influence my world, being obedient to the Great Commandment (Mark 12:30–31) and the Great Commission (Matthew 28:19–20).

177

HISTORICAL SKETCH AND PRIMARY SOURCES

All of the Western religions—Judaism, Islam, Catholicism, and Protestantism—contain sects and movements that embrace religious conservatism. Woman's scriptural place is in the home as obedient servant to
her husband. Jewish and Christian conservatives find support for their
views in the Old Testament, Genesis 3:16, wherein men are made masters
of women, a sentiment echoed in the Koran. Evangelical and fundamentalist Christians also draw upon the books of the New Testament, especially Ephesians 5:22–33, where wives are urged to submit to their husbands, and 1 Corinthians 11:3, 7–9, where women are told that men were
not created for women but women were created for men.

The most visible movement of religious conservatives in the United
States and Canada is the Promise Keepers, an evangelical Christian men's
movement begun in 1990 by former University of Colorado football coach
Bill McCartney. From a local fellowship of seventy-two men that featured
prayer, fasting, and mutual encouragement, this movement has grown
exponentially in the 1990s. Its first regional gathering in the University of
Colorado Events Center attracted 4,200 men. In its first national meeting
in 1992 there were 22,000 men gathered in the university's Folsom Stadium, and in 1993 50,000 filled the same stadium. In 1994 278,600 men
gathered at seven sites around the country, and by the end of the summer
of 1995, 726,890 men had gathered at thirteen sites around the country.
And 1996 looks to be equally as dynamic; preenrollments are high and
the cost of attending a conference is even higher.

The phenomenal growth of Promise Keepers is not as remarkable when
a number of factors are considered. No other men's movement has had in
place such a large number of national and local organizations made up of
people who share in large part a common way of looking at the world.
These organizations include the Christian Coalition, Focus on the Family,
and the 700 Club, not to mention local churches and councils. No other
movement has had antecedent traditions of massive rallies for individuals of that perspective, whereas Promise Keepers maintains a format in its
rallies that is commonly found in other evangelical gatherings, such as
the Billy Graham crusades. Since the early 1970s Christian crusaders such
as Edwin Louis Cole have been specifically organizing Christian men and
holding separate retreats for them. Cole's book *Maximized Manhood* (1982)
is a forerunner of current Promise Keepers ideology, and Cole is a frequent speaker at Promise Keepers conferences.

Furthermore, this movement is not totally new in the history of American evangelism. In the first two decades of this century William A. Sunday, a former major league baseball player for the Chicago White Stock-

ings, led hundreds of huge evangelistic rallies in different cities around the United States. These rallies were remarkably similar to the Promise Keepers rallies of today: They were often for men only; they involved a series of promises very similar to those of today; Jesus was held up as the model of masculinity, the most manly man; and society was viewed as suffering from a moral crisis brought on by a lack of masculine leadership (Ashley 1961; McLoughlin 1959).

Promise Keepers has been able to use these preexisting structures and practices along with a carefully coordinated hierarchy. Each state, region, and community (local church) has a designated leader in a carefully trained and prescribed chain of command that conforms to preexisting structures. The "ambassador," for example, "introduces the ministry of Promise Keepers to churches in his community"; the "point man," under the authority of his pastor, is the leader of the men's group in his church.

The thematic content of this movement, however, goes beyond traditional evangelistic ideas. There is definitely a gesture in the direction of feminism with the central idea that men have not kept their promises to women: Men have not been good providers and protectors, and men have not treated women, especially their wives, with respect. But other themes of concern to the men's movement also surface. Issues of male-female relationships, male friendships, racial prejudice, balancing work and family, learning from other men, and appropriate masculine behavior are common topics for the many lecturers who address conferences around the country. Some of the writers in this movement have read the later Farrell, Gilder, Goldberg, and Bly (Hicks 1993).

The Promise Keepers movement has produced a vast literature, including a magazine entitled *New Man* and many books by the leadership of the movement. In addition to *New Man,* our three primary sources will be Bill McCartney's *What Makes a Man?* (1992), Robert Hicks's *The Masculine Journey* (1993), and the collection of essays *Seven Promises of a Promise Keeper* (1994). McCartney's book is really a collection of essays by the founding leadership of the Promise Keepers. An early book, it discusses twelve promises. Hicks's book is of special interest because of his ability to relate the evangelical Christian men's movement to the more secular men's movements that have appeared in the United States and Canada since 1970. And the essays in *Seven Promises* reflect the thinking of the Promise Keepers leadership today.

DESCRIPTION AND EXPLANATION OF MALE REALITY

Promise Keepers is a form of religious conservatism; hence, its theological foundations are basic to its understanding of male reality. Evangelical

Christians are a trinitarian form of Protestantism that takes the Bible in its original manuscript to be literally true, that believes the Holy Spirit is active in believers and in the new birth of an unbeliever, and that regards each human as a sinner whose redemption can be achieved only through faith and Christ's death (What is a Promise Keeper? 1996). Evangelicals believe in present-day miracles as well as in the miracles of the virgin birth and the Resurrection of Jesus. Jesus will return to earth bringing power and glory. The great commandment and great commission that are referred to in promise seven are to acknowledge that there is only one God and one truth, and to spread the word of that truth.

As this ideology applies to men, there are three basic premises that guide the movement. The first theological premise is the doctrine that men are sinners. Men are not only sinners in the sense that there was original sin in the Garden of Eden, but men are also sinners who have free will and are tempted into the worst kinds of debauchery (Hicks 1993:38, 41). Hicks speaks of "the savagery of the soul" and the "insanity in our hearts" (Hicks 1993:41, 43). Cole once began a men's gathering with these words: "If you are here tonight and committing adultery, fornication, homosexuality, incest, or habitual masturbation; indulging in pornography; gratifying yourself with sexual fantasies or any other kinds of sex sin, I command you in the name of Jesus Christ of Nazareth to repent, and be restored to a right relationship with God the Father by being reconciled through Jesus Christ and the power of the Holy Spirit" (Cole 1982:15).

The third promise is a promise of spiritual, moral, ethical, and sexual purity. Sexual purity is especially a focus at rallies and in the literature (cf. Cole 1982; Hicks 1993; Hart 1994). The need to stress sexual purity is the religious conservative's version of the sociobiological theme that men are naturally promiscuous and of the moral conservative's view that male nature is barbaric and given to short-term gratification. Hart notes that "most Christian men face a lifelong struggle controlling their sexuality. The struggle is basically between their hormones and higher aspirations, between their bodies and their fallenness" (Hart 1994:38). Hicks praises Arab cultures for keeping the flesh covered and argues "our failure to observe these basic regulations about nakedness has created . . . a society that is outwardly sexually compulsive but inwardly bored" (Hicks 1993:65).

Women, too, are equally guilty of original sin; it is because of woman's role in the Fall, according to Genesis, that women were ordered to obey man. Yet in Promise Keepers conferences women are excused, in a sense, from their contribution to original sin by the fact that they are "the weaker vessel" (O'Neal 1995). Thus, the first reality for men is that they are sinners particularly tempted by sexual sin and caught up in a society that exploits their own nature and provides relentless temptation.

The second major premise of Promise Keepers male reality is that it is tough to be a man, especially a Christian man. Christian men face not only the sexual temptations of a permissive society but they also face the risks of living in a society that is hostile to their Christian values. McCartney is deliberately vague in his warning about the "Adversary" of the Christian man: "Christian men all over our nation and around the world are suffering because they feel they are on a losing streak and they can't break the pattern. The Adversary has us where he wants us—feeling defeated. It need not be that way" (McCartney 1992b:13). And Randy Phillips, president of Promise Keepers, notes: "Satan has declared war on us and our families, on our churches and communities" (Phillips 1994). One gets the feeling that the Adversary, or Satan, is nothing less than society as a whole. Promise Keepers literature and speeches are filled with metaphors of cultural war. It is the Christian life and Christians against culture. McCartney's call to battle is a known crowd pleaser at the rallies—to "deafening cheers and standing ovations" Coach McCartney states: "We're calling men of God to battle—we will retreat no more. We're going to contest anything that sets itself up against the name of Jesus Christ" (Gilbreath 1995:26).

Culture is described as in "moral collapse," in "moral decline," "AIDS-infested," "fatherless," without ethics, at a crossroads (Oliver 1992:177; Hicks 1993:57, 87; Ford 1992:21; Marian 1995:50; Evans 1994:73). The details of the moral decline are obvious—there are sexual promiscuity, single-parent families, pornography, divorce, homosexuality, and too many men have left the church and abandoned their relationship with Jesus.

The third and final premise is that men are special and essentially different from women. This belief is central to the Promise Keepers program for change through the assertion of masculine leadership. Promise Keepers followers believe that men, by nature, have "a personal relationship with Christ" (Hicks 1993:35). Men are dependent on God, "made in God's image" and "His representatives on earth," His "vice-regents" (Hicks 1993:33). Unless one understands the special place for men in creation, one will not understand the evangelical claims of "how men experience their humanness in contrast to women" (Hicks 1993:32). God created men and women with different biologies and with different scriptural mandates, which gives the justification for male leadership within the family (Dobson 1995; Hicks 1993:35). Men are in the image of God and Jesus, who is the paradigm of masculinity for men to emulate (Hicks 1993:18). Larry Crabb defines "masculinity": "Masculinity, I suggest, might therefore be thought of as the satisfying awareness of the substance God has placed within a man's being that can make an enduring contribution to God's purposes in this world and will be deeply valued by others . . . as a reliable source of wise, sensitive, compassionate, and decisive involvement" (Crabb 1992:49).

McCartney's book especially is a blend of prescription and description creating the message that Christian men *are* "Christ-like" and *should be* "Christ-like" (Smalley and Trent 1992:39ff; Yates 1992:37–38). Like Farrakhan, moral conservatives, and biological conservatives, Promise Keepers believe men are especially equipped to rule—with the added twist that masculine rule is scripturally, and therefore morally, mandated.

Finally, if biological conservatives treat men as genetically driven, religious conservatives treat men as spiritually and biologically driven. For evangelical Christians, men are creations of an active deity. Christian men may be caught in a society that is sex-obsessed and containing values contrary to their Christian teaching, but the Holy Spirit is active in each man, although each man is not always open to a personal relationship with Jesus. True happiness is difficult at best in this world, but without contact with Jesus it is certainly impossible. How men can be Christlike in an un-Christlike world seems to be the prevailing concern of the Promise Keepers.

Feminism

When feminism is mentioned in Promise Keepers literature it is rarely defined, and it is never seen as positive. Promise Keepers holds a thinly veiled belief that if only men would be kind and beneficent heads of families, feminism would simply go away, because feminism is largely "the result of the misuse of [men's] authority" according to Promise Keepers president Randy Phillips (Minkowitz 1995:69). Furthermore, feminism may be to blame for much of the adverse social reality that afflicts men, especially Christian men.

> Some in the women's movement have not only neutered Christ but would call for the castration of all men in the name of rape prevention. (Hicks 1993:24)

> The feminist era has made all gender differentiation into political discrimination. Therefore, when some feminists read the Bible all they see is the sexual discrimination that they believe dominated the biblical writer's instruction. (Hicks 1993:49)

> In spite of overwhelming research to the contrary, some anti-gun lobbyists, some feminists, and most of those who would totally dismantle our military under the guise of peace condemn the warrior. (Hicks 1993:75)

The antifeminist bent of Promise Keepers is not surprising. Liberal feminists champion marriage without leadership or marriage in which leadership is decided upon by those involved. And none of the feminist movements favors traditional roles for men and women.

When Hicks, for example, consults other perspectives in the men's movement, he looks exclusively at antifeminist writers such as George Gilder or Warren Farrell or nonfeminists such as Robert Bly and Robert Moore. Profeminist writers are virtually ignored. Cole asserts that "the feminist movement left its most vocal supporters empty and bitter. The fact is, any movement that ignores God is headed for trouble" (Black 1994:66). The suggestion is clear that feminism is a godless movement; therefore, it contributes to the godlessness of contemporary society. It has also failed to deliver on its promises to its supporters. Hicks hints at what those failed promises might be. For all the promotion by feminists of nontraditional roles, women still favor their traditional role in the family and favor men who are traditional males (Hicks 1993:65, 73). Feminism can only disappoint these primary needs of men and women.

In contradiction of the claim that the feminist movement is godless, a regular theme in Promise Keepers is that men have left the church because women (Christian feminists?) have taken it over. A major reason for the origin of Promise Keepers was to take the church back for men and to make men comfortable in church (Gilbreath 1995:24). Men are less likely to attend church regularly than are women, and Promise Keepers has an explanation for this difference (Gilbreath 1995:24). In an essay entitled "Why Men Feel So Out of Place at Church," Hicks writes: "I have seen too many good men leave the church, or church leadership, because they were tired of playing the games and they saw a lot of what the church was doing as a waste of time. We must recapture the church for men, defeminize it, and make our appeals to men where it will cost them something more than their money or their time. Christ wants their lives" (Hicks 1992:155). Consistent with the concern that men have abdicated their family leadership role is the thesis that men have abdicated their role as religious leaders. Promise Keepers is staking its future on the willingness and need to reassert "masculine leadership" in both areas (Marian 1995:50).

The followers of Promise Keepers, like mythopoetics, find themselves in a feminized world, particularly in the spiritual domain that is most central to them. Mythopoetics worry about women's perceived greater spirituality; Hicks notes that Christian men have a "deep-seated inferiority complex about spiritual things" and "in most men's minds, the standard is whatever their wives are into, so that makes the standard feminine" (Gilbreath 1995:24). Feminism only makes things worse: The feminist movement is not a Christian movement; feminism challenges men's biblical command to lead the family; feminism challenges men's biblical command to be warriors in protecting the family; feminism thereby casts doubt on the literal truth of the Bible, a cardinal principle of faith for Promise Keepers.

ASSESSMENT OF MALE REALITY AND AGENDA FOR CHANGE

As with many of the earlier perspectives, these descriptions and explanations of male reality carry with them a clearly implied assessment of that reality. In this section we turn to a further articulation of the Promise Keepers assessment of male reality and look at its prescriptions based on that assessment.

We have already noted that Promise Keepers see North American society as a culture in crisis. Promise Keeper essays often begin with dire warnings. For example:

Today we face a culture in steady decline. (Boone 1994:25)

It is painfully apparent that America is losing its families. (Evans 1994:73)

In our culture ethics have become almost a joke. (McCartney 1992b:21)

Adultery in America is an epidemic of staggering proportions. (Farrar 1992:80)

I am convinced that the primary cause of this national crisis is the *feminization* of the American male. . . . I'm trying to describe a misunderstanding of manhood that has produced a nation of "sissified" men who abdicate their role as spiritually pure leaders, thus forcing women to fill the vacuum. (Evans 1994:73)

The answer to these and other moral crises, such as abortion, out-of-wedlock births, drugs, crime, and pornography—to name a few—is the spiritual renewal of the North American man. Thus, while others may approach these "problems" as political, Promise Keepers are explicit in denying that theirs is a political movement. Instead, they insist that it is a spiritual movement whose only purpose is to help men to become more Christlike and more God-centered in their lives. As one essayist put the matter, Promise Keepers is "not a social club. It's not a political force. What God is doing among men is a transformation of the heart" (Black 1994:64).

Phillips illustrates the power of such a spiritual renewal with a story about a skinhead who came to disrupt a Martin Luther King Jr. parade, but who found himself "surrendering" his heart to Jesus and being counseled by a "converted Jew, a Black man, an Hispanic man, and an Anglo man. . . . They huddled, with arms around each other, as this young man surrendered his heart to Jesus. He left the skinhead lifestyle that night and continues to be a minister of reconciliation today" (Phillips 1994:8). Phillips concludes with "only a unified team with the same mission will advance . . . our common mission [and] prevent our common menace, Satan, from turning this wonderful mission into a mere monument" (Phillips 1994:8).

Thus, consistent with their Statement of Faith, Promise Keepers put great store in the work of the Holy Spirit to create miracles and to transform lives. Clearly, men who support one another and who create an environment of faith enhance the work of this spirit. At one level, then, the Promise Keepers answer to the moral crisis that it has identified in society is a religious renewal among men that makes them more Christlike, committed to church and family, and committed to helping other men of different denominations and races. Mass media accounts of the Promise Keepers commonly pick up on this theme: "Promise Keepers—with its message that men have failed to be spiritual leaders in the home, church and community—is attracting wide-eyed attention across the country" (Housewright 1994).

Probably no prescription of the Promise Keepers has attracted more attention than their suggestion that what is needed is male (masculine) leadership in the home and the community. Frequently quoted in this regard is Tony Evans's advice to men returning from a gathering:

I can hear you saying, "I want to be a spiritually pure man. Where do I start?" The first thing you do is sit down with your wife and say something like this; "Honey, I've made a terrible mistake. I've given you my role. I gave up leading this family, and I forced you to take my place. Now I must reclaim that role."

Don't misunderstand what I'm saying here. I'm not suggesting that you *ask* for your role back, I'm urging you to *take it back*. (Evans 1994:79)

Critics have been quick to argue that such a prescription amounts to putting women back in a subservient role and to a restoration of patriarchal dominance in the family and society. Thus, Christian and non-Christian critics alike often express concern that Promise Keepers is simply an attempt to restore men to patriarchal dominance in the home, thus undoing years of growth toward greater equality in marriage (Housewright 1994; Gilbreath 1995; Wagenheim 1995; O'Neal 1995). But Promise Keepers consistently argue that their message is to honor women. Love your wife as Jesus loved the Church (Housewright 1994; O'Neal 1995).

Articles in *New Man,* probably in response to such criticisms, frequently attempt to draw a distinction between being a leader and being a boss

(Maxwell 1995). Bosses fix blame, leaders fix mistakes; bosses rely on authority, leaders rely on cooperation. Maxwell argues that "Christian leadership principles can and will work at home, in your church and on the job" (Maxwell 1985:78). The principles of Christian leadership are grounded in relationships with people, not in authority over them; built on responsibilities, not on rights over others; focus on the leader's obedience to God rather than on the nonleader's obedience to the leader (Maxwell 1995:81; cf. Eble 1995). If that is how "leadership" is construed, then indeed there is a misunderstanding between the Promise Keepers and their critics concerning the message of man as head of the family. Yet everyone avoids talking about the hard cases; for instance, what is to be done in the family when children or wives are not cooperative, not willing to follow the Promise Keepers role model, and the differences are irreconcilable? Is it then the man's role in these cases to make the decision and the woman's to obey? And why is it that women cannot lead? Is it because of a defect of nature or a lack of ability? If it is only the biblical injunction that men should lead, then are women not as capable as men of leadership?

The Promise Keepers claim to be a purely spiritual organization, as contrasted with a political organization, is untenable given the presence of so many political organizations at Promise Keepers conferences. Outside each Promise Keepers stadium venue is a large space dedicated to selling a wide range of Promise Keepers books, shirts, caps, and tapes. But most of this space is taken up with booths from various political organizations. *World* magazine, distributed free at its booth, offers "to help Christians apply the Bible to their understanding of and response to everyday current events" (*"World* Mission Statement"). In this publication life insurance advertisements are headlined "Traditional Christian Faith and Values vs. Welfarism and Big Government." Articles espouse Star Wars technology, note the "ruination of family vacations" on Gay Weekend at Disney World, attack Time Warner, embrace Clarence Thomas as the "soul of the conservative wing of the court," denounce the "once-proud Navy" for allowing women in combat, and seem to endorse virtually every Republican budget agenda (*World* June 17/14 1995; *World* July 1/8 1995).

Christian family movements such as Focus on the Family, its president and publisher, James C. Dobson, and the National Center for Fathering advocate traditional male-headed families and work politically to maintain father-centered families by promoting books and articles by authors such as David Blankenhorn, who also appears in *New Man* (February 1995). Focus on the Family Publishing now serves as publisher for the Promise Keepers organization. Chuck Colson's book *Breakpoint* from Focus on the Family features articles identifying feminism as an "extremist ideology";

argues that God has created a female chemical and hormonal balance that women who have abortions disrupt, thereby risking breast cancer; and endorses Blankenhorn's ideas. Colson notes that what went wrong was that "the nineteenth-century strategy of defining family virtues as 'women's work' guaranteed that men would eventually reject them. After-all, no self-respecting man will submit to standards he regards as unmanly" (Colson 1995:14). Colson also urges Christian men to "use this booklet in your church and Bible-study groups" (Colson 1995:12).

Another group, Exodus International, is "a Christian referral and resource network founded in 1976. Our primary purpose is to proclaim that freedom from homosexuality is possible through repentance and faith in Jesus Christ as Savior and Lord".

In short, the space allocated to political causes and messages at Promise Keepers gatherings is substantive. The organizations represented are part and parcel of the right-wing war against culture, which is a central component of the Promise Keepers message.

The third promise is a promise of sexual purity, and perhaps no other gets more weight in Promise Keepers conferences and literature. We have already alluded to the focus on male sexuality and the commonly expressed suggestion that it is out of control. Promise Keepers begin early to attend to the issue of teen males. It is not uncommon at rallies for young men to make a pledge to remain virgins until their marriages. Teenage males stand in front of the rallies and take vows of virginity. At a Texas rally, Cole states: "What a thing for a man on his wedding night!—to take his wife in his arms, standing in the hotel room, she in her white satin nightgown, he in his blue silk pajamas . . . and say, 'Darlin', I love you, you're God's gift to me; tonight I want to give you something no other woman in the whole world will have. Tonight I want to give you the gift of my manhood" (Stoltenberg 1995:28).

Josh McDowell, a leader in the evangelical organization Campus Crusade for Christ, advises parents to instill Christian values in their children, and he attacks the public school system for promoting sexual permissiveness by trying to be "value free and morally neutral" (McDowell 1995:54). Although the extreme preoccupation with male sexuality does not commit the Promise Keepers to the proposition defended by Gilder that men are barbarians, there *is* a strong suggestion that men are the problem, that the problem is sexual, and that women, through marriage, are the civilizers of men. In an echo of Gilder, Dobson writes: "The reproductive capacity of women results in a greater appreciation of stability, security, and enduring human relationships. In other words, females are more future-oriented because of their concern for children" (Dobson 1995:37). Women, Hicks notes, read *Good Housekeeping, Better Homes and Gardens,* and *Family Circle*—men read *Playboy* (Hicks 1993:65).

Although Promise Keepers literature is consistently unfavorable to feminism and the feminist agenda, there is also a kind of sensitivity to issues of concern to women that is only possible in the light of feminism. For example, there is a strong theme that men have not respected their wives; they have not been good fathers, they have not been good providers, and they have not been the protectors of their families. Although these concerns predate the twentieth century, they are also concerns that have been noted in different language by feminist critics of the family. Included in this analysis is a concern that men work too much and, therefore, do not have time for their families. As one man confesses, his drive for success led him to work twenty hours a day: "As I listened, I repented over and over. I realized I was not loving my wife as Jesus loves the church" (Halbrook 1995:94). In an article published in *New Man*, Judith Couchman warns against being a Christian chauvinist—someone who uses condescending language to women, listens more to men than to women, sets different standards for women than for men, and supports the boy's club by sharing information with men but not women (Couchman 1995:100–101). And as we have noted, being a leader in Promise Keepers literature means listening to and respecting those who are led— wives and children as well as employees.

The Promise Keepers agenda for change closely parallels movements like the Million Man March. There is at the outset a call for each man to get right with God, in this case to accept Jesus Christ. Then there are a series of vows to go back to the community and the family and to take one's responsibility and assume one's God-given leadership. The theme of leadership is blended with one of respecting women, or at least not disrespecting them. All of this takes place within a larger context of a market economy that supports black business, or Christian business in the case of the evangelical movement. There is great reliance on role modeling, and both programs encourage the leadership of prominent athletes. Each is essentially conservative in outlook; each depends upon the encouragement of charismatic leaders through whom God operates. Clearly, institutional practices and economic forces are secondary to spiritual motivation and the authority of the church.

CRITIQUE: CRITICISMS AND RESPONSES

Criticism 1

The theme of "honoring" one's wife is left vague and is sometimes insulting to women—just beneath the rhetoric of honoring one's wife is the implication that men must be the protectors, spiritual guides, moral guides, and leaders in the family because women are weaker and less capable of performing such tasks (Compare Stoltenberg 1995:28). When Gary Smalley spoke to the Seattle Promise Keepers gathering on July 7, 1995, Jennifer O'Neal made the following observations after hearing that speech:

> Smalley said that his goal was for every man in attendance there today to return home with a greater desire to treasure his wife. Despite the obvious differences between men and women. . . . "Honor," he said, "is the beginning of all wisdom. It is the greatest word I know of. What did you do when you saw Bill McCartney [whose presence at the rally was just revealed]? You gasped, didn't you? You said 'Wow!' That is honor. Now the next time you wake up in the morning and see your wife, I want you to respond just like you did just now. 'Wow! I can't believe how lucky I am to be here in this bed with you!' " The men listening laughed out loud. . . . But then he sneaked something in as he read a passage from the Bible, a passage about the weaker vessel. "Now you need to realize," Smalley paused from his reading, "that 'weaker vessel' is an expression of honor." Then he continued reading. No additional comment upon how exactly this phrase constituted an expression of honor. . . . After a while I grew tired of sitting and listening to jokes about wives—about their astounding ability to remember something negative their husband did ten years ago, about the heat they give their husbands when they do something wrong. (O'Neal 1995)

And Dobson notes that "because of the fragile nature of the male ego and a man's enormous need to be respected, combined with female vulnerability and a woman's need to be loved . . . it is a mistake to tamper with the time-honored relationship of a husband as loving protector and wife as recipient of that protection (Dobson 1995:39).

Response

The Bible is clear that male leadership is required in society. 1 Timothy 2:11–14 is clear that "a woman should learn in quietness and full submission . . . she must be silent. For Adam was formed first, then Eve. And Adam was not the one deceived; it was the woman who was deceived and became a sinner." And 1 Corinthians 11:7–9 states, "A man . . . is the image and glory of God; but the woman is the glory of man. For man was not made from woman, but woman from man. Neither was man created for woman, but woman for man." But this biblical mandate does not mean male dominance. As Chad Hammond, southeast regional director for Promise Keepers notes: "That's not the message at all. . . . The last thing we want to do is come off sounding like we're not honoring women. Christ said, Love your wife as I have loved the Church" (House-wright 1994).

Criticism 2

As evidenced by the large amount of right-wing literature given away at its gatherings, Promise Keepers is inseparable from that agenda. In the words of Carol J. Adams, a graduate of Yale Divinity School who teaches at Southern Methodist University's Perkins School of Theology: The Promise Keepers are "part of the religious right's agenda to mobilize and maintain men's control over culture, interpretation and the Bible. As long as they maintain that control, then dissenting points of view—such as views about varieties of ways of being a family—are not seen as part of how we live as Americans today" (Housewright 1994). Thus, the Promise Keepers claim that the organization is not political because it does not endorse candidates or back one party over the other is disingenuous (Stoltenberg 1995:26).

Response

The whole message of the Promise Keepers is consistent with applying Christian principles in making political decisions. But Promise Keepers is not political in the sense that what goes on in the conference is attention to Christian principles. How each member applies those principles politically is left to the individual.

Criticism 3

Promise Keepers, like the mythopoetics and men's rights gatherings, has created a forum that is virtually free of diversity—it is almost exclusively white middle-class male—free of women, free of feminist criticism, free of men who might disagree. As Stoltenberg notes: "These guys have discovered that conservative 'sexual purity' is a better basis for male bonding than the 'sexual revolution' could ever be (what with liberals fronting for pornographers and extolling hot sex with virtually anything that moves). And these guys have discovered that unless males are reliably in league as men, male supremacy can no longer claim credible authority over females one-on-one" (Stoltenberg 1995:29).

Response

It is important to have a male-only gathering, and non-Christian men are not going to be comfortable or capable of participation in Promise

Keepers. This gathering is not a discussion group or even a democracy. It is about each man learning to go back to his own community and find a "faith partner" with whom he can share his fears, sins, and secrets. It is about men becoming accountable to one another and keeping their promises (cf. Woodward and Keene-Osborn 1994). These goals require a Christian-men-only gathering, which is a right under freedom of religion. Conferences are racially diverse, although this varies from one part of the country to another (Minkowitz 1995).

Criticism 4

Promise Keepers is a movement obsessed with the threat of male sexuality. Its publications are filled with warnings of male sexuality out of control. And yet at rallies the group continues to exploit sexuality. Consider the following description from a Dallas rally, by John Stoltenberg:

> Then Dr. Ed Cole (founder and president, Christian Men's Network) propounds his own paean to procreation: "God gave us creatures power in our loins. . . . When a man and woman who are married engage in an intimate physical relationship, they are actually celebrating the covenant of marriage. . . . Why does God want a man and a woman to be virgins at the time of marriage?" The crowd hangs on Cole's every syllable as he graphically describes how a virginal young man and woman "consummate their marriage with sexual intimacy, and in that act, when she is a virgin, when the hymen is broke, and it causes the shedding of blood, when that blood flows over the man's part, in that act of intercourse, when that blood blows over the man's part, to God that is a sign that they have entered into the sacred covenant. . . ." The heady mix of patriarchal social contract and carnality rarely gets more pulse-pounding than this mental gang-bang: a sixtyish man of the cloth inviting 45,000 other men to picture the coital puncturing of a woman's hymen in the mind's eye simultaneously. (Stoltenberg 1995:28)

Response

Although Cole's speech may be a bit heavy on the rhetoric, others have noted that "most of the speeches are not about the evil of the other, but about how to refrain from abusing others" (Minkowitz 1995).

Criticism 5

The pursuit of sexual purity promises a holy war and disenfranchisement of gay men and lesbian women. McCartney endorsed Colorado's notorious Amendment 2, calling homosexuality "an abomination of almighty God" (Wagenheim 1995:81). Tony Evans declared at the Dallas rally: "It's been too long that three percent of homosexuals control our moral majority" (Stoltenberg 1995:51). The Promise Keepers' insistence on loving the sinner but hating the sin is hypocritical. Endorsement of legislation like Amendment 2 would strip individuals who have not been convicted of any crime, but who are considered sinful, of protection of their basic citizens' rights of nondiscrimination in housing, insurance, and even voting. Only in a theocracy is sin identified with a loss of basic citizens' rights. And no other group of "sinners" is so singled out for rights deprivation; indeed, *everyone* is a sinner according to the Promise Keepers, so why are gay men and lesbians singled out for legalized discrimination?

Response

> I am opposed to any kind of gay-bashing, and I am deeply concerned that we will be losing to AIDS a large and talented resource of human creativity, energy, and contribution that lies in our gay communities. (Heterosexuals will be lost, too.) Having said this, I must speak out of my own observation, research, counseling experience, and spiritual conviction. From this passage in Leviticus [18:22], it couldn't be clearer what God's opinion is about a man's use of his phallus. The penis has no place *in* another man. (Hicks 1993:59)

SUMMARY AND CONCLUSIONS

Many themes converge at Promise Keepers conferences. There is the historical tradition of evangelism and gatherings of men who need spiritual renewal. The demand for renewal comes from the fact that men are sinners and the sins of the body are and have been a focus for evangelist throughout the history of North American evangelism. But just as Billy Sunday's rallies drew on issues of temperance, suffrage for women, and the lessening participation of men in church life, so today's conferences address issues that are topical, such as the new assertiveness of women, the increasing number of families headed by women, male violence, and the lessening participation of men in church life. And just as Billy Sunday took stands on various political issues and political candidates, so does today's Promise Keepers offer a place for political action consistent with its view of social reality. Sunday's rallies were enormously successful for a few years—thousands of men attended—but they quickly died out. The issues changed with World War I, and men tended to lose interest in hearing the same general message over and over. Today's Promise Keepers probably faces a similar fate. Its message is a very generalized one that keeps being repeated over and over. And if in fact there has been a gender revolution by which young men and women move toward greater equality in society and in the home, Promise Keepers may well be a dying voice calling for a reinstitution of a traditional patriarchy that has already been abandoned by young Christians and non-Christians alike.

SUGGESTED READING

For historical reasons it is worth looking at Edwin Cole's *Maximized Manhood: A Guide to Family Survival* (1982) and William G. McLoughlin's *Modern Revivalism: Charles Grandison Finney to Billy Graham* (1959). Otherwise, a wide variety of literature is available from Promise Keepers: P.O Box 103001, Denver, CO 80250-3001.

▪ TEN ▪

Looking from the Past to the Future

Men live their lives, learn their social roles, and, inspired perhaps by feminist analysis, sometimes come to struggle with the idea of the kind of men they want to be. It is during this reflective process that they develop a perspective on masculinity, a theory about the forces that are acting on them and about the changes they would like to make. Each of the perspectives described in this book represents, in one way or another, a struggle with our socially inherited ideas about masculinity. Even the conservative perspective is a defense of this legacy. Each perspective is a paradigm through which men can try to understand—and change—their reality. But these paradigms are incompatible at times, and they require different choices with serious consequences. They ask us to make judgments about the worth of our economic system, the oppression of women, and the oppression of men by economic, racial, and religious factors. Each perspective also promises to achieve a better reality; it holds out strategies that men *ought* to pursue in the name of either social justice or personal well-being. In this chapter we look to the future—to the promises of these perspectives and to questions that remain unanswered.

PREDICTIONS

In the 1990s the secular men's movement is on the wane. The circulation of major publications is down, and the number of men attending conferences is either stagnant or declining. The International Men's Conferences held in Austin, Texas, in 1991–1993 declined from 700 men to a little over 200 men. M&M conferences under the auspices of NOMAS continue to attract a steady 350 to 450 participants. Leaders of wisdom groups report declining attendance, and the August 1995 conference of the National Coalition of Men and Children disappointed its leadership.

Wingspan, the national journal for mythopoetic men, hit a high circulation of about 150,000 around 1990, ceased publication shortly after, and now has resumed publication with a circulation of about 20,000. *Changing Men* is having financial problems and has, at least temporarily, ceased publication. *Man!* magazine, a publication that ranged over mythopoetic, men's rights, and profeminist perspectives, after a promising beginning in 1990 ceased publication in 1993. At the same time, men seem to be embracing conservative perspectives; in the 1994 general election men voted Republican in far greater numbers than did women, and Promise Keepers seems to be the only men's movement in the 1990s with vitality and potential for growth. In the following sections I explore some of the reasons for these tendencies; I also speculate about the long-term success or failure of the different sociopolitical perspectives discussed in this book.

The Conservative Perspective

The goal of conservatism is the restoration of the traditional nuclear family with the husband as breadwinner and the wife as homemaker. The 1990s would seem to be a time of conservative ascendancy: Everyone is promoting family values; Congress and the presidency are solidly conservative in that regard. Christian conservatives endorse candidates at all levels who have either been elected or are campaigning to be elected. Conservative men no longer apologize for claiming the right to be heads of their families; Promise Keepers, Louis Farrakhan, and both national political parties are calling for men to return to traditional masculine leadership roles. And as we have seen, conservative attacks on affirmative action, gay rights, abortion, and public education are at an all-time high.

Yet in spite the visibility of conservatives, they are experiencing a notable lack of success. Except for the defeat of the ERA as a constitutional amendment, which has nevertheless basically been adopted by all the states, the major elements of the conservative social agenda have not been achieved. Conservative forces have not gained a constitutional amendment banning abortion, a constitutional amendment permitting officially sponsored prayers in school, or a family protection act that would require school curricula to promote traditional gender roles. Conservatives have been unable to stem the tide of violence on television, of obscenity in music, of teen pregnancy, of gains in gay rights, or of the increasing numbers of women who are going to work (Mishel and Bernstein 1994:61).

The reasons for this failure amid such prominence is that modern conservatism is at odds with itself. On the one hand, it seeks to hold onto the traditional family with its male breadwinner. On the other, it embraces a market capitalism that drives down real wages, makes many workers redundant, and refuses to pay a family wage, thus forcing more and more families to have multiple breadwinners. In other words, capitalism produces the very conditions that prevent the traditional family from surviving. In other arenas, the conservative struggle against pornography has been countered by a free-market industry worth billions of dollars; and the conservative struggle to grant full human rights to the fetus has encountered resistance from manufacturers of birth control pills, which cause fertilized eggs to be aborted.

The conservative agenda harms itself in another way as well. The 1980s and 1990s have seen dramatic cuts in entitlements for the most vulnerable elements of society, especially women and children (Mishel and Bernstein 1994:279–296; Henwood 1995; Cunningham and Reed 1995). This decline of the social safety net together with lack of work, especially work that pays a family wage, has led to a significant increase in poverty throughout much of the 1980s and 1990s (Mishel and Bernstein 1994). And poverty is the best predictor of family disintegration (Coontz 1992:258–260). Thus, families continue to disintegrate while surrounded by rhetoric calling for the preservation of the family. Historians of the family note that the heyday of the stable nuclear family in the 1950s was also one of the most heavily subsidized periods, where U.S. families enjoyed extensive entitlements for education, housing, insurance, health care, and utilities (Coontz 1992:68ff). Thus, the very agenda the conservative politicians call into being only leads to more poverty, more fatherless children, and less stable families and communities. In short, the conservative agenda has virtually no chance of long-term success; the restoration of the traditional family is not compatible with market-driven capitalism and decreasing entitlements for families. Simply stated, the conservative agenda of nuclear-family restoration is incompatible with the interests of contemporary capitalism, which seeks to pay fewer benefits, lower wages, and especially to avoid paying *family* wages (Cunningham and Reed 1995; Henwood 1994).

The Profeminist Perspective

The goal of the men's movement is to create a substantial social movement that will encourage and support men in their abandonment of a masculinity that is oppressive to women and harmful to themselves. The activists in this movement have worked hard to lessen violence against women and homophobia among men. They have created an impressive number of men's studies courses, have conducted national meetings, and have written extensively. But the future of men's studies, as independent programs, is likely to be limited by budgets that are expanding in other directions. And the fear within established women's studies programs that men's studies could become a forum for men's rights groups, as some already have, will probably limit the support of women's programs for such courses. Furthermore, success in academia is not necessarily a sign of success for a movement. As Judith Stacey has noted, "For in the same period in which academic feminism flourished, many feminist political struggles outside the university have been resisted and contained" (Stacey 1993:713). Profeminist men's studies are tied to the fate of feminism, and certainly there is evidence that the men's movement is becoming a largely academic discipline, complete with esoteric methodologies, while its political activism fades from sight.

Although NOMAS continues to hold national conferences that attract a few hundred men and women, it has failed in its efforts to become a substantial movement. Its membership is largely restricted to "converts" among academics, students, and professional-class psychologists. Some observers believe that the movement exists largely because it meets the personal needs of its members rather than because it features a profeminist agenda (Gross, Smith, and Wallston 1983; Doyle 1989:306–313). Others argue that formal membership and growth in size should not be a measure of the influence of such a movement (Goldberg 1985:306; Shiffman 1987:300). The problem with the latter argument is the lack of good evidence to support it. In fact, much of the evidence that American men are changing remains anecdotal, although Gerson makes a case for change (Gerson 1993).

We have already noted the dilemma confronting the profeminist men's movement. Indeed, the conflict between its two feminist wings has seemingly precluded its growth into a mass movement. Liberal profeminists are inviting men to join a movement that promises to let women participate in society on an equal basis, thus producing more competition for jobs in an economy of lessening opportunities and more power sharing—this in a society where many men already feel relatively alienated and controlled. Radical profeminists, meanwhile, are inviting men to join a movement in which men are distrusted and from which they have been excluded because their masculinity is believed to be premised on violence and woman-hating. It is difficult if not impossible to build a substantial men's movement grounded in both these theories. The distance between most men and the women's movement is further exacerbated by the movement's near-exclusive focus on the problems of owning- and professional-class white males.

The Men's Rights Perspective

The goals of the men's rights perspective are to create an awareness of the hazards of being male and to build a substantial movement among men that recognizes the costs and discriminations of being masculine.

Much of what has been said about the profeminist men's movement also applies to the men's rights movement. The latter, too, seems to be a movement that meets the needs of its members, who feel victimized in some way. But its growth, its national conferences, and its publications are even more erratic than the comparable structures in the relatively weak profeminist movement. And the split between those interested in fathers' rights and those who prefer to pursue a more general agenda remains unresolved.

The men's rights movement has been successful in keeping its focus on the discriminations against men and the very real costs of being masculine. It has achieved some legal victories and even managed to influence NBC's 1988 special on men ("NBC-TV May Upset Feminists" 1988). In addition, most states have seen the formation of men's rights lobbies, which are working toward new custody and divorce laws.

The strategic problem confronting this movement is that it is trying to make a case for male oppression in a social reality of male privilege. The lack of oppressive structures aimed at men makes it difficult to politicize men. When the women's movement started, there were many laws, policies, and scientific theories in existence that either assumed the inferiority of women or explicitly advanced it. Indeed, gross inequities still favor men. The fact that the men's rights movement lacks such; targets is recognized by some of its advocates (Goldberg 1976:4; Farrell 1993; Kimbrell 1995). And what efforts have been made to create the impression of male disadvantage, in a society where the reality of male privilege is widely accepted, have not been successful. Indeed, a society that values and depends on wealth is unlikely to equate the poverty of women with the burden for men of being breadwinners. Hence the efforts to create a sense of male "oppression" have given the movement an aura of narcissism and self-pity (Hooks 1984:79).

The men's rights movement is likely to continue to fragment. It not only lacks the dynamism of genuinely oppressed groups but, except for Richard Doyle, is sufficiently at odds with the conservative tradition that it cannot draw on what could be its greatest alliance against the feminist agenda—conservative men. After all, conservatism offers a clear antifeminist alternative that has none of the pitfalls of the men's rights position. For example, at a time when there is a shortage of employment, the men's rights perspective is arguing that women, too, should be given the right to good jobs so that men will not have to support them. But to many conservative men this looks like an invasion of the traditionally privileged male workplace. The conservative view is certainly self-interested: Women should be at home in part to create a climate in which men can be providers. Thus, the advocates of the men's rights position occupy an ideological "no-man's" land. They want the support of antifeminist conservatives for a liberal agenda item—equal opportunity—that undermines the traditional male role.

The rise of conservative thinking has affected the men's rights movement significantly. Conservative radio talk shows are now the major forum for antifeminist rhetoric. And men's rights advocates have had to give ground in their opposition to traditional masculinities. In its earlier forms this movement regarded traditional masculinity as the coffin that swallows men; it is the provider role that leads men to die younger and suffer the deprivation of family. Yet the 1995 National Congress for Men and Children called for the freedom of men to choose to be traditionally masculine. To hold up such a "choice" when in fact much of the literature argues that men do not have this choice is a genuflection in the direction of conservative allies, as was the refusal to take up gay rights as an issue. Other alliances between conservatives and men's rights advocates are also short-lived. Conservatives want to be tough on deadbeat dads and welfare mothers, men's rights advocates want to be tough on welfare mothers and soft on deadbeat dads, and what starts out as an alliance on welfare reform (cutting benefits) often ends up in a battle to make men pay child support (Zimmerman 1996).

The Spiritual Perspective

Logically speaking, the goal of the mythopoetic perspective must be the restoration of appropriate male initiation rites. Male violence, lack of male vitality, and poor father-son and male-female relations are, from this perspective, caused by the absence of male initiations. Boys need a path into manhood that allows them to come to terms with their wounds and their shadow selves. John Rowan's objective, for instance, is to help men make a spiritual adjustment that will enable them to enter the profeminist men's movement or, at least, to support its agenda.

Men's counseling networks and individual counselors have incorporated these Jungian ideas into their work with some success. But apart from these therapeutic uses, a few rather expensive workshops, and the occasional men's conference, there are few opportunities through which men can receive the appropriate initiations and inspirations. The men attracted to this perspective seem to come mostly from other parts of the men's movement as well as from new-age groups. But its appeal is unlikely to transcend the limited pools represented in these populations.

As a theory of personal development, the Jungian framework is scientifically unacceptable and naive. It provides little insight into how masculinity is formed or how it can be changed, and it seems to lack a willingness to explore historical or cultural differences. As a tool for further exploration of masculinity, it is therefore less attractive than the more social science-oriented liberal movement.

The Socialist Perspective

The short-term goals of socialist feminism are greater worker control in wage labor and a major reduction in men's control over women's labor. The long-term goal of socialism is the end of the class division between workers and owners.

Socialist ideas affecting worker control have been and continue to be incorporated into nonsocialist political and social approaches. According to Edward Rice, "Marx's various platforms, such as trade unionism, the abolition of child labor, equal rights for women, free education for all, old-age pensions, and social security ... [are accepted by] virtually all capitalist countries ... as a matter of course" (Rice 1977:2). Historically, socialism's success in furthering its agenda has come at those times when people's common problems were so apparent that collective action was required; and each success was followed by a period of retrenchment by owning-class interests (Piven and Cloward 1979).

Today, socialism faces several problems. First, many people identify socialism with political tyranny (Stalinism). Second, there is a history of sexism within traditional socialist and labor organizations. Third, socialist thought is alien to the dominant liberalism of the major feminist and men's organizations in the United States. And, finally, the job ghettoization of minority women, white women, and minority men has separated them from the situation of white working males. Until these problems are overcome, the working class (which is well over half female, black, Latino, and gay or lesbian) will remain divided.

Certain recent developments may help to alleviate these problems. Repressive Stalinist regimes are currently being dismantled and may be replaced with democratic socialist or mixed structures. Moreover, socialist feminism and civil rights movements have significantly influenced socialist and labor organizations in the United States and Canada, rendering them less sexist and less racist. Finally, the real wages of men are declining while real wages for women are on the rise, thus reducing one major difference between men and women in the area of work. If these trends continue, the possibility of collective action will increase, because men and women within the working class will face more problems in common. And if feminists are correct in their assessment that the economic inequalities between men and women and the differences in the kinds of work they do exacerbate other social and political inequalities, then as men and women are equalized at work, alliances between them on other issues should become easier to create. There is also some evidence to suggest that demands for greater worker control are increasing and being perceived more favorably, especially among new and previously unorganized workers (Center for Popular Economics 1986:85–89). Thus, the hold of liberalism and conservatism over modern ideology may weaken as growing class-conscious organizations reject their tolerance of class inequalities.

Gay and Black Perspectives

These group-specific perspectives have much to say not only about the conditions of the "outside" groups themselves but also about the creation of society at large. But this perspective must continually struggle to move from a position of invisibility to one of recognition. Our look at gay and black viewpoints on masculinity has revealed a battle for visibility on two fronts. One is the struggle of gay and black men within society at large; the other is the struggle within the men's movement, the socialist feminist movement, and so on. Obviously these struggles are linked.

For profeminist gay men, the struggle against homophobia within particular perspectives has had mixed success. Gay men have won a place in the profeminist men's movement but have been virtually excluded from the men's rights perspective. Socialist groups have been increasingly open to the agenda of gay liberation (Cliff 1984:221–223). The claim that homophobia is a primary underlying cause of masculinity has become a recognized perspective in its own right.

The success of the gay liberation movement may hinge to some extent on what happens outside of it. For example, if the AIDS panic should deepen institutional and individual homophobia, gay men may find their perspective discounted and their agenda abandoned. Currently, some communities consider sexual affection to be protected by civil rights legislation, and some schools teach courses in gay and lesbian studies. Yet there remain ominous countervening forces that feed on and encourage homophobia—forces such as conservative legislation that blocks gay men and lesbian women from adopting children, civil rights laws that fail to include gay men and lesbian women, laws that ban gays and lesbians from military service, and insurance companies that attempt to limit and deny payments to AIDS victims. There is also a growing level of street violence against gay men and lesbian women.

For those concerned with exploring black masculinity, the immediate goal is to stop the decimation of black men. The long-term goal is to greatly lessen the antiblack racism that so insidiously afflicts American society. In society at large and within men's organizations, at least some progress has been made. Jesse Jackson ran a popular and progressive campaign in 1984, and other black politicians continue to make gains in municipal and state elections. Feminist and profeminist groups are seemingly more open to the issues of black women and men. The National Organization for Changing Men is maintaining its efforts to include black men in the movement, to acknowledge the leadership of black men who have been profeminist, and to sponsor antiracist workshops. The socialist agenda almost always addresses the special issues that affect black workers. And the men's rights perspective claims that its agenda serves men of all races.

These successes may contribute little, however, if Robert Staples is correct in his observation that dying capitalism is prepared to take black men with it (Staples 1986), or if Manning Marable is accurately concerned that "the racist/capitalist state . . . has proceeded down a public policy road which could inevitably involve the complete obliteration of the entire Black reserve army of labor and sections of the Black working class" (Marable 1983:252). In other words, black males are not being brought into wage labor in numbers sufficient to prevent their decimation. The concern is that society has fundamentally ceased to care about the human consequences of racism and has left a large percentage of black men to struggle against drugs, poverty, and personal and institutionalized violence. Thus, for black men the harsh reality of social oppression may eclipse the successful articulation of their group-specific perspective.

CONCLUSIONS

The perspectives in the preceding chapters offer us distinct analyses of masculinity. Conservatives see masculinity as primarily the result of men's intrinsic nature or as civilization's triumph over that nature. Profeminists see masculinity as the result of social ideals and stereotypes. For men's rights groups masculinity is an effort to cope with double binds and the relative powerlessness of men. The spiritual perspective attributes masculinity to the working out of archetypical patterns. Socialists see masculinity as having been formed by the relations of production. From the gay standpoint, homophobia is a principal cause of masculinity, whereas black theorists call attention to the role of racism.

In the face of these conflicting theories we may be tempted to slide into either cynicism or skepticism. We become cynics if we take these theories to be mere self-interested rationalizations for political interest groups. We become skeptics if we conclude that no one perspective is more right than any other.

We are more likely to avoid these alternatives, however, if we, first, improve our conceptual clarity regarding masculinity, and, second, improve the research about men and masculinity.

This book is an attempt to gain that conceptual clarity. In the process of clarifying perspectives, we not only come to understand the basic ideas upon which they rest but we also discover which ideas need further examination. We have seen in the previous chapter, for example, that our understanding of masculinity itself needs work. We started out with the claim that the components of masculinity—roles, stereotypes, and ideals—are historically situated and relative to specific groups. But that is just a beginning. What factors need to be included in these categories? And to which group(s) are they relevant? How, for example, are we to ascertain the content of the masculine gender role? The stereotypes and ideals themselves may be inaccurate or misleading. And the men under study are not all masculine in the same sense. Finally, even the criteria by which we can distinguish masculinities need to be defined. Ultimately, we must yet provide a satisfactory understanding of masculinity for any particular historically situated group of men.

Closely related to the question of understanding masculinity is the issue of what causes and maintains it. Could it be that each perspective we have discussed has grasped only a partial cause of masculinity? Maybe stereotypes, ideals, homophobia, racism, the relations of production, and even genetic tendencies and / or archetypes each play a role in producing the masculinity of any group or of any age? But not all of these can be *the* underlying or primary cause, if there is one. Thus, it is important to decide if there is an underlying cause. If so, how accessible is it to change? If not, what are the multiple causes and how accessible are they to change? Without a clear causal explanation of masculinity, we have little hope of arriving at an effective agenda for altering men's reality.

Power is another focal concept in need of clarification. It is the power relations that are built into the social roles of masculinity that most perspectives find problematic. Profeminists object to male power over women. Men's rights groups object to women's power over men. Conservatives are concerned about maintaining a balance of power between the masculine and feminine roles. Socialist feminists object to men's power over women's labor and owners' power over workers. Adherents of the spiritual perspective are concerned about the balance of energy (power?) between men and women. And the group-specific perspective is concerned about the power differences between dominant masculinity and other masculinities.

The second task, which is dependent on the above clarifications, is to back up these perspectives with empirical research. So much of the current writing about men and masculinity is anecdotal; that is, it either tells of individual experience or generalizes upon individual experience and draws conclusions about men in general. We have already seen the danger inherent in this type of writing. When the experiences of men of a certain class and set of choices are generalized, a false universality is created that undermines or ignores the realities of men differently situated. Alternatively, even the "scientific" theories of masculinity are biased, outdated, and poorly conceptualized (Pleck 1981; Brod 1987c; Kimmel 1987c; Carrigan, Connell, and Lee 1987; Clatterbaugh 1996). Fortunately, the literature on men and masculinity has been greatly improved by the establishment of scholarly publications such as *masculinities, The Journal of Men's Studies,* and the *Journal of African American Male Studies.*

At this point, I must reiterate the fact that these perspectives are so-cio*political* perspectives. Each perspective is in a political confrontation with the others. Each originated with a need to confront the political realities of feminist theory and practice. Thus, political values and commitments will always enter into the descriptions, explanations, assessments, and agendas of each perspective. There will never be a final perspective on masculinity that is free of political bias and thus completely objective. Such a perspective—or dogma, as the case may be—is not even desirable. But this is not to say that our theories about masculinity cannot be improved. My point is simply that we must be as aware as possible of the values and assumptions underlying our theories. Equally important, we must acknowledge that clearer ideas about masculinity and its causes are potentially achievable through better research.

POSTSCRIPT

The reader will note that this book begins with conservative resistance to feminism and ends with a booming conservative movement, Promise Keepers. The completion of this circle is symbolic of the overall direction of the men's movement. The *first* "wave" of men's response was negative; men generally were derisive of feminism. The *second* wave, which came at about the same time as the first, was profeminist. These men genuinely believed that feminism was right and just and that it was their duty to change themselves and other men. The *third* wave welcomed feminist ideas such as ending traditional roles, but it rejected feminism as a means to that end. And the third wave took up a theme also found in profeminist writing—that men, too, were oppressed, discriminated against, and restricted by society. The third wave just took this idea further and argued that perhaps it was men who were the more powerless and the more oppressed, and more importantly, that feminism lied when it claimed that men were privileged relative to women. This third wave has made a cottage industry of talking about the oppression and victimization of men. The *fourth* wave of the men's movement came in the late 1980s and early 1990s. This movement was mystical, Jungian, and apolitical. In many ways mythopoetics came to lionize traditional masculine activities—

hunting, boxing, and drumming. At the same time they valued poetry and expressions of feeling among men. But this fourth wave also picked up on the victimization of men in its constant talk about the wounds men suffer. The *fifth* wave, the evangelical Christian, seeks a total restoration of traditional forms of masculinity. It operates on the thinly veiled premise that if only men will keep their promises, women will stop being feminists. And this wave, too, picks up the theme of how tough it is to be a man. Thus we have traveled in a full circle from traditional masculinity to traditional masculinity, in the course of which feminist ideas and basic assumptions have been largely abandoned. This journey reveals the historical effect, to date, of the overall men's movement: namely, the restoration of patriarchy. Each successive wave asked less and less change of men; each wave moved closer and closer to an exoneration of traditional masculinities. This is not unfair to the profeminists who resisted this historical tendency while being a part of the aggregate movement any more than it is unfair to say that the U.S. Supreme Court has drifted to the right even though it has contained dissenters like Thurgood Marshall and William O. Douglas.

At the same time, we must be aware that many men's lives are *not* being determined by men's movements. Men are changing for many reasons: declining wages, which makes families dependent upon two incomes; the fact that men must take up some of the slack of childcare and homemaking; and because many men hold deeply embedded feminist values that lead to expectations along these lines. Thus, although conservatism is the final chapter, it is not the last word.

· Bibliography ·

Abbott, Franklin, ed. 1987. *New Men, New Minds*. Freedom, Calif.: Crossing.

Abron, J. M. 1990. The image of African Americans in the U.S. Press. *Black Scholar* 21:49–52.

Adam, Barry D. 1995. *The Rise of a Gay and Lesbian Movement*, rev. ed. Boston: Twayne Publishers.

Adams, M. 1985. Female emotion and feminist logic. In *Men Freeing Men*, ed. Francis Baumli, p. 289. Jersey City, N.J.: New Atlantis.

Alterman, Eric. 1996. The right brothers. *The Nation* 262:9 (March 4):7, 24.

Altman, Dennis. 1972. *Homosexual: Oppression and Liberation*. Sydney: Angus & Robertson.

———. 1982. *The Homosexualization of America, the Americanization of the Homosexual*. New York: St. Martin's.

———. 1986. *AIDS in the Mind of America: The Social, Political and Psychological Impact of a New Epidemic*. New York: Anchor.

"A Men's Group Experience." 1974. In *Men and Masculinity*, eds. Joseph H. Pleck and Jack Sawyer, pp. 159–161. New York: Prentice Hall.

American Fathers Coalition. 1995. Welfare reform—no room for daddy? Insert. *Network* 9:1.

Andrews, William L. 1994. The black male in American literature. In *The American Black Male: His Present Status and His Future*, eds. Richard G. Majors and Jacob U. Gordon, pp. 59–68. Chicago: Nelson-Hall.

Andrezejewski, Julie. 1996. *Oppression and Social Justice: Critical Frameworks*. 5th ed. Needham Heights, Mass.: Simon and Schuster.

Aptheker, Herbert, 1938. *The Negro in the Civil War*. New York: International.

———. 1978. *The Unfolding Drama*. New York: International.

Ashley, William. 1961. *The Billy Sunday Story*. Grand Rapids, Mich.: Zondervan.

A Simple Matter of Justice. n.d. *Program Guide, 1993 March on Washington for Lesbian, Gay, and Bi Equal Rights and Liberation*.

Astrachan, Anthony. 1986. *How Men Feel: Their Response to Women's Demands for Equality and Power*. New York: Doubleday.

Balance. 1994. Statement of purpose. (Spring).

Barash, David P. 1979. *The Whispering Within*. New York: Elsevier.

———. 1982. *Sociobiology and Behavior*. New York: Elsevier.

Barker-Benfield, G. J. 1976. *The Horrors of the Half-Known Life*. New York: Harper & Row.

Barnhouse, Ruth Tiffany. 1988. Foreword. In *He! Understanding Masculine Psychology Based on the Legend of Parsifal and His Search for the Grail, and Using Jungian Psychological Concepts,* ed. Robert Johnson, pp. v–vi. New York: Harper & Row.

Bartkey, Sandra. 1992. Foucault, feminity, and the modernization of patriarchal power. In *Feminist Philosophies,* ed. Janet A Kourany, James P. Sterba, and Rosemarie Tong, pp. 103–118. New Jersey: Prentice Hall.

Bartolome, Fernando. 1974. Executives as human beings. In *Men and Masculinity,* eds. Joseph H. Pleck and Jack Sawyer, pp. 100–106. New York: Prentice Hall.

Basow, Susan A. 1986. *Gender Stereotypes: Traditions and Alternatives.* 2d ed. Monterey, Calif.: Brooks/Cole.

Bauer, Bob, and Daphne Bauer. 1985a. Men hide their pain. In *Men Freeing Men,* ed. Francis Baumli, p. 292. Jersey City, N.J.: New Atlantis.

———. 1985b. Visitation lawsuit. In *Men Freeing Men,* ed. Francis Baumli, p. 167. Jersey City: New Atlantis.

Baumli, Francis, ed. 1985. *Men Freeing Men: Exploding the Myth of the Traditional Male.* Jersey City, N.J.: New Atlantis.

Beall, Anne E., and Robert J. Sternberg, eds. 1993. *The Psychology of Gender.* New York and London: Guilford Press.

Beam, Joseph. 1986. No cheek to turn. *Changing Men* 17 (Winter):9–10.

Beane, Jeff. 1992. First loves. *Changing Men* 24 (Summer/Fall):26–29.

———. 1993. Beane responds. *Changing Men* 26 (Winter/Spring):5.

Bell, Donald H. 1982. *Being a Man.* Lexington, Mass.: Lewis Publishing Co.

Bell, Tony. 1986. Black men in the white men's movement. *Changing Men* 17 (Winter):11–12, 44.

Benevento, Nicole, ed. 1981. *Building Feminist Theory.* New York: Longman.

Bennett, William J. 1988. We hold these truths. *National Review* (September 16):39.

Bereano, Philip L. 1996. Mystique of the phantom "gay gene." *Seattle Times* (February 25).

Berkeley Men's Center. 1974. Berkeley men's center manifesto. In *Men and Masculinity* eds. Joseph H. Pleck and Jack Sawyer, pp. 173–174. New York: Prentice Hall.

Binder, Brad. 1989. Wild men and warriors. *Changing Men* 20 (Winter–Spring):46.

Black, Jim Nelson. 1994. The heart of the new man. *New Man* (November/December):65–68.

Blankenhorn, David. 1995. *Fatherless America: Confronting Our Most Urgent Social Problem.* New York: HarperCollins.

Blood, Peter, Alan Tuttle, and George Lakey. 1983. Understanding and fighting sexism: A call to men. In *Off Their Backs . . . And on Our Own Two Feet,* pp. 9–23. Philadelphia: New Society Publishers.

Bly, Carol. 1991. The charismatic men's movement: Warrior wannabes, unconscious deals, and psychological booty. *Omni* (March):6.

Bly, Robert. 1981. *The Man in the Black Coat Turns.* New York: Doubleday.

———. 1985. "Men and the Wound." Cassette, Human Development Associates, Inc., 4913 North Newhall Street, Milwaukee, WI 53217.

———. 1987. *The Pillow and the Key: Commentary on the Fairy Tale of Iron John, Part One.* St. Paul, Minn.: Ally Press.

———. 1988. *When a Hair Turns Gold: Commentary on the Fairy Tale of Iron John, Part Two.* St. Paul, Minn.: Ally Press.

———. 1990. *Iron John.* New York: Addison-Wesley Publishing Co. Inc.

———. n.d. Interview. *The Sun* 96:12.

Bly, Robert, and Deborah Tannen. 1992. Where are women and men today? *New Age Journal* (January/February):28–33, 92–97.

Bly, Robert, and Michael Meade. 1990. "Men and the Life of the Soul, Grief, and Desire." 8 Cassettes (F885–F892), Audio Productions, Seattle, Washington.

Boone, Willington. 1994. Why men must pray. In *Seven Promises of a Promise Keeper,* pp. 25–31. Colorado Springs, Colo.: Focus on the Family Publishing.

Booth, William, ed. 1987. *A Little Book on the Human Shadow.* New York: Harper & Row.

Borgmann, Albert. 1992. *Crossing the Postmodern Divide.* Chicago and London: The University of Chicago Press.

Boston, T. D. 1988. *Race, Class and Conservatism.* Winchester, Mass.: Unwin Hyman.

Bottigheimer, Ruth B. 1989. *Grimms' Bad Girls and Bold Boys.* New Haven, Conn.: Yale University Press.

Bowen, Asta. 1989. Sexism toward men has everything to do with money. *Seattle Post-Intelligencer* (October 18).

Boyd, Billy Ray. 1992. *Circumcision: What It Does.* Santa Cruz, Calif.: C. Olson and Co.

Brannon, Robert. 1987. Strange bedfellows. *Brother* 6:1 (December):5.

Brittan, Arthur. 1989. *Masculinity and Power.* New York: Basil Blackwell.

Brod, Harry. 1985. Feminism for men: Beyond liberalism. *Brother* 3:3 (June):2, 5.

———. 1986. Unlearning racism, valuing our differences. *Changing Men* 17 (Winter):13.

———, ed. 1987a. *The Making of Masculinities.* Boston: Allen & Unwin.

———. 1987b. Introduction: Themes and theses of men's studies. In *The Making of Masculinities,* ed. Harry Brod, pp. 1–17. Boston: Allen & Unwin.

———. 1987c. The case for men's studies. In *The Making of Masculinities,* ed. Harry Brod, pp. 39–62. Boston: Allen & Unwin.

———, ed. 1988. *A Mensch Among Men: Explorations in Jewish Masculinity.* Freedom, Calif.: Crossing.

———. 1994. Review of *The Myth of Male Power: Why Men Are the Disposable Sex. Masculinities* 2:2 (Summer):84–87.

Brod, Harry, and Michael Kaufman, eds. 1994. *Theorizing Masculinities.* Thousand Oaks, Calif.: Sage Publications.

Brown, Laura. 1992. Essian lies: A dystopian vision of the mythopoetic men's movement. In *Women Respond to the Men's Movement,* ed. Kay Leigh Hagan, pp. 93–100. San Francisco: Harper.

Burant, Christopher X. 1988. Of wild men and warriors. *Changing Men* 19 (Spring/Summer):7–9, 46.

Burton, Roger V., and John W. M. Whiting. 1961. The absent father and cross-sex identity. *Merrill-Palmer Quarterly* 7.

Byne, William. 1994. The biological evidence challenged. *Scientific American* 270:5 (May):50–55.

Calamai, Peter. 1988. Conservatives want to extend the Reagan revolution. *Seattle Post-Intelligencer* (March 25).

California Anti-Sexist Men's Political Caucus. 1980. *Male Pride and Anti-Sexism.*

Candell, Peter. 1974. When I was about fourteen. In *Men and Masculinity*, eds. Joseph H. Pleck and Jack Sawyer, pp. 14–17. New York: Prentice Hall.

Carlson, Robert Arthus. 1987. The transitional man. *The New Times.* Mimeograph.

Carrigan, Tim, Bob Connell, and John Lee. 1987. Toward a new sociology of masculinity. In *The Making of Masculinities*, ed. Harry Brod, pp. 63–100. Boston: Allen & Unwin.

Center for Popular Economics. 1986. *Economic Report to the People.* Boston: South End.

Chappel, Steve, and David Talbot. 1990. *Burning Desires.* New York: Simon and Schuster.

Churchill, Ward. 1994. *Indians Are Us? Culture and Genocide in Native North America.* Monroe, Maine: Common Courage Press.

Clatterbaugh, Kenneth. 1986. Are men oppressed? *Changing Men* 17 (Winter):17–18.

———. 1988. Masculinist perspectives. *Changing Men* 20 (Winter–Spring):4–6.

———. 1992. The oppression debate in sexual politics. In *Rethinking Masculinity: Philosophical Explorations in Light of Feminism*, eds. Larry May and Robert Strickwerda, pp. 169–190. Lanham, Md.: Littlefield, Adams.

———. 1994. Men and masculinity: A guide to selected journals, magazines, and newsletters from the men's movements. *Serials Review* 20 (November):25–30.

———. 1995a. Mythopoetic foundations and new age patriarchy. In *The Politics of Manhood*, ed. Michael S. Kimmel, pp. 44–63. Philadelphia: Temple University Press.

———. 1995b. Whose keepers, what promises? *M.E.N. Magazine* 6:10 (October 1995):1, 16–19.

———. 1996. What is problematic about masculinities. *masculinities* (forthcoming).

Cliff, Tony. 1984. *Class Struggle and Women's Liberation: 1640 to the Present Day.* London: Bookmarks Publishing Co-operative.

Coalition of Free Men. n.d. Mimeographed material.

Cohen, Jon. 1992. Feminist allies or anti-feminist backlash: Analyzing (the) men's movement. *Nonviolent Activist* 9:2 (March):709.

———. 1993. Letter to the NOMAS leadership collective and the activist men's caucus. *Activist Men's Journal* 5:6:38–39.

Cohen, Mitchell, and Dennis Hale, eds. 1966. *The New Student Left: An Anthology.* Boston: Beacon.

Cole, Edwin Louis. 1982. *Maximized Manhood: A Guide to Family Survival.* Springdale, Pa.: Whitaker House.

Collins, Patricia Hill. 1991. *Black Feminist Thought: Knowledge, Consciousness, and the Politics of Empowerment.* New York: Routledge.

Colson, Chuck. 1995. *Breakpoint: Special Edition.* Washington, D.C.: Prison Fellowship Ministries.

Connell, R. W. 1993. The big picture: Masculinities in recent world history. *Theory and Society* 22:597–623.

———. 1995. *Masculinities.* Berkeley and Los Angeles: University of California Press.

Conway, David. 1987. *A Farewell to Marx.* Middlesex: Penguin.

Coontz, Stephanie. 1992. *The Way We Never Were: American Families and the Nostalgia Trap*. New York: Basic Books.

Cose, Ellis. 1995. *A Man's World: How Real Is Male Privilege—and How High Is Its Price?* New York: HarperCollins.

Cote, Rick, Michael Biernbaum, and Peter Bresnick. 1993. A statement from the editors and publisher. *Changing Men* (Winter/Spring):7–8.

Couchman, Judith. 1995. Christian chauvinists? *New Man* (May/June):100–101.

Crabb, Larry. 1992. Masculinity. In *What Makes a Man? Twelve Promises That Will Change Your Life*, ed. Bill McCartney, pp. 48–49. Colorado Springs, Colo.: Navpress.

Craft, Nikki. 1993. So much slime, so little time: The transgression of profeminism. *Changing Men* 26 (Winter/Spring):18–23.

Crawford, Mary, and Margaret Gentry, eds. 1989. *Gender and Thought: Psychological Perspectives*. New York and Berlin: Springer-Verlag.

Cunningham, Michael. 1993. Themes in the life views of older and younger African American males. *Journal of African American Male Studies* 1:1:15–29.

Cunningham, Shea, and Betsy Reed. 1995. Balancing budgets on women's backs: The World Bank and the 104th U.S. Congress. *Dollars and Sense* 202 (November/December):22–25.

Curry, George E. 1996. Million man messenger: Can Farrakhan deliver on the march's promise? *emerge* 7:4:36–48.

Daly, Tom. 1990/1991. Claiming the spear in the nuclear age. *Wingspan: Journal of the Male Spirit* (December-March):10–11.

———. 1992. At a men's dance. *Wingspan: Journal of the Male Spirit* (January-March):7.

Dansky, Steven, John Knoebel, and Kenneth Pitchford. 1977. The effeminist manifesto. In *A Book of Readings for Men Against Sexism*, ed. Jon Snodgrass, pp. 116–120. Albion, Calif.: Times Change Press.

David, Deborah S., and Robert Brannon, eds. 1976. *The Forty-Nine Percent Majority*. New York: Random House.

Davis, Angela. 1981. *Women, Race, and Class*. New York: Random House.

———. 1988. *Women, Culture, and Politics*. New York: Random House.

Deckard, Barbara S. 1975. *The Women's Movement: Political, Socioeconomic, and Psychological Issues*. New York: Harper & Row.

DeCrow, Karen. 1982. Men's Rights Incorporated, "News Release" (October).

Diamond, Jed. 1983. *Inside Out: Becoming My Own Man*. San Raphael, Calif.: Fifth Wave.

———. 1985a. Liberating the woman in me. In *Men Freeing Men*, ed. Francis Baumli, p. 80. Jersey City, N.J.: New Atlantis.

———. 1985b. What good are men? In *Men Freeing Men*, ed. Francis Baumli, p. 105. Jersey City, N.J.: New Atlantis.

1988. Wife beaters, wimps, and warriors. *Men Talk* 12:3 (Fall):9.

———. 1994. *The Warrior's Journey Home: Healing Men, Healing the Planet*. Oakland, Calif.: New Harbinger Publications, Inc.

Diamond, Sara. 1989. *Spiritual Warfare: The Politics of the Christian Right*. Boston: South End Press.

DiMascio, William M. 1995. *Seeking Justice: Crime and Punishment in America*. Edna McConnel Clark Foundation.

Dobash, R. E., R. P. Dobash, M. Wilson, and M. Daly. 1992. The myth of sexual symmetry in marital violence. *Social Problems* 39:71–91.

Dobson, James C. 1995. Biology determines gender roles. In *Male/Female: Opposing Viewpoints*, pp. 32–39. San Diego: Greenhaven Press.

Donahue, Phil. 1992. Men's sensitivity movement, part I and part II. Transcripts 3514, 3515. Multimedia Entertainment, Inc., New York.

Donaldson, Mike. 1993. What is hegemonic masculinity? *Theory and Society* 22:643–657.

Doty, William G. 1993. *Myths of Masculinity*. New York: Crossroad.

Dovidia, John F., and Samuel L. Gaertner, eds. 1986. *Prejudice, Discrimination, and Racism*. Orlando, Fla.: Academic.

Dowsett, G. W. 1993. I'll show you mine, if you'll show me yours: Gay men, masculinity research, men's studies, and sex. *Theory and Society* 22:697–709.

Doyle, James. 1984. *The Male Experience*. Dubuque, Iowa: Wm. C. Brown.

———. 1989. *The Male Experience*. 2d ed. Dubuque, Iowa: Wm. C. Brown.

———. 1995. *The Male Experience*. 3rd ed. Dubuque, Iowa: Wm. C. Brown.

Doyle, Richard. 1976. *The Rape of the Male*. St. Paul, Minn.: Poor Richard's Press.

———. 1985. Divorce. In *Men Freeing Men*, ed. Francis Baumli, p. 166. Jersey City, N.J.: New Atlantis.

Dubbert, Joe L. 1979. *A Man's Place*. Englewood Cliffs, N.J.: Prentice Hall.

DuBois, W.E.B. 1935. *Black Reconstruction in America*. New York: Harcourt, Brace.

Dworkin, Andrea, and Catharine MacKinnon. 1985. Model anti-pornography law. *Changing Men* 15 (Fall):23.

Dyson, Michael. 1989. The plight of black men. *Zeta Magazine* (February):51–56.

Easlea, Brian. 1987. Patriarchy, scientists, and nuclear warriors. In *Beyond Patriarchy*, ed. Michael Kaufman, pp. 195–215. Toronto: Oxford University Press.

Easton, Billy. 1985. Voices from the heart: Tenth national men's conference. *Changing Men* 15 (Fall):39.

Eble, Diane. 1995. Reason to rejoice. *New Man* (March/April):80–81.

Edwards, Tim. 1994. *Erotics and Politics*. London and New York: Routledge.

Ehrenreich, Barbara. 1983. *The Hearts of Men*. New York: Doubleday.

Ehrlich, Carol. 1977. The reluctant patriarchs: A review of *Men and Masculinity*. In *A Book of Readings for Men Against Sexism*, ed. Jon Snodgrass, pp. 141–145. Albion, Calif.: Times Change Press.

Ellis, John M. 1983. *One Fairy Story Too Many: The Brothers Grimm and Their Tales*. Chicago: University of Chicago Press.

Ellis, Johnathan. 1982. The meaning of gay rights. *M.* 9 (Summer–Fall):12, 29.

Ellison, Ralph. 1952. *Invisible Man*. New York: Random House.

Engels, Friedrich. 1972. *The Origin of the Family, Private Property, and the State*. New York: International Publishers.

Evans, Tony. 1994. Spiritual purity. In *Seven Promises of a Promise Keeper*, pp. 73–81. Colorado Springs, Colo.: Focus on the Family Publishing.

Faludi, Susan. 1991. *Backlash: The Undeclared War Against American Women*. New York: Crown Publishers.

Farrakhan, Louis. 1995. Speech. Million Man March, Washington, D.C., October 16.

Farrar, Steve. 1992. Real men don't. In *What Makes a Man? Twelve Promises That Will Change Your Life,* ed. Bill McCartney, pp. 80–81. Colorado Springs, Colo.: Navpress.

Farrell, Warren. 1975. *The Liberated Man.* New York: Bantam.

———. 1986. *Why Men Are the Way They Are.* New York: McGraw-Hill.

———. 1993. *The Myth of Male Power: Why Men are the Disposable Sex.* New York: Simon and Schuster.

Fast, Julius. 1971. *The Incompatibility of Men and Women and How to Overcome It.* New York: M. Evans.

Fasteau, Marc Feigen. 1974a. *The Male Machine.* New York: McGraw-Hill.

———. 1974b. Why aren't we talking? In *Men and Masculinity,* eds. Joseph H. Pleck and Jack Sawyer, pp. 19–21. New York: Prentice Hall.

Fausto-Sterling, Anne. 1985. *Myths of Gender.* New York: Basic Books.

Fathers for Equal Rights. 1988. How to choose an attorney. *Transitions* 8:4 (July–August):14–17.

Feminist Anti-Censorship Task Force. 1985. Feminism and censorship: Strange bedfellows. *Changing Men* 15 (Fall):12.

Ferguson, Ann. 1977. Androgyny as an ideal for human development. In *Feminism and Philosophy,* eds. Mary Vettereling-Braggin, Frederick A. Elliston, and Jane English. Totowa, N.J.: Littlefield, Adams.

Fernbach, David. 1981. *The Spiral Path.* Boston: Alyson.

Finkelhor, David, and Kersti Yllo. 1985. *License to Rape: Sexual Abuse of Wives.* New York: Holt, Rinehart & Winston.

Ford, Leighton. 1992. Defining a promise keeper. In *What Makes a Man? Twelve Promises That Will Change Your Life,* ed. Bill McCartney, pp. 17–25. Colorado Springs, Colo.: Navpress.

Foreman, Ann. 1977. *Femininity as Alienation: Women and the Family in Marxism and Psychoanalysis.* London: Pluto.

Franklin, Clyde W. II. 1987. Surviving the institutional decimation of black males: Causes, consequences, and intervention. In *The Making of Masculinities,* ed. Harry Brod, pp. 155–169. Boston: Allen & Unwin.

———. 1988. *Men and Society.* Chicago: Nelson-Hall.

———. 1994a. Men's studies, the men's movement, and the study of black masculinities: Further demystification of masculinities in America. In *The American Black Male: His Present Status and His Future,* eds. Richard G. Majors and Jacob U. Gordon, pp. 3–19. Chicago: Nelson-Hall.

———. 1994b. "Ain't I a man?" The efficacy of black masculinities for men's studies in the 1990s. In *The American Black Male: His Present Status and His Future,* eds. Richard G. Majors and Jacob U. Gordon, pp. 271–283. Chicago: Nelson-Hall.

Freeman, Gregory. 1990. Group aims efforts at black males. *St Louis Post Dispatch* (July 29).

Friedan, Betty. 1963. *The Feminine Mystique.* New York: Dell.

———. 1992. Their turn: How men are changing. In *Men's Lives,* 2nd ed., eds. Michael S. Kimmel and Michael A. Messner, pp. 572–579. New York: Macmillan.

Frye, Marilyn. 1983. *The Politics of Reality: Essays in Feminist Theory.* Trumansburg, N.Y.: Crossings Press.

Gaquin, D. A. 1977/1978. Spouse abuse: Data from the National Crime Survey. *Victimology* 2:632–634.

Gardner, Gerald. 1959. *The Meaning of Witchcraft.* New York: Magickal Childe.

Gary, Lawrence E. 1987. Predicting interpersonal conflict between men and women: The case of black men. In *Changing Men: New Directions in Research on Men and Masculinity,* ed. Michael S. Kimmel, pp. 232–243. Newbury Park, Calif.: Sage.

Gawthrop, Dan. 1992. Gay and seeking a place in the community of men. *Vancouver Sun* (January 11).

Gerson, Kathleen. 1993. *No Man's Land: Men's Changing Commitment to Family and Work.* New York: Basic Books.

Gertner, Douglas M., and Jeff E. Harris, eds. 1994. *Experiencing Masculinities: Exercises, Activities, and Resources for Teaching and Learning About Men.* 4th ed. Denver: Everyman Press.

Gerzon, Mark. 1982. *A Choice of Heroes: The Changing Face of American Manhood.* Boston: Houghton Mifflin.

Gibbs, Jewelle T. 1988. *Young, Black and Male in America: An Endangered Species.* Dover, Del.: Auburn House.

Gibson, James William. 1994. *Warrior Dreams: Violence and Manhood in Post-Vietnam America.* New York: Hill and Wang.

Gilbreath, Edward. 1995. Manhood's great awakening. *Christianity Today* (February 6, 1995):21–28.

Gilder, George. 1973. *Sexual Suicide.* New York: Bantam.

———. 1981. *Wealth and Poverty.* New York: Basic Books.

———. 1986. *Men and Marriage.* London: Pelican.

Gilmore, Brian. 1996. After Chico. *The Nation* (February 12):22–24.

Gilmore, David D. 1990. *Manhood in the Making: Cultural Concepts of Masculinity.* New Haven: Yale University Press.

Goldberg, Herb. 1976. *The Hazards of Being Male: Surviving the Myth of Masculine Privilege.* New York: Signet.

———. 1979. *The New Male.* New York: Signet.

———. 1985. Why the men's movement is not happening. In *Men Freeing Men,* ed. Francis Baumli, p. 306. Jersey City, N.J.: New Atlantis.

———. 1987. *The Inner Male: Overcoming Roadblocks to Intimacy.* New York: New American Library.

Goldberg, Steven. 1974. *The Inevitability of Patriarchy.* New York: William Morrow & Co.

———. 1993. *Why Men Rule: A Theory of Male Dominance.* Chicago and La Salle: Open Court.

Goodman, Gerre, George Lakey, Judy Lashof, and Ericka Thorne. 1983. *No Turning Back: Lesbian and Gay Liberation for the 1980s.* Philadelphia: New Society Publishers.

Goodnow, Cecilia. 1992. Time doesn't heal division over this issue: Research revives age-old debate: To cut or not? *Seattle Post-Intelligencer* (August 18).

Gordon, Jacob U. 1994. Introduction. In *The American Black Male: His Present Status and His Future,* eds. Richard G. Majors and Jacob U. Gordon, pp. ix–xii. Chicago: Nelson-Hall.

Gordon, John. 1982. *The Myth of the Monstrous Male—and Other Feminist Fables.* New York: Playboy Press.

————. 1985. I have a fantasy. In *Men Freeing Men,* ed. Francis Baumli, pp. 269–279. Jersey City, N.J.: New Atlantis.

Gornick, Vivian, and Barbara K. Moran, eds. 1971. *Women in Sexist Society.* New York: Mentor.

Gould, Robert E. 1974. Measuring masculinity by the size of a paycheck. In *Men and Masculinity,* eds. Joseph H. Pleck and Jack Sawyer, pp. 96–100. New York: Prentice Hall.

Gould, Stephen Jay. 1977. *Ever Since Darwin.* New York: Norton.

————. 1981. *The Mismeasure of Man.* New York: Norton.

————. 1994. Curveball. *The New Yorker* (November 28): 139–149.

Gray, John. 1986. *Liberalism.* Minneapolis: University of Minnesota Press.

Gray, Stan. 1987. Sharing the shop floor. In *Beyond Patriarchy,* ed. Michael Kaufman, pp. 216–234. Toronto: Oxford University Press.

Gribbin, William J. 1986. Washington abandons the family. *National Review* (July 18):33–35, 61.

Hay, Harry. 1987a. Towards the new frontiers of fairy vision . . . subject-SUBJECT consciousness. In *New Men, New Minds,* ed. Franklin Abbott, pp. 196–202. Freedom, Calif.: Crossing.

————. 1987b. A separate people whose time has come. In *Gay Spirit: Myth and Meaning,* ed. Mark Thompson, pp. 279–291. New York: St. Martin's.

Hayman, Andrea S. 1976. Legal challenges to discrimination against men. In *The Forty-Nine Percent Majority,* eds. Deborah S. David and Robert Brannon, pp. 297–320. New York: Random House.

Hayward, Frederick. 1985a. The male unpaid role: Body guard and protector. In *Men Freeing Men,* ed. Francis Baumli, p. 238. Jersey City, N.J.: New Atlantis.

————. 1985b. We who are about to die. In *Men Freeing Men,* ed. Francis Baumli, pp. 239–240. Jersey City, N.J.: New Atlantis.

————. 1985c. Our lady of maternity church of the woman I serve. In *Men Freeing Men,* ed. Francis Baumli, pp. 173–174. Jersey City, N.J.: New Atlantis.

————. 1987. A shortage . . . of good women. *Single Scene Magazine* (September):12.

————. 1988. Play mr. for me. *Spectator* (April 22–28).

Hearn, Jeff, and David L. Collinson. 1994. Theorizing unities and differences between men and between masculinities. In *Theorizing Masculinities,* eds. Harry Brod and Michael Kaufman, pp. 97–118. Thousand Oaks, Calif.: Sage Publications.

Hearn, Jeff, and David Morgan, eds. 1990. *Men, Masculinities, and Social Theory.* London: Unwin Hyman.

Henwood, Doug. 1994a. Women working. Left Business Observer 65:4–5.

————. 1994b. RIP, Dems? *Left Business Observer* 67:1–2.

————. 1995. The cleaver. *Left Business Observer* 70:8.

Herbert, Bob, Hugh Price, Joseph Marshall, Patrick Day, and John Singleton. 1994. Symposium: Black men, is America their land of opportunity? *Seattle Post-Intelligencer* (December 4).

Herrnstein, Richard J., and Charles Murray. 1994. *The Bell Curve: Intelligence and Class Structure in American Life.* New York: Free Press.

Hicks, Robert. 1992. Why men feel out of place at church. In *What Makes a Man? Twelve Promises That Will Change Your Life*, ed. Bill McCartney, pp. 154–156. Colorado Springs, Colo.: Navpress.

———. 1993. *The Masculine Journey: Understanding the Six Stages of Manhood.* Colorado Springs Colo.: Navpress.

Hillman, James. 1980. *Facing the Gods.* Irving, Calif.: Spring.

———. 1987. The wildman in the cage: Comment. In *New Men, New Minds*, ed. Franklin Abbott, pp. 182–186.

Hills, Virendra. 1983. The courage to let go. *Soluna* 4:4:4–10, 25–27.

Hooks, Bell. 1981. *Ain't I a Woman: Black Women and Feminism.* Boston: South End.

———. 1984. *Feminist Theory from Margin to Center.* Boston: South End.

Horn, Patricia. 1992. To love and to cherish: Gays and lesbians lead the way in redefining the family. In *Men's Lives*, eds. Michael S. Kimmel and Michael A. Messner, pp. 515–521. New York and Toronto: Macmillan.

Hornacek, Paul Carlo. 1977. Anti-sexist consciousness-raising groups for men. In *A Book of Readings for Men Against Sexism*, ed. Jon Snodgrass, pp. 123–129. Albion, Calif.: Times Change Press.

Housewright, Ed. 1994. Spirited success: Christian men's movement draws converts, critics. *Dallas Morning News* (October 27).

Houtz, Jolayne. 1995. In her face!! *Seattle Times* (January 10).

Hubbard, Ruth, and Marian Lowe, eds. 1979. *Genes and Gender II.* New York: Gordian.

Hutchinson, Earl Ofari. 1994. *The Assassination of the Black Male.* Los Angeles: Middle Passage Press.

Icard, Larry. 1986. Black gay men and conflicting social identities: Sexual orientation versus racial identity. In *Social Work Practice in Sexual Problems*, eds. J. Gripton and M. Valentich, pp. 83–93. New York: The Haworth Press.

Interrante, Joe. 1982. Dancing along the precipice: The men's movement in the 80's. *M.* 9 (Summer–Fall):3–6, 20–21.

———. 1983. Dancing along the precipice: The men's movement in the 80's. *M.* 10 (Spring):3–5, 32.

Jaggar, Alison M. 1983. *Feminist Politics and Human Nature.* Totowa, N.J.: Rowman & Allanheld.

Jeffords, Susan. 1989. *The Remasculinization of America: Gender and the Vietnam War.* Bloomington: Indiana University Press.

Johnson, Robert. 1988. *He! Understanding Masculine Psychology, Based on the Legend of Parsifal and His Search for the Grail, and Using Jungian Psychological Concepts.* New York: Harper & Row.

Jones, Charles L., Lorne Tepperman, and Susannah J. Wilson. 1995. *The Futures of the Family.* Englewood Cliffs, N.J.: Prentice Hall.

Joseph, Gloria. 1981. The incompatible ménage a trois: Marxism, feminism, and racism. In *Women and Revolution*, ed. Lydia Sargent, pp. 91–107. Boston: South End.

Jourard, Sidney M. 1974. Some lethal aspects of the male role. In *Men and Masculinity*, eds. Joseph H. Pleck and Jack Sawyer, pp. 21–29. New York: Prentice Hall.

Jung, Carl Gustav. 1977. *C. G. Jung Speaking*, eds. William McGuire and R.F.C. Hull. Princeton, N.J.: Princeton University Press.

Kaplan, Morris B. 1994. Intimacy and equality: The question of lesbian and gay marriage. *The Philosophical Forum* 25:4:333–360.

Kamenetsky, Christa. 1984. *Children's Literature in Hitler's Germany: The Cultural Policy of National Socialism.* Columbus: Ohio University Press.

Kammer, Jack. 1992. "Male" is not a four letter word. In *Wingspan: Inside the Men's Movement,* ed. Christopher Harding, pp. 62–71. New York: St. Martin's.

Katz, Barbara J. 1976. Saying goodbye to superman. In *The Forty-Nine Percent Majority,* eds. Deborah S. David and Robert Brannon, pp. 291–296. New York: Random House.

Kaufman, Michael, ed. 1987a. *Beyond Patriarchy.* Toronto: Oxford University Press.

———. 1987b. The construction of masculinity and the triad of men's violence. In *Beyond Patriarchy,* ed. Michael Kaufman, pp. 1–29. Toronto: Oxford University Press.

———. 1994. Men, feminism, and men's contradictory experiences of power. In *Theorizing Masculinities,* eds. Harry Brod and Michael Kaufman, pp. 142–163. Thousand Oaks, Calif.: Sage Publications.

Keith, Jeff. 1974. My own men's liberation. In *Men and Masculinity,* eds. Joseph H. Pleck and Jack Sawyer, pp. 81–88. New York: Prentice Hall.

Kennedy, Tom. 1977. Homophobia on the left. In *A Book of Readings for Men Against Sexism,* ed. Jon Snodgrass, pp. 166–176. Albion, Calif.: Times Change Press.

Kilhefner, Don. 1987. Gay people at a critical crossroad: Assimilation or affirmation. In *Gay Spirit: Myth and Meaning,* ed. Mark Thompson, pp. 121–130. New York: St. Martin's.

Kimball, Gale. 1983. *50/50 Marriage.* Boston: Beacon Press.

Kimbrell, Andrew. 1995. *The Masculine Mystique.* New York: Ballantine.

Kimmel, Michael S. 1987a. The contemporary "crisis" of masculinity in historical perspective. In *The Making of Masculinities,* ed. Harry Brod, pp. 121–153. Boston: Allen & Unwin.

———, ed. 1987b. *Changing Men: New Directions in Research on Men and Masculinity.* Newbury Park: Sage.

———. 1987c. Rethinking "masculinity." In *Changing Men: New Directions in Research on Men and Masculinity,* ed. Michael S. Kimmel, pp. 9–24. Newbury Park, Calif.: Sage.

———. 1987d. Judaism, masculinity and feminism. *Changing Men* 18 (Summer–Fall):15.

———. 1990. *Men Confront Pornography.* New York: Crown.

———. 1992. Introduction. In *Men's Lives,* eds. Michael S. Kimmel and Michael A. Messner, pp. 1–11. New York: Macmillan.

———. 1993. The politics of accountability. *Changing Men* 26 (Summer/Fall):3–4.

———. 1994. Masculinity as homophobia: Fear, shame, and silence in the construction of gender identity. In *Theorizing Masculinities,* eds. Harry Brod and Michael Kaufman, pp. 119–141. Thousand Oaks, Calif.: Sage Publications.

———, ed. 1995. *The Politics of Manhood: Profeminist Men Respond to the Mythopoetic Men's Movement (and the Mythopoetic Leaders Answer).* Philadelphia: Temple University Press.

Kimmel, Michael S., and Michael A. Messner, eds. 1992. *Men's Lives.* 2nd ed. New York: Macmillan.

Kimmel, Michael S., and Thomas E. Mosmiller, eds. 1992. *Against the Tide: Pro-Feminist Men in the United States, 1776–1990, a Documentary History.* Boston: Beacon Press.

Kinsman, Gary. 1987. Men loving men: The challenge of gay liberation. In *Beyond Patriarchy*, ed. Michael Kaufman, pp. 103–119. Toronto: Oxford University Press.

Kipnis, Aaron R. 1991. *Knights without Armor: A Practical Guide for Men in Quest of Masculine Soul.* Los Angeles: Jeremy P. Tarcher, Inc.

Kitcher, Philip. 1985. *Vaulting Ambition, Sociobiology and the Quest for Human Nature.* Cambridge: MIT Press.

Kleinberg, Seymour. 1987. The new masculinity of gay men, and beyond. In *Beyond Patriarchy*, ed. Michael Kaufman, pp. 120–138. Toronto: Oxford University Press.

Kokopeli, Bruce, and George Lakey. 1983. More power than we want: Masculine sexuality and violence. In "Off Their Backs . . . and on Our Own Two Feet," pp. 1–8. Philadelphia: New Society Publishers.

Korda, Michael. 1973. *Male Chauvinism: How It Works.* New York: Random House.

Lamm, Bob. 1977a. Learning from women. In *A Book of Readings for Men Against Sexism*, ed. Jon Snodgrass, pp. 49–56. Albion, Calif.: Times Change Press.

———. 1977b. Men's movement hype. In *A Book of Readings for Men Against Sexism*, ed. Jon Snodgrass, pp. 153–157. Albion, Calif.: Times Change Press.

Langley, Roger, and Richard C. Levy. 1980. *Wife Beating: The Silent Crisis.* New York: E. P. Dutton.

LaRossa, Ralph. 1992. Fatherhood and social change. In *Men's Lives*, eds. Michael S. Kimmel and Michael A. Messner, pp. 521–535. New York and Toronto: Macmillan.

Lawrence, Ken. 1994. Klansmen, nazis, and skinheads: Vigilante repression. In *The American Black Male: His Present Status and His Future* eds. Richard G. Majors and Jacob U. Gordon, pp. 21–37. Chicago: Nelson-Hall.

Lee, Richard, and Richard Daly. 1987. Man's domination and woman's oppression: The question of origins. In *Beyond Patriarchy*, ed. Michael Kaufman, pp. 30–44. Toronto: Oxford University Press.

Lee, Virginia. 1984. Danaan Parry: Discovering the warrior within. *Yoga Journal* (March–April).

Lehne, Gregory K. 1976. Homophobia among men. In *The Forty-Nine Percent Majority*, eds. Deborah S. David and Robert Brannon, pp. 66–88. New York: Random House.

Leibowitz, Lila. 1979. "Universals" and male dominance among primates: A critical examination. In *Genes and Gender II*, eds. Ruth Hubbard and Marion Lowe, pp. 35–48. New York: Gordian.

Levant, Dr. Ronald F. 1995. *Masculinity Reconstructed.* New York: Dutton.

LeVay, Simon, and Dean H. Hamer. 1994. Evidence for a biologial influence in male homosexuality. *Scientific American* 270:5 (May):44–49.

Levin, Michael. 1980. The feminist mystique. *Commentary* 70:6 (December):25–30.

Levine, Martin P. 1992. The status of gay men in the workplace. In *Men's Lives*, eds. Michael S. Kimmel and Michael A. Messner, pp. 251–266. New York and Toronto: Macmillan.

Levine, Stan. 1974. One man's experience. In *Men and Masculinity*, eds. Joseph H. Pleck and Jack Sawyer, pp. 156–159. New York: Prentice Hall.

Levy, Charles, J. 1992. ARFN as faggots: Inverted warfare in Vietnam. In *Men's Lives*, eds. Michael S. Kimmel and Michael A. Messner, pp. 183–197. New York and Toronto: Macmillan.

Litewka, Jack. 1977. The socialized penis. In *A Book of Readings for Men Against Sexism*, ed. Jon Snodgrass, pp. 16–35. Albion, Calif.: Times Change Press.

Logan, Dan. 1985. Some thoughts about my feelings. In *Men Freeing Men*, ed. Francis Baumli, pp. 19–21. Jersey City, N.J.: New Atlantis.

Lyman, Peter. 1992. The fraternal bond as a joking relationship: A case study of the role of sexist jokes in male group bonding. In *Men's Lives*, eds. Michael S. Kimmel and Michael A. Messner, pp. 143–154. New York: Macmillan.

Lyttelton, Ned. 1987. Men's liberation, men against sexism and major dividing lines. In *Women and Men: Interdisciplinary Readings on Gender*, ed. Greta Hofmann Nemiroff, pp. 472–477. Markham, Ontario: Fitzhenry & Whiteside.

Maccoby, E. E., and C. N. Jacklin. 1974. *The Psychology of Sex Differences*. Stanford, Calif.: Stanford University Press.

MacLeod, Jay. 1987. *Ain't No Makin' It*. Boulder, Colo.: Westview Press.

Madison Men's Organization. 1991. Report on Wisconsin's equal justice task force. Xerox.

Majors, Richard. 1986. Cool pose: The proud signature of black survival. *Changing Men* 17 (Winter):5–6.

———. 1994. Conclusion and recommendations: A reason for Hope—an overview of the new black movement in the United States. In *The American Black Male: His Present Status and His Future*, eds. Richard G. Majors and Jacob U. Gordon, pp. 300–315. Chicago: Nelson-Hall.

Majors, Richard, and Janet Mancini Billson. 1992. *Cool Pose: The Dilemmas of Black Manhood in America*. New York: Lexington Books.

Majors, Richard, Richard Tyler, Blaine Peden, and Ron Hall. 1994. Cool pose: A symbolic mechanism for masculine role enactment and coping by black males. In *The American Black Male: His Present Status and His Future*, eds. Richard G. Majors and Jacob U. Gordon, pp. 59–68. Chicago: Nelson-Hall.

Majors, Richard G., and Jacob U. Gordon, eds. 1994. *The American Black Male: His Present Status and His Future*. Chicago: Nelson-Hall.

MacDonald, Sally. 1995. Father and father. *Seattle Times* (Sunday, June 25).

Male/Female Roles: Opposing Viewpoints. 1995. San Diego: Greenhaven Press.

Mann, Patricia S. 1994. *Micro-Politics: Agency in a Postfeminist Era*. Minneapolis and London: University of Minnesota Press.

Marable, Manning. 1983. *How Capitalism Underdeveloped Black America*. Boston: South End.

———. 1994. The black male: Searching beyond stereotypes. In *The American Black Male: His Present Status and His Future*, eds. Richard G. Majors and Jacob U. Gordon, pp. 69–77. Chicago: Nelson-Hall.

Marian, Jim, and Lynne Marian. 1995. Greg Laurine touches his generation. *New Man* (January/February):44–50.

Martin, Del. 1976. *Battered Wives*. San Francisco: Glide.

Marx, Karl. 1964a. *The Economic and Philosophic Manuscripts of 1844*, ed. Dirk J. Struik. New York: International.

————. 1964b. Estranged labor. In *The Economic and Philosophical Manuscripts of 1844*, ed. Dirk J. Struik, pp. 106–117. New York: International.

————. 1964c. The meaning of human requirements. In *The Economic and Philosophical Manuscripts of 1844*, ed. Dirk J. Struik, pp. 147–164. New York: International.

Marx, Karl, and Friedrich Engels. 1984. *The German Ideology*, ed. C. J. Arthur. New York: International.

Mason, Dawn. 1995. House GOP robs kids of a future. *Seattle Post-Intelligencer* (March 30).

Mauer, Marc. 1994. A generation behind bars: Black males and the criminal justice system. In *The American Black Male: His Present Status and His Future*, eds. Richard G. Majors and Jacob U. Gordon, pp. 245–259. Chicago: Nelson-Hall.

Maxwell, John C. 1995. Secular vs. spiritual leadership. *New Man* (May/June):78–83.

May, Larry, and Robert Strikwerda, eds. 1992. *Rethinking Masculinity: Philosophical Explorations in Light of Feminism*. Lanham, Md.: Littlefield, Adams.

McCartney, Bill, ed. 1992a. *What Makes a Man? Twelve Promises That Will Change Your Life*. Colorado Springs, Colo.: Navpress.

————. 1992b. It's time for men to take a stand. In *What Makes a Man? Twelve Promises That Will Change Your Life*, ed. Bill McCartney, pp. 9–13. Colorado Springs, Colo.: Navpress.

McDowell, Josh. 1995. Josh McDowell: Rescuing teen-agers. *New Man* (March/April):53–57.

McLeod, Michael. 1986. Singles' stories. *Seattle Times* (November 30).

McLoughlin, William G. 1959. *Modern Revivalism: Charles Grandison Finney to Billy Graham*. New York: The Ronald Press Company.

McMahon, Anthony. 1993. Male readings of feminist theory: The psychologization of sexual politics in the masculinity literature. *Theory and Society* 22:675–695.

McMillen, Neil R. 1989. *Dark Journey: Black Mississippians in the Age of Jim Crow*. Champaign: University of Illinois Press.

McNeely, R. L., and Gloria Robinson-Simpson. 1987. The truth about domestic violence: A falsely framed issue. *Social Work* (November–December):485–490.

————. 1988. The truth about domestic violence revisited: A reply to Saunders. *Social Work* (March–April):184.

Menner, Michael A. 1993. "Changing men" and feminist politics in the United States. *Theory and Society* 22:723–737.

Men's Rights Incorporated. 1985. Are men's problems serious? Mimeograph.

————. "News Release," various dates.

————. Mimeographed material, various dates.

Miedzian, Myriam. 1991. *Boys Will Be Boys*. New York: Doubleday.

————. 1992. "Father hunger": Why "soup kitchen" fathers are not good enough. In *Women Respond to the Men's Movement*, ed. Kay Leigh Hagan, pp. 127–131. San Francisco: HarperSanFrancisco.

Mill, John Stuart. 1988. *The Subjection of Women*, ed. Susan M. Okin. Indianapolis: Hackett.

Miller, Richard W. 1984. *Analyzing Marx: Morality, Power and History*. Princeton, N.J.: Princeton University Press.

Millett, Kate. 1970. *Sexual Politics*. New York: Ballantine.

Minkowitz, Donna. 1995. In the name of the father. *MS* 6:3 (December):64–71.

Mirandé, Alfredo. 1988. Qué gacho es ser macho: It's a drag to be a macho man. *Astlan*, 17:2:63–89.

Mishel, Lawrence, and Jared Bernstein. 1994. *The State of Working America 1994–95*. Armonk, N.Y.: M. E. Sharpe.

Mohr, Richard D. 1992. *Gay Ideas: Outing and Other Controversies*. Boston: Beacon Press.

————. 1994. *A More Perfect Union: Why Straight Americans Must Stand Up for Gay Rights*. Boston: Beacon Press.

Moore, Robert. 1990. Robert Moore interview: Decoding masculine initiation. *Wingspan* (Spring):1, 10–12.

Moore, Robert, and Douglas Gillette. 1990. *King, Warrior, Magician, Lover: Rediscovering the Archetypes of the Mature Masculine*. San Francisco: HarperSanFrancisco.

Montana senate eliminates gays from sex-offender bill. 1995. *Oregonian* (Friday, March 24).

Morgan, Robin. 1978. *Going Too Far*. New York: Vintage.

Munoz, Carlos Jr. 1989. *Youth, Identity and Power*. London: Verso.

Muwakkil, Salim. 1988. Getting black males off the endangered species list. *In These Times* 12:28 (June 22–July 5):7.

Nardi, Peter M. 1992. The politics of gay men's friendships. In *Men's Lives*, eds. Michael S. Kimmel and Michael A. Messner, pp. 394–398. New York and Toronto: Macmillan.

National Advisory Commission on Civil Disorders. 1968. *Report of the National Advisory Commission on Civil Disorders*. New York: Bantam.

"National Conference on Homophobia." 1988. *Brother* 6:2 (March):7.

National Organization for Changing Men. n.d. Various mimeographs.

National Organization for Men Against Sexism. 1990. Statement of principles. In *Men's Lives*, eds. Michael S. Kimmel and Michael A. Messner, p. 553. New York: Macmillan.

National Organization for Women, Inc. n.d. Who cares about women's rights? Leaflet.

"NBC-TV May Upset Feminists." 1988. *Transitions* 8:3 (May–June):1, 23.

Neirenberg, John. 1987. Misogyny: Gay and straight. In *New Men, New Minds*, ed. Franklin Abbott, pp. 130–133. Freedom, Calif.: Crossing.

Nemiroff, Greta Hofmann, ed. 1987. *Women and Men: Interdisciplinary Readings on Gender*. Markham, Ontario: Fitzhenry & Whiteside.

New Society Publishers. 1983. "Off Their Backs . . . and on Our Own Two Feet." Philadelphia: New Society Publishers.

Nichols, Jack. 1975. *Men's Liberation*. London: Penguin.

Nisbet, Robert. 1986. *Conservatism*. Minneapolis: University of Minnesota Press.

Novak, James. 1991. Patriarchy *is* civilization. *The Liberator* 17:10:1, 8.

Nussbaum, Martha. 1992. The softness of reason. *The New Republic* (July 13 and 20): 26, 27, 30, 32, 34–35.

Oliver, Gary. 1992. Moral collapse. In *What Makes a Man? Twelve Promises That Will Change Your Life*, ed. Bill McCartney, pp. 176–179. Colorado Springs, Colo.: Navpress.

O'Neal, Jennifer. 1995. In the stadium proper: A "weaker vessel" among the Promise Keepers. Unpublished paper.

Parrish, Geov. 1993. Male supremacy and the men's pro-feminist movement: The dubious legacy of the National Organization for Men Against Sexism. Open letter to subscribers of the *Activist Men's Journal* (January).

Pascal, Eugene. 1992. *Jung to Live By*. New York: Time Warner.

Pelka, Fred. 1991. Robert Bly and Iron John. *On the Issues* (Summer):17–19.

Penner, Naomi. 1985. What's a woman like me doing in a men's movement like this? In *Men Freeing Men*, ed. Francis Baumli, pp. 303–305. Jersey City, N.J.: New Atlantis.

Phillips, Randy. 1994. A monument or a mission? *Men of Action* (Fall):8.

Pierce, Chester M., and Wesley E. Profit. 1994. Racial group dynamics: Implications for rearing black males. In *The American Black Male: His Present Status and His Future*, eds. Richard G. Majors and John U. Gordon. Chicago: Nelson-Hall.

Pierce, Christine. 1971. Natural law language and women. In *Women in Sexist Society*, eds. Vivian Gornick and Barbara K. Moran, pp. 242–258. New York: Mentor.

Piven, Frances, and Richard A. Cloward. 1979. *Poor People's Movements*. New York: Random House.

Pleck, Joseph H. 1981. *The Myth of Masculinity*. Cambridge: MIT Press.

———. 1992a. Men's power with women, other men, and society: A men's movement analysis. In *Men's Lives*, eds. Michael S. Kimmel and Michael A. Messner, pp. 19–27. New York: Macmillan.

———. 1992b. Prisoners of manliness. In *Men's Lives*, eds. Michael S. Kimmel and Michael A. Messner, pp. 98–107. New York: Macmillan.

Pleck, Joseph H., and Jack Sawyer, eds. 1974. *Men and Masculinity*. New York: Prentice Hall.

Price, Joyce. 1993. Activists visit White House to call for father's rights in divorce cases. *Washington Times* (October 8).

Rabinowitz, Fredric E., and Sam V. Cochran. 1994. *Man Alive: A Primer of Men's Issues*. Pacific Grove, Calif.: Brooks/Cole.

Raymond, Janice. 1981. The illusion of androgyny. In *Building Feminist Theory*, ed. Nicole Benevento, pp. 59–66. New York: Longman.

"Recovery Fails Latinos." 1989. *Dollars and Sense* 151 (November):19–21.

Reed, Adolph Jr. 1994. Looking backward. *The Nation* (November 28):654–665.

Reed, Ishmael. 1989. The black pathology biz. *The Nation* (November 20):597–598.

Reinisch, June Machover, Leonard A. Rosenblum, and Stephanie A. Sanders, eds. 1987. *Masculinity/Femininity: Basic Perspectives*. New York and Oxford: Oxford University Press.

Rhodes, Elizabeth. 1991. New ties that bind. *Seattle Times* (July 21).

Rice, Edward. 1977. *Marx, Engels, and the Workers of the World*. New York: Four Winds.

Richardson, Laurel. 1988. *The Dynamics of Sex and Gender*. New York: Harper & Row.

Rix, Sara E., ed., for the Women's Research and Education Institute of the Congressional Caucus for Women's Issues. 1987. *The American Woman 1987–88*. New York: W. W. Norton.

Robinson, Cedric J. 1983. *Black Marxism: The Making of the Black Radical Tradition.* London: Zed Press.

Rochlin, Gregory. 1980. *The Masculine Dilemma.* Boston: Little, Brown.

Roszak, Betty, and Theodore Roszak, eds. 1969. *Masculine/Feminine.* New York: Harper & Row.

Rotundo, E. Anthony. 1993. *American Manhood: Transformations in Masculinity from the Revolution to the Modern Era.* New York: Basic Books.

Rowan, John. 1983. *The Reality Game: A Guide to Humanistic Counseling and Therapy.* London: Routledge & Kegan Paul.

————. 1987. *The Horned God.* New York: Routledge & Kegan Paul.

Rowbotham, Sheila. 1973. *Woman's Consciousness, Man's World.* Middlesex: Penguin.

Rubin, Gayle. 1969. Woman as nigger. In *Masculine/Feminine,* eds. Betty Roszak and Theodore Roszak, pp. 230–240. New York: Harper & Row.

Russell, Diana E. H. 1982. *Rape in Marriage.* New York: Macmillan.

Ryan, Jon. 1988. Adoption's real fathers. *Transitions* 8:6 (November–December):1–2.

Sabo, Don. 1992. Pigskin, patriarchy and pain. In *Men's Lives,* eds. Michael S. Kimmel and Michael A. Messner, pp. 158–161. New York: Macmillan.

Sacco, V. F., and H. Johnson. 1990. *Patterns of Criminal Victimization.* Ottawa: Statistics Canada.

Sargent, Lydia, ed. 1981. *Women and Revolution.* Boston: South End.

Satzman, Freda. 1979. Aggression and gender: A critique of the nature-nurture question for humans. In *Genes and Gender II,* eds. Ruth Hubbard and Marian Lowe, pp. 71–89. New York: Gordian.

Saunders, Daniel G. 1988. "Other truths" about domestic violence: A reply to McNeely and Robinson-Simpson. *Social Work* (March–April):182.

Sawyer, Jack. 1974. On male liberation. In *Men and Masculinity,* eds. Joseph Pleck and Jack Sawyer, pp. 170–173. New York: Prentice Hall.

Schein, Leonard. 1977a. All men are misogynists. In *A Book of Readings for Men Against Sexism,* ed. Jon Snodgrass, pp. 69–74. Albion, Calif.: Times Change Press.

————. 1977b. Dangers with men's consciousness-raising groups. In *A Book of Readings for Men Against Sexism,* ed. Jon Snodgrass, pp. 123–129. Albion, Calif.: Times Change Press.

Schenk, Roy. 1982. *The Other Side of the Coin: Causes and Consequences of Men's Oppression.* Madison: Bioenergetics Press.

Schoenberg, B. Mark. 1993. *Growing Up Male: The Psychology of Masculinity.* Westport, Conn.: Bergin & Garvey.

Schuenemann, Jim. 1990. Me and my shadow dance. *Wingspan: Journal of the Male Spirit* (Spring):14–15.

Schwalbe, Michael. 1996. *Unlocking the Iron Cage: The Men's Movement, Gender Politics, and American Culture.* New York and Oxford: Oxford University Press.

Schwartz, M. D. 1987. Gender and injury in spousal assaults. *Sociological Focus* 20:61–75.

Schwarz, Joel. 1995. Parenting: One size or style doesn't fit all, researcher says. *University Week* (November 9):8.

Segal, Lynne. 1990. *Slow Motion: Changing Masculinities, Changing Men.* New Brunswick, N.J.: Rutgers University Press.

———. 1993. Changing men: Masculinities in context. *Theory and Society* 22:625–641.

Seidler, Victor J., ed. 1991. *The Achilles Heel Reader: Men, Sexual Politics and Socialism.* London: Routledge.

Seven Promises of a Promise Keeper. 1995. Colorado Springs, Colo.: Focus on the Family Publishing.

Seventh National Conference on Men and Masculinity. 1982. "Reweaving Masculinity." Mimeographed material.

Shiffman, Michael. 1987. The men's movement: An exploratory empirical investigation. In *Changing Men: New Directions in Research on Men and Masculinity,* ed. Michael S. Kimmel, pp. 285–314. Newbury Park, Calif.: Sage.

Shilts, Randy. 1987. *And the Band Played On: Politics, People, and the AIDS Epidemic.* New York: St. Martin's.

———. 1993. *Conduct Unbecoming: Lesbians and Gays in the U.S. Military, Vietnam to the Persian Gulf.* New York: St. Martin's.

Shostak, Arthur. 1988. Men vs. abortion: What are their rights? *Transitions* 8:5 (September–October):1–2.

Shostak, Arthur B., and William Gomberg, eds. 1965. *Blue-Collar World.* Englewood Cliffs, N.J.: Prentice Hall.

Sides, Robert. 1984. What is the free man?—Two views. *American Man* 2:3 (Spring):2.

———. 1985a. Men's liberation and humanism. In *Men Freeing Men,* ed. Francis Baumli, p. 296. Jersey City, N.J.: New Atlantis.

———. 1985b. Women's responsibility and the E.R.A. In *Men Freeing Men,* ed. Francis Baumli, p. 268. Jersey City, N.J.: New Atlantis.

Silverstein, Olga, and Beth Rashbaum. 1994. *The Courage to Raise Good Men.* New York: Viking.

Simon, Jim. 1994. Gay-rights fight takes national stage. *Seattle Times* (May 29).

Simpkinson, Charles H. 1986. Healing "the grief our fathers lived": A weekend with Robert Bly. *The Common Boundary* 4:4 (July–August):1, 13.

Small, Fred. 1985. Pornography and censorship. *Changing Men* 15 (Fall):7–8, 43–45.

Smalley, Gary, and John Trent. 1992. The promises you make to your self. In *What Makes a Man? Twelve Promises That Will Change Your Life,* ed. Bill McCartney, pp. 39–47. Colorado Springs, Colo.: Navpress.

Smolowe, Jill. 1995. Marching home. *Time* 146:18 (October 30):40–50.

Snodgrass, Jon, ed. 1977a. *A Book of Readings for Men Against Sexism.* Albion, Calif.: Times Change Press.

———. 1977b. Men and the feminist movement. In *A Book of Readings for Men Against Sexism,* ed. Jon Snodgrass, pp. 6–11. Albion, Calif.: Times Change Press.

Solicitor General of Canada. 1985. Female victims of crime. *Canadian Urban Victimization Survey Bulletin* 4. Ottawa: Programs Branch/Research and Statistics Group.

Sowell, Thomas. 1985. *Civil Rights: Rhetoric or Reality?* New York: Morrow, William.

————. 1993. *Is Reality Optional? and Other Essays*. Stanford: Hoover Institution Press.

Speyer, Rob. 1994. Decoy police to pose as gays. *New York Daily News* (May 10).

Stacey, Judith. 1993. Toward kinder, gentler uses of testosterone. *Theory and Society* 22:711–721.

Staples, Robert. 1986. Black male sexuality. *Changing Men* 17 (Winter):3–4, 46.

Starhawk. 1979. *The Spiral Dance: A Rebirth of the Ancient Religion of the Great Goddess*. San Francisco: Harper & Row.

Stein, Harry. 1994. The post-sensitive man is coming! The post-sensitive man is coming! (And boy is he pissed.). *Esquire* (May):57–63.

Stevens, William K. 1981. A congress of men asks equality for both sexes. *New York Times* (June 15).

Stewart, James B. 1994. Neoconservative attacks on black families and the black male: An analysis and critique. In *The American Black Male: His Present Status and His Future*, eds. Richard G. Majors and Jacob U. Gordon, pp. 39–58. Chicago: Nelson-Hall.

Stoltenberg, John. 1977. Toward gender justice. In *A Book of Readings for Men Against Sexism*, ed. Jon Snodgrass, pp. 74–83. Albion, Calif.: Times Change Press.

————. 1985a. Speech to brotherstorm demonstration. *Brother* 4:1 (November):8–9.

————. 1985b. Pornography and freedom. *Changing Men* 15 (Fall):15–16, 46–47.

————. 1995. Male virgins, blood covenants & family values. *On The Issues: The Progressive Woman's Quarterly* 4:2 (Spring):25–29, 51–52.

Straton, Jack. 1991. Where are the ethics in men's spirituality. *Changing Men* 23 (Fall/Winter):10–12.

————. 1993. What NOMAS conspiracy? *Activist Men's Journal* 5:6 (April):41–49.

————. 1994. The myth of the "battered husband syndrome." *masculinities* 2:4 (Winter):79–82.

Suzuki, David. 1988. *Metamorphosis*. Toronto: General Paperbacks.

Takaki, Ronald T. 1979. *Iron Cages: Race and Culture in 19th Century America*. Seattle: University of Washington Press.

Tartar, Maria. 1987. *The Hard Facts of the Grimms' Fairy Tales*. Princeton: Princeton University Press.

Tavris, Carol. 1992. *The Mismeasure of Woman*. New York: Simon and Schuster.

Tavris, Carol, and Carole Wade. 1986. *The Longest War: Sex Differences in Perspective*. 2nd ed. New York: Harcourt Brace Jovanovich.

Taylor, Ronald. 1994. Black males and social policy: Breaking the cycle of disadvantage. In *The American Black Male: His Present Status and His Future*, eds. Richard G. Majors and Jacob U. Gordon, pp. 147–166. Chicago: Nelson-Hall.

Terkel, Studs. 1984. *Working*. New York: Random House.

Terry, Don. 1995. In the end, Farrakhan has his day in the sun. *New York Times National* (October 17, 1995).

Tewksbury, Richard. 1995. Sexuality of men with HIV disease. *The Journal of Men's Studies* 3:3:205–228.

"The counter-attack of God." 1995. *The Economist* (July 8):19–21.

Thomas, Lee. 1961. *The Billy Sunday Story: The Life and Times of William Ashley Sunday, D.D.* Grand Rapids, Mich.: Zondervan Publishing House.

Thompson, Keith. 1987. What men really want: An interview with Robert Bly. In *New Men, New Minds*, ed. Franklin Abbott, pp. 166–181. Freedom, Calif.: Crossing.

Thompson, Mark, ed. 1987a. *Gay Spirit: Myth and Meaning.* New York: St. Martin's.

———. 1987b. This gay tribe: A brief history of fairies. In *Gay Spirit: Myth and Meaning*, ed. Mark Thompson, pp. 260–278. New York: St. Martin's.

———. 1987c. Harry Hay: A voice from the past, a vision for the future. In *Gay Spirit: Myth and Meaning*, ed. Mark Thompson, pp. 182–199. New York: St. Martin's.

Thurow, Lester C. 1987. A surge in inequality. *Scientific American* 256:5 (May):30–37.

Tieger, Todd. 1980. On the biological basis of sex differences in aggression. *Child Development* 51:943–963.

Tolson, Andrew. 1977. *The Limits of Masculinity.* New York: Harper & Row.

Tong, Rosemarie. 1989. *Feminist Thought: A Comprehensive Introduction.* Boulder, Colo.: Westview Press.

Treadwell, Perry. 1985. Men's dreams of bonding. In *Men Freeing Men*, ed. Francis Baumli, pp. 302–303. Jersey City, N.J.: New Atlantis.

Turner, Jonathan H., Royce Singleton, Jr., and David Musick. 1984. *Oppression: A Socio-History of Black-White Relations in America.* Chicago: Nelson-Hall.

Ulbrich, David J. 1995. A male-conscious critique of Erich Maria Remarque's *All Quiet on the Western Front. The Journal of Men's Studies* 3:3:229–240.

Unbecoming Men. 1971. Washington, N.J.: Times Change Press.

United States Citizens Alliance. n.d. Statement of Principles.

Van Cleve, Janice. 1994. New York cops to decoy as gays to flush out gay-bashers. Hands Off the University of Washington (handsoff@u.washington.edu.) (May 11).

van den Berghe, Pierre L. 1979. *Human Family Systems—An Evolutionary View.* New York: Elsevier.

van den Berghe, Pierre, and David P. Barash. 1977. Inclusive fitness and human family structure. *American Anthropologist* 79:809–821.

Vetterling-Braggin, Mary, Frederick A. Elliston, and Jane English, eds. 1978. *Feminism and Philosophy.* Totowa, N.J.: Littlefield, Adams.

Wagenheim, Jeff. 1995. Among the Promise Keepers. *New Age Journal* (April):78–81, 126–129.

Wagner, Sally Roesch. 1985. Suffrage in the 1870's and anti-pornography in the 1980's. *Changing Men* 15 (Fall):26–27.

Walters, Marianne. 1993. The codependent Cinderella and Iron John. *The Family Therapy Networker* (March/April):60–65.

Wandachild, Gary Mitchell. 1977. Complacency in the face of patriarchy. In *A Book of Readings for Men Against Sexism*, ed. Jon Snodgrass, pp. 83–97. Albion, Calif.: Times Change Press.

Washington Coalition for Family Rights. 1988. Mimeographed material.

Wasserstrom, Richard. 1980. *Philosophy and Social Issues.* Notre Dame: University of Notre Dame Press.

Weeden, Larry. 1995. Josh McDowell talks about purity (an interview). *New Man* (March/April):53–57.

Weisberger, Bernard A. 1958. *They Gathered at the River: The Story of the Great Revivalists and Their Impact upon Religion in America.* Boston: Little, Brown.

Weiss, Michael. 1974. Unlearning. In *Men and Masculinity*, eds. Joseph H. Pleck and Jack Sawyer, pp. 162–170. New York: Prentice Hall.

Weissman, Andy. 1977. Labor pains. In *A Book of Readings for Men Against Sexism*, ed. Jon Snodgrass. Albion, Calif.: Times Change Press.

West Hills Counseling Center. 1989. Leaving the father and seeking the king. Leaflet.

What is Promise Keepers? 1996. *Break down the walls: Promise Keepers' men's conferences*. Leaflet.

Wheat, Tom. 1985. NOCM is no answer. *Brother* 3:3 (June):2–3.

White, K. 1992. *The First Sexual Revolution: The Emergence of Male Heterosexuality in Modern America*. New York: New York University Press.

Whitehead, Barbara Dafoe. 1993. Dan Quayle was right. *Atlantic Monthly* 271:4 (April):47–84.

Williams, Patricia J. 1995. The million man atonement: Different drummer please, marchers! *The Nation* (October 30):493–494.

Williamson, Tom. 1985a. Homophobia. In *Men Freeing Men*, ed. Francis Baumli, p. 104. Jersey City, N.J.: New Atlantis.

———. 1985b. A history of the men's movement. In *Men Freeing Men*, ed. Francis Baumli, pp. 308–324. Jersey City, N.J.: New Atlantis.

Wilson, Edward O. 1975. *Sociobiology: The New Synthesis*. Cambridge: Harvard University Press.

———. 1976. *On Human Nature*. Cambridge: Harvard University Press.

Winner, F. D. 1983. *Genetic Basis of Society*. Dunedin, Fla.: Shakespeare Publishing Co.

Wolfe, Alan. 1973. *The Seamy Side of Democracy: Repression in America*. New York: David McKay.

Woodward, Kenneth L., and Sherry Keene-Osborn. 1994. The gospel of guyhood. *Newsweek* (August 29).

World. P.O. Box 2330, Asheville, N.C. 28802.

Worrall, A., and K. Pease. 1986. *Patterns in Criminal Homicide: Evidence from the 1982 British Crime Survey*. Philadelphia: University of Pennsylvania Press.

"Write Bill Moyers About the Myth of Male Power." 1994. *The Backlash!* (1994):13.

Yates, John. 1992. Whose man? In *What Makes A Man? Twelve Promises That Will Change Your Life*, ed. Bill McCartney, pp. 36–38. Colorado Springs, Colo.: Navpress.

Young, Iris. 1981. Beyond the unhappy marriage: A critique of the dual systems theory. In *Women and Revolution*, ed. Lydia Sargent, pp. 43–69. Boston: South End.

Zaretsky, Eli. 1976. *Capitalism, the Family, and Personal Life*. New York: Harper & Row.

Zimmerman, Rachel. 1996. New chance for deadbeat dads penalties. *Seattle Post-Intelligencer* (February 24).

Zinn, Maxine Baca. 1992. Chicano men and masculinity. In *Men's Lives*, eds. Michael S. Kimmel and Michael A. Messner, pp. 67–77. New York and Toronto: Macmillan.

Zipes, Jack, ed. and trans. 1989. *Fairy Tales and Fables from Weimar Days*. Hanover, Conn.: University Press of New England.

▪ About the Book ▪
and Author

What is social reality for men in modern society? What maintains or explains this social reality? What condition might we imagine that would be better for men? How might we achieve this better condition?

These are the questions Kenneth Clatterbaugh brings to seven different visions of men in modern society considered in this book. In clear and insightful language, Clatterbaugh surveys not just conservative, liberal, and radical views of masculinity but also the alternatives offered by the men's rights movement, spiritual growth advocates, and black and gay rights activists. Each of these is explored both as a theoretical perspective and as a social movement, and each offers distinctive responses to the questions posed.

This is the first book to survey the range of responses to feminism that men have made, and it is also the first to put political theory at the center of men's awareness of their own masculinity. Clatterbaugh treats all views with fairness as he develops and defends a vision of men and masculinity consistent with feminist ideals and a just society.

Kenneth Clatterbaugh is professor of philosophy and adjunct professor in Women's Studies at the University of Washington. He has written and lectured widely on men's movements.

· Index ·